Riches for
the Poor

Other books by Earl Shorris

FICTION

Ofay
The Boots of the Virgin
Under the Fifth Sun: A novel of Pancho Villa
In the Yucatán

NON-FICTION

The Death of the Great Spirit: An Elegy for the American Indian
The Oppressed Middle: Scenes from Corporate Life
Jews Without Mercy: A Lament
Power Sits at Another Table: Aphorisms
While Someone Else Is Eating (editor)
Latinos: A Biography of the People
A Nation of Salesmen: The Tyranny of the Market and the Subversion of Culture
New American Blues: A Journey Through Poverty to Democracy

Earl Shorris

Riches for the Poor

The Clemente Course

in the Humanities

W. W. Norton & Company

New York ■ *London*

For information about permission to reproduce selections from this book, write to Permissions,
W. W. Norton & Company, Inc., 500 Fifth Avenue, New York, NY 10110

The text and display of this book are composed in Garamond 3.
Composition by Allentown Digital Services Division of R.R. Donnelley & Sons Company

Library of Congress Cataloging-in-Publication Data
Shorris, Earl, 1936–
    Riches for the poor : the Clemente Course in the Humanities / Earl Shorris.
        p.   cm.
    Rev. ed. of: New American blues. 1997.
    Includes bibliographical references and index.
    ISBN 0-393-32066-9 (pbk.)
        1. Poor—United States. 2. Poverty—United States. I. Shorris, Earl, 1936– . New
    American blues. II. Title.

HV4045 .S464 2000
362.5'0973—dc21

                                                                              00-035676

W. W. Norton & Company, Inc., 500 Fifth Avenue, New York, N.Y. 10110
                            www.wwnorton.com

W. W. Norton & Company Ltd., 10 Coptic Street, London WC1A 1PU

1 2 3 4 5 6 7 8 9 0

This book is dedicated to
my intrepid museum-going companion Tyler Sasson Shorris;

it is indebted to
our professors and social service providers
and most especially to Martin Kempner, Leon Botstein, and Robert Martin.
Sylvia Shorris was there at the birth of this project
and she has been there every day since;
it was she who suggested the course be offered
to American Indians and Alaska Natives.

Mr. Rich Man, Mr. Rich Man, open up
your heart and mind.
Mr. Rich Man, Mr. Rich Man, open up
your heart and mind.
Give the poor man a chance, help stop
these hard, hard times.

— BESSIE SMITH

Contents

The Clemente Course in the Humanities has continued and grown thanks to the interest and support of

The National Endowment for the Humanities and the state humanities commissions of Alaska, Florida, Illinois, Massachusetts, New Jersey, Oklahoma, Oregon, Washington, and Wisconsin

The Fund for the Improvement of Post-Secondary Education of the U.S. Department of Education

The Open Society Institute

AKC Foundation

Alaska Department of Health and Social Services, Division of Juvenile Justice

Alaska Rural Community Action Program (RuralCAP)

Alaska Rural Systemic Initiative/Alaska Federation of Natives

Kenneth and Marleen Alhadeff Charitable Foundation

Brooklyn Union Gas (KeySpan)

CBS/Westinghouse

Centro de la Raza (Seattle)

Cherokee Nation

Cherokee National Historical Society

Chevak Traditional Council

Children's Board of Hillsborough County, Florida

The Door

Fales Foundation Trust

Grace Jones Richardson Trust

Hearst Foundation

Hispanic Federation of New York

Instituto Technologico y de Estudios Superiores de Monterrey–Campus Morelos

Darv Johnson

John S. and James L. Knight Foundation

Kongsgaard-Goldman Foundation

Starling Lawrence

Stephen and May Cavin Leeman Foundation
Library of America and Lawrence Hughes
Henry Luce Foundation
J. Roderick MacArthur Foundation
Middlesex County Economic Opportunities Corp.
Marilyn and Philip Napoli
Anne Navasky
New Jersey Community Services Block Grant
New York City Board of Education
New York State/OASAS
New York Times Foundation
Northside Mental Health Center (Tampa)
Martin and Anne Peretz
Roberto Clemente Family Guidance Center
Daniel J. and Mary Ann Rothman
Tucker Anthony Incorporated
United Nations Development Program (Yucatán, Mexico)
U.S. Department of Health and Human Services/Head Start Quality
    Improvement Grant
Universidad Iberoamericana
University Community Resource Center—Tampa
University of Alaska at Anchorage
University of British Columbia
University of South Florida
W. W. Norton & Company
Walter Chapin Simpson Center for the Humanities at the
    University of Washington
Tom and Margo Wycoff
Yupiit School District, Alaska

Intentions

ACCORDING TO ISAIAH BERLIN, Alexander Herzen "had a natural gift for criticism—a capacity for exposing and denouncing the dark sides of life." And only a few paragraphs later, Berlin added, "As if to restore the equilibrium of his moral organism, nature took care to place in his soul one unshakable belief, one unconquerable inclination. Herzen believed in the noble instincts of the human heart."

This work seeks to offer an explanation of long-term poverty by placing the unfairness of force, "the dark side of human life," in contrast to the inclusiveness of legitimate power, which is one of "the noble instincts of the human heart." It examines and denounces the dark side and suggests a triumph of the noble instincts.

Riches for the Poor

I.

Richer Than Rockefeller

In autumn of 1999, more than four hundred students attended the Clemente Course, a rigorous, university-level course in the humanities. It was not what the world had expected of them, nor what they had expected for themselves. They were all poor, most worked at low-paying jobs, some collected welfare, some were homeless, some had been to prison, more than a few were single parents. Many had not completed high school.

The majority of the students lived in cities: New York, Seattle, Anchorage, Philadelphia, Tampa, Vancouver, Los Angeles, Poughkeepsie, New Brunswick, and Holyoke. Others lived in remote villages in the Yucatán and the Yukon/Kuskokwim Delta. The students were mainly young adults, most of them in their twenties, and even though they were poor, untrained and uneducated, they now entertained the possibility that their lives were not over.

The faculty could have taught at any first-rate college or university, and in fact, many of them did. They ranged in age and experience from university deans to young scholars. In addition to college professors, there were poets, city historians, artists, a well-known critic, and the former chairman of the fifty-six Yup'ik Eskimo villages. No one worked as a volunteer, for a university faculty is not best made of volunteers; the faculty were paid at the rate of adjunct professors at the best universities, for that was the level of effort and knowledge expected of them.

It was the fifth year of the course in the United States, the third year in Canada, the second year in the Yucatán, and work was underway at the Universidad Iberoamericana, the National Autonomous University of Mexico, and the Instituto Technologico y de Estudios Superiores de Monterrey to begin courses in central Mexico. The course was taught in English, Spanish, Yucatecan Maya, Cup'ik Eskimo, and would soon be taught in Kiowa and Cherokee in association with the University of Science and Arts of Oklahoma.

Twenty-three students in New York City who had already completed the course were enrolled in a second-year "Bridge" Course (between the end of the Clemente Course and the start of college), taught by Stuart Levine, dean of Bard College. In San Antonio Sihó, Yucatán, they were reading Maya classical literature in Maya with Miguel Angel May May, whose stories and criticism were beginning to win a national reputation. In Seattle, Lyall Bush, who had come to the course from the Washington Humanities Council, had replaced the Logic section of the course with a broader view he preferred to call Critical Thinking. Martin Kempner, national director of the Bard College Clemente Course in the Humanities, kept in constant touch with his directors at a dozen sites, pushing the academic level up and the attrition rate down.

Although the course had expanded to seventeen sites from the original experiment on the Lower East Side of New York, its aims had remained the same: through the humanities to enable poor people to make the journey into the public world, the political life as Pericles had defined it, beginning with family, and going on to neighborhood, community, and state. To do this successfully required an entirely different view of poverty and poor people. The old ideas about the poor had been proved wrong, or if not wrong, at least not very useful in assisting people out of multigenerational poverty. In truth, the poor had often lifted themselves out of poverty, but other than immigration and such obvious factors as equal justice before the law, how they did it was not well known.

The Clemente Course originated in a single idea: Force and power are not synonymous in a democratic society. The idea led to years of traveling across the United States, listening to the poor, trying to understand whether the distinction between force and power worked in practice as it did in theory, and if it worked in practice, what else might be learned about poverty from the poor themselves? If they were not understood as cases to be managed, if one could sit at the feet of the poor, and listen; if one could be a student in the school of their lives, of what had befallen them, was there not something more to be learned? Starling Lawrence, with whom I first raised the question of force and power, added still another issue to the project: What was to be done?

Of itself, the Clemente Course does not answer the question. It is only a manifestation of the answer. The course is the Greek answer, and even though it operates in Maya and Cup'ik as well as Western/European culture, its Athenian roots are old and very deep. If any one person can be singled out as its founder, it must be Socrates, for he not only gave the course a method, he was the first to exemplify the connection between the political world and the humanities.

Behind the facade of the great ironist, Socrates lived the engaged life. As a young man, he put on the armor of a hoplite and went to war in defense of Athens. Later, in the role of teacher, he explored the question of what a person ought to do, although never in the sense of developing a doctrinal position as in a religion. The gods and the rules for living attributed to them were of no interest to him; he was above all a political man, a humanist, one who held human beings responsible for human thoughts and actions, which as we know may have been part of the reason or rationalization for his death sentence.

The deep connection he made between the humanities and politics was his own life: He did not, as we say, *do* philosophy, he *was* a philosopher. For Socrates, who upon consideration of his imminent death was comforted by the thought that he would either sleep or spend his afterlife in the company of such people as the poet Homer, the humanities and political life were of a piece.

Although there is no bald statement of the relation of the humanities to politics that we can attribute to Socrates, no one who thinks about him can fail to comprehend the importance of the connection. Moreover, the connection did not arise from the mind of Socrates alone; it is bound up in the development of the Greek *polis,* intimately connected to the democratic conduct of the city-state. While the Platonic notion of a philosopher-king was never realized, something even more astonishing occurred in ancient Athens, the philosopher-citizen; that is, the person who thought reflectively about the management of the internal and external affairs of state.

That this happened concurrent with the rise of Greek poetry, drama, art, philosophy, mathematics, and history is not in question. If one holds to the separation of the humanities and the public life, and there are many who do, the concurrence can only be explained as coincidence. Democracy lasted but briefly, they will say, adding that neither Plato nor Aristotle cared much for it. Nonetheless, one might ask of the separatists what other state invented democracy, where individual freedom was considered before Athens. That democratic institutions could have arisen without the intellectual impetus of the humanities is unlikely.

Of course, the humanities also exist in undemocratic societies; it was profoundly disturbing to the liberal thinker Isaiah Berlin to find that his beloved Akhmatova could produce beautiful poetry despite living under a totalitarian dictatorship. The real question, the one raised by listening to the poor, is whether or not a democracy, which we think of as the most political form of government, can exist in full without the humanities.

It is not my purpose here to explore a definition of freedom, but even so, given our most general notions of freedom, is thoughtless freedom possible? Or is freedom in such circumstance merely chaos?

Where freedom found its first clear expression, in ancient Athens, the separation of the humanities from the public world was not possible; the humanities and the polis needed each other for their very existence. Only much later, after St. Paul relocated freedom inside the mind, was it possible to separate the humanities from life: Philosophy moved to the monastery and painting to the interior of the church. Compare the actions of the great philosopher of the Enlightenment, Immanuel Kant, and Socrates. When Socrates came up against the unreasonable judgement of the state, he chose to die rather than abandon his principles, as we learn from his refusal to accept Crito's offer to escape from Athens.

After Kant published *Religion and the Bounds of Mere Reason* and caused a stir in 1793, the king of Prussia asked his subject in Königsberg to promise never again to write about religion. Kant gave and kept his promise. The contrast with Socrates could not be much more clear. The philosopher who said, "The unexamined life is not a fit life for man," refused to recant on pain of death. The philosopher who boiled the great questions down to "What can I know? How shall I live? What may I hope?" and then gave us the categorical imperative did as he was told.

One lived in a monarchy and the other, although he died during a troubled period, in a democracy. It would be foolish to compare the work of Kant, important as it is, with that of Socrates. Both men were concerned with beauty as well as truth and virtue; yet Kant was able to live apart from the world and Socrates was the most worldly of men.

In the contemporary world, one may also live apart. It is possible to be quite comfortable inside what the French literary critic Sainte-Beuve called "the ivory tower," and to imagine that the humanities exist only for those in the ivory tower or even to think that the humanities are in some way an ivory tower unto themselves: ". . . art for art's sake," as the nineteenth-century Frenchman Victor Cousin said, and M-G-M motion pictures studios agreed.

The humanities do not languish, useless and wasteful, when they exist apart from the intercourse of the public life, but they do not have their full effect. One might argue, as William Gass has done, that art need not be moral, but if the full range of the humanities were outside the moral realm in a democratic society, where would the society seek its moral self? The members of the society would have to look to the Prince or the Church. But when church and state are separate, as in an open, democratic society, the alternative is the humanities. That is the Greek notion on which the Clemente Course was founded.

Despite its Greek legacy, the course was born an orphan, and if my friends and colleagues and I are dogged in the pursuit of our beliefs, it will remain an orphan. The course is a political idea with no partisan political affiliation. Although I think of myself as a man of the left, the course belongs not to me but to the Renaissance idea of the humanities as defined by Petrarch, and in the cultural arena that would qualify it as conservative. If there is a political bias in the course, it is against mobilization and for autonomy.

With seventeen sites in three countries, the Clemente Course has become an institution, but it owns nothing—not a desk, not a chair, not a scrap of paper. Although a part of the course, the heart of it, has a guardian in Bard College, it remains, with the help of its guardian, outside the clans of partisan political affiliation and academe, an orphan in the private world, a citizen of the public world.

The course seeks to be what it hopes its students will become. It has, in short, adopted for its practice what I believe to be one of the great human discoveries: autonomy. Like all self-governing citizens, the Clemente Course has established order for itself: a general approach to the curriculum; a teaching method; standards, principles, and procedures, and a system of rewards for work; all of which will be discussed in succeeding chapters.

Such a course could also be taught to the rich and middle classes, but the humanities have fallen out of favor in many, perhaps most, colleges and universities now, replaced by the rich man's version of welfare-to-work training programs, although a few institutions of higher education remain devoted, at least in part, to education.

This fall from education to training in the universities highlights the basic distinction between the Clemente Course and most other efforts to assist people who want to escape from poverty: If the humanities have ceased to be utilized by the rich, why foist them upon the poor?

The loss to students and to society that comes of failing to teach the humanities in high schools and colleges merits not one book but many books of diagnosis and prescription. How long a country that forsakes the ethical and intellectual strength of reflective thinking can continue to prosper is open to question. Whether such a nation can maintain a position of leadership is doubtful.

Before the general abandonment of the humanities and the downgrading of post-secondary schooling from education to "preparation," education and more specifically the study of the humanities was thought to be the province of the rich. The children of the Rockefellers (or currently the Gates) would have been expected to know something about history, art, literature, and philosophy. Even today their schooling tends toward the more complex, less repetitive kind of work. The poor, on the other hand, have always been trained to perform simpler tasks, usually less cognitively demanding and consequently less remunerative than the trades.

Whenever the nation becomes interested, for whatever reason, in alleviating the suffering of the poor, the method is always the same: training. Some programs also attempt to teach the poor to wear more appropriate clothing, others to give them the habit of rising early, and so on. In most such programs, including those suggested by the Welfare Reform Act of 1996, both promise and punishment have a role. These policies result from the idea that the poor are different from the rest of the people, either less able or less deserving or both.

If one holds to that view, the idea of educating poor people is absurd. They should be trained, if they are capable even of that. Such a policy has certain obvious advantages for the rest of the society: it enables them to use the poor to do the whatever the non-poor want to avoid and to pay them very little for their labor.

The other, less obvious, advantage involves power: the uneducated poor have neither the economic nor the intellectual resources to take and hold their fair share of power in a democratic society.

By training the poor while keeping education in the humanities beyond their reach, the rich and the middle classes maintain the poor in the role of the meek. The poor may rob or even kill someone now and then, usually each other, but the uneducated poor pose no economic or political threat to those who hold power.

How the humanities affect the poor, why they are deserving of such riches, and why it is to the benefit of the general society to teach the humanities to the poor all depend upon a different understanding of poverty. In an earlier version of this book, *New American Blues: A Journey Through Poverty to Democracy,* I described visits with many of the eight hundred or more poor people from whom I learned how to think about their situation. There are no narratives of those visits here; this book is about the Clemente Course.

Nonetheless, as I talked about the Clemente Course to people around the United States, and in Mexico, Canada, Australia, Greece, and France over the last five years, I learned that unless I speak in detail about the theory of poverty that gave rise to the course, the idea of teaching the humanities to the poor seems unfounded, so far from the common view of what the poor need as to seem capricious.

When speaking to prospective students, I tell them: "I will make you as rich as Rockefeller, richer, because not all Rockefellers have studied the humanities. If you study the humanities, you will have the riches you deserve." Neither I nor the directors and professors who give the courses tell the students that the humanities will make them political, citizens in the truest sense. There is no need to do that now, as there was no need in ancient Greece for Aeschylus or Sophocles or Euripides to explain the eventual political effect of their work. Nor did Pericles feel the need to tell Athenian mourners about the art, literature, and philosophy of their polis; it was understood, for he spoke to an audience of citizens.

In the succeeding chapters that lead up to the idea for the Clemente Course, which came not out of the ivory tower but from a conversation in a maximum-security prison, a theory of poverty will be presented. The theory appears to hold, the course appears to work, yet we ask each other many questions: How is the integration of the disciplines best accomplished? What is gained and what is lost by establishing a core syllabus for each section of the course? What can be done about the calamities that befall our students and cause them to drop out of the course? One of the greatest successes of the course has been in Yucatán, but will that apply to urban Mexico? Can the Greek idea, which Laszlo Versényi called "socratic humanism," be applied in non-European cultures? And not do harm either to the idea of the humanities or to an American culture considered through an ancient Greek lens?

A great deal remains to be learned about the course in all of its aspects. Dr. Martin Kempner, Dean of Graduate Studies Robert Martin of Bard, and everyone else connected to the course continue to examine the methods. Difficult and useful questions have been posed by Peter Steinberger, Dean of Students at Reed College, which is contemplating a course for Portland, Oregon. In Mexico, the faculties of Instituto Technologico y de Estudios Superiores de Monterrey, Universidad Iberoamericana, and the National Autonomous National University of Mexico have raised the issue of the portability of the concept. Am Johal is pursuing a variation of the course at the University of British Columbia. As Socrates would have it, nothing about the operation of the course is fixed, dead; it exists in dialogue, which begins with the idea that the poor are human and that the proper celebration of their humanity is in the public world, as citizens. In the chapters between this and those that describe the history and operation of the Clemente Course, I will attempt to explain why.

For the reader who prefers to begin with the practice and then consider the theory behind it, the first evidence of the connection between the humanities and the problem of poverty appears in Chapter XI. The development of the course; its growth in the United States, Canada, and Mexico; and its extension to include indigenous American languages begins with Chapter XIII and continues until the final chapter, which is a summary. There is some risk in reading the book in this way, however: Without the ideas that gave rise to the course, the need for reflective thinking as a precursor to the political life, and even the value of the political life itself, may not be very clear. The Clemente Course might appear to be no more than a college preparatory program for underprivileged people, and that would diminish the celebration of the humanities and the possibilities of the human spirit that are the joy of the work.

II.

A Game of Poverty: Definitions

Them that's got shall have.
Them that's not shall lose.

— BILLIE HOLIDAY

THE KIND OF POVERTY known in the United States belongs to the modern world. In Neolithic societies, which Rousseau said were "the youth of the world," wealth generally belonged to the entire social unit. Chieftains may have had more wives to enjoy or fewer onerous tasks to perform, but in these societies, governed by ritual, equality rather than inequality was the rule. Bad hunting or drought affected the entire social unit on a more or less equal basis.

As Neolithic societies grew larger and farming and husbandry replaced hunting and gathering, the concept of private property developed, and inequalities became more pronounced. Property extended beyond the limits of memory or common knowledge, and owners had to find some way to describe their cattle and mark the boundaries of their land. This new inequality led to the invention of writing and the emergence of the modern world some four or five thousand years ago in Mesopotamia.

With inequality came other changes in society. Ritual, which had brought people together, binding them by the memory of some common and therefore equalizing experience, broke down and was replaced by contests. The Olympic Games spring immediately to mind, but that formalization came late. By the time of the Trojan War, according to Homer, contests had become institutionalized.[1] Simple board games were played in Egypt at least a thousand years earlier. The precise timing does not matter so much as the loss of equality inherent in a game: The players begin as equals and end as unequals; games establish differences between the players.

The making of poverty in a rich country like the United States has the same structure as a game, because the players begin as equals in nature and end up as unequals in society. Capitalism probably accounts for much of this, but games played according to slightly different rules exist in all modern societies.[2]

The game of the modern world as it was played in ancient Greece is revealed in the concept of *pleonexia,* which the OED defines as "covetousness, avarice, greed." Gregory Vlastos, in his *Platonic Studies* (Princeton, NJ: Princeton University Press, 1981), has a more extensive explanation: ". . . gaining some advantage for oneself by grabbing what belongs to another—his property, his wife, his office, and the like—or by denying him what is (morally or legally) due him—fulfillment of promises made to him, repayment of monies owed to him, respect for his good name and reputation and so forth." (p. 116) In a

---

[1] The solid date in ancient Greece is 776 B.C., the first Olympic Games. No certain date can be given for Homer, although approximately 700 B.C. is now widely accepted. The funerary games described in the *Iliad* may have taken place as early as 1220 B.C. The question then arises whether Homer's reference to wrestling contests refers to his own time or to the date of the historical event in Troy. In either case, the evidence shows the game as a very early component of modern civilization. Musical contests probably took place at Delphi as early as 1500 B.C., and Egyptian board games, like Hounds and Jackals, were played at least three hundred years earlier. It was the athletic contest, however, that most clearly delineated the change in status of the players.

[2] See Claude Lévi-Strauss, The Savage Mind (Chicago: University of Chicago Press, 1966). In this, as in much of his social thought, Lévi-Strauss brings to mind the arguments of Rousseau's Discourse on the Origins of Inequality.

footnote, he adds: "I despair of an adequate English translation. Its occurrence in [Aristotle's *Nicomachean Ethics*] is rendered by 'self-advantage' in Shorey . . . Cornford's 'self-interest' is intolerably loose: only when self-interest is sought at the expense of others and in contravention of . . . [equity, fairness] would the Greeks speak of *pleonexia*." (ibid.) Certainly the old Soviet Union was such a place. Thorstein Veblen, who preceded the structuralist Lévi-Strauss by half a century, claimed the rules of American economic society were formed on the playing fields of colleges. Veblen's words echo now in the use of the term "player" among the wealthiest Americans, for whom it describes a man or woman who wins on such a scale as to be able to determine who among the rest of society, including his or her peers, will also win. Or lose.

If the choice of words among the most powerful Americans is apt and the theories of the social scientists are correct—and it surely seems so on the face of it—the goal of modern society is not wealth but inequality.

Lewis H. Lapham, the editor and essayist, once wrote with uncharacteristic bluntness that for every person who eats caviar someone must eat dog food. Lapham, who chooses his words carefully, did not speak of beef or chicken at one end of the continuum and rice and beans at the other; he chose extremes, winners and losers, the game of the modern world, the American way.

According to the Organization for Economic Cooperation and Development (OECD),[3] Lapham knew what he was talking about: The

---

[3] Quoted in the *New York Times*, Oct. 27, 1995. The countries studied, from the lowest to the greatest income gap, were Finland, Sweden, Belgium, the Netherlands, Norway, West Germany, Luxembourg, Switzerland, New Zealand, France, Britain, Australia, Canada, Italy, Ireland, and the United States. Even in Finland, however, people at the 10th percentile earned a little more than half the median while those at the 90th percentile earned more than 1.5 times the median. The difference between the United States and Finland was significant: The rich earned 2.59 times as much as the poor in Finland and 5.9 times as much in the United States. It is important to keep in mind that the study dropped out the very richest and the very poorest 10 percent in making the comparisons.

United States had a greater income gap between rich and poor than any of fifteen other industrialized countries the group studied. In the richest country in the world, measured according to gross domestic product, the contest had produced the greatest inequality.

The game of modern civilization does not require that the loser suffer privation. It has no interest in desperate poverty; the OECD studied poverty at the 10th percentile, not the 99th. At the far end of the scale, the 99th or even the 98th percentile, there is no contest, for the winners must assume that those people were never equals, not even in nature; either they were born lacking normal mental, emotional, or physical abilities or they came into the world in impossible circumstances, without sufficient food or even the most meager educational opportunities. According to the rules of the game, the participants must begin as putative equals.[4]

No sense of fairness should be inferred from this, however; equals cannot logically mean exact equals. If that were the case, every contest would end in a draw. And the game of modern society never ends in a draw, even in the most rigorously socialistic societies.

Precisely what do I mean by "equal"? This is not the place to explore the question in depth, but it may be the place to admit the vagueness of the concept and the likelihood that its main use in contemporary America is to validate the game of winners and losers, feeding the pride of the winners and the shame of the losers by keeping the results from appearing to be preordained.

Over the last quarter of a century the game has been played with great ferocity in America; the income gap between rich and poor grew faster during the Reagan, Bush, and Clinton administrations than it

---

[4] Immigrants who come to the United States for economic reasons have a different understanding of the game. Although they come with little or no money or real capital, they consider themselves winners compared to those they left behind. If this sense of relative wealth and the ability to make a new social contract in a new homeland enables them to move into the middle, where the illusion can be continued, they and their children prosper. If they do not move into the middle within a generation, their children understand themselves as relatively poor rather than relatively rich, and suffer the bitterness of losers in the American game.

had during any period in recent history, reversing the trend of the preceding twenty years when the gap had narrowed.[5] And it is not absolute income that defines the game, but the gap between the 10th and the 90th or the 15th and the 85th percentiles. The middle represents only the inefficiency of the game, which was devised to sort the winners from the losers.[6]

In democratic societies, the middle group creates an illusion of efficiency by allying itself with the rich or the poor. When the middle allies itself with the rich, as in the recent past, members of the group declare themselves winners—perhaps not winners of the blue ribbon, but winners of the red or the gold. During the Depression, what remained of the middle allied itself with the poor, defining anything but the blue ribbon as a loss. This may account for the different definitions of poverty then and now.

Since unequals must be produced in order to have a game, the de-

[5] *New York Times,* June 20, 1996, reporting U.S. Census Bureau data. Changes in the methods of gathering and analyzing income data may account for some of the rate of increase during the Clinton administration, but the trend remained constant. In one analysis, household income for the highest quintile increased from $73,754 to $105,945 on an inflation-adjusted basis between 1968 and 1994. During the same period, income for the lowest quintile increased from $7,202 to $7,762.

The next day, figures compiled by the University of Michigan in a longitudinal study of seven thousand families were reported. The figures, all adjusted to 1996 dollars, follow:

	1984		1994	
	Avg. Net Worth	Share of Wealth	Avg. Net Wealth	Share of Wealth
Poorest 20%	$-3,282	-0.44%	-7,075	-0.64%
Poorest 10%	-7,777	-0.52	-15,467	-0.70
Next Poorest 20%	12,151	1.64	17,503	1.58
Middle 20%	47,760	6.44	61,777	6.56
Next Richest 20%	114,881	15.49	141,778	12.77
Richest 20%	570,050	76.84	871,463	78.47
Richest 10%	918,633	61.32	1,482,698	66.76

[6] In *The Savage Mind,* Lévi-Strauss equates winners and losers in the game with the killers and the killed in ancient situations. Veblen's use of the playing field seems more correct, especially in the industrialized world where the suffering of the losers has been mitigated to some extent by the welfare state.

finition of "winners" and "losers" becomes of paramount importance. As in war, the power to define the terms belongs to the winners. The exact point at which a person passes from the middle to winning is of little interest except to those who live near the dividing line, which is always blurred by illusion.

More serious thought has been given to defining poverty. On the one hand, naming the losers has always been one of the comforts, if not the pleasures of the rich, and on the other it measures the extent of the social, political, moral, and economic failing of the modern world. How one defines poverty depends on one's view of the game. There are at least five different ways to understand the origins of inequality in America:

1. If the definer pretends that a game among equals has taken place, he or she may decide that the great variable in the game is moral; that is, the losers are not the moral equals of the winners. The game was played that way long before the birth of John Calvin, and it will continue to be played that way after the demise of Bill Clinton, Newt Gingrich, and William Bennett, but Calvin was the Hoyle of the game, and Clinton, Gingrich, Edward C. Banfield, William Bennett, Ken Auletta, Pat Robertson, et al. have fought hard to maintain the canon. Played by such rules, the game leads to the idea of an *underclass,* defined by Auletta in a book with that word for a title, or a *culture of poverty,* a phrase coined by sociologist Oscar Lewis.

2. If the definer pretends that a game of equals produces equal results, he must argue that the losers were unequal in nature. This argument in defense of the game has a long and distasteful history: slavery of various forms, Gobineau, the Nazi philosophers, and in more recent times the work of Charles Murray and William Shockley.

3. The game itself is flawed. But to prove that view, the outcome must be shown to be flawed; the losers will have to be equal to or greater than the winners in every way but the outcome of the game. Socialism, communism, and what is now commonly known as liberalism result from this view. Conservators of capitalism, like

Franklin Delano Roosevelt and Lyndon Baines Johnson, subscribe to this view when they believe it is necessary.

4. In the late 1950s and 1960s, a syncretic view was widely held by the liberal wing of the Democratic Party. It resulted in the War on Poverty, which was based on the idea that both the poor and the game were flawed, but emphasized the need to improve the former.

5. The belief that the winners are flawed belongs largely to saints, savioúrs, and a few monks. Communists, socialists, and even liberal Democrats are often accused of holding this view, but one has only to look at the comforts enjoyed by the winners among them to understand the frivolity of the accusation.

For the most part, poverty in the United States is described as a percentage of the total population. In 1989, it was 11.7 percent, although in 1960 it was much higher. At the end of the twentieth century, much is being made of a fall in the poverty rate from 13.3 percent in 1997 to 12.7 percent in 1998. Those who claim that "a rising tide lifts all boats" take comfort in the accomplishment of this apparent decline in poverty. The mirage of percentages please them, for it agrees with their view. It is, however, only a mirage.

People are poor one household, one family at a time. The real measure should be the absolute number of people in poverty. Since there were 248,500,000 people in the United States at about the time poverty hit its low of 11.7 percent, the number of poor then was about 29 million. If the poverty rate were to fall to 11.7 percent in 2000, it would describe about 32 million people. The point the celebrants of welfare reform and Reaganomics would prefer to avoid is that the rate of poverty will decline faster than the rate of population growth if *real,* rather than mere statistical, improvement takes place.

Every view depends in large measure upon the definition of poverty and each view has a different definition. Poverty was not codified until the beginning of the twentieth century, when Charles Booth completed his massive study of the poor in London. He concluded that a third of the people were living in poverty; that is, having income below the level needed for bare subsistence. An official poverty level was not set in the United States until the 1960s, when Mollie Orshansky, an employee of the Social Security Administration, put the poverty level at three times the cost of a subsistence diet. She based her formula on a Department of Agriculture study showing that the average family spent a third of its income on food.

Orshansky claimed that her estimate of poverty for the Social Security Administration should never have been used for that purpose, according to Michael Katz in *The Undeserving Poor.* Orshansky said that the number of poor people in 1975 should have been 36 or 37 million, about 10 million more than the commonly used figure. Using the same ratio, the number of poor people in 1992, officially estimated at 38 million, would have been closer to 53 million.

Estimates by established academics and demographers of the number of people living in poverty in the mid-1990s range from 14.5 percent to 18 or 19 percent. As the effects of the 1996 Welfare Reform Bill begin to push large numbers of children and old people into poverty, the number will undoubtedly increase. At the upper end of the scale, some radical groups claim that one-third of the entire population lives in poverty, the same proportion that Booth found in London at the turn of the last century. If that estimate seems outrageous, it should be compared with the figures for New York City teased out of U.S. Census Bureau reports by the Community Service Society of New York: The society found that 27 percent of the people in the city lived below the federal poverty level in 1993.[7] By 1998, it had fallen

---

[7] *New York Times,* July 14, 1995. Since the people not counted by the census mainly comprise the very poor, undocumented persons, the homeless, and the physically and mentally disabled, it is probably safe to assume a slightly higher true percentage, bringing the prevalence of poverty in contemporary New York City even closer to London at the end of the nineteenth century.

Projections of the number of people who will be forced into poverty by the Welfare Reform Act of 1996 may be overstated, especially for cities like New York, where local and state governments may attempt to ameliorate the effects of the act. However, there can be no doubt that the number of poor will increase, perhaps surpassing the percentage of poor who lived in London a century earlier.

to 24.3 percent, but the figure of $16,600 for a family of four was more absurd than ever.

But the idea of what anybody means by "poor" is still not clear. Did Booth and Orshansky choose to describe absolute or relative poverty? Who determined the subsistence level in London at the end of the nineteenth century or in the United States in the middle of the next century?

If poverty were merely a matter of subsistence, objective means could be used to define it: indoor temperatures in winter, the presence of insects or rodents, the absence of hot and cold running water, and so on, for housing. Minimal proper nutrition can be measured, as can the availability and quality of health care. Clothing, especially for children, presents a problem, because some children outgrow clothes faster than others and some climates require more expensive winter clothing. But food, shelter, and clothing may not be all the components worth considering. We know exactly what a cow needs, but a six-year-old girl and her twenty-two-year-old mother have sensibilities considerably more complex than those of a cow.

At the end of the twentieth century, the debate over the definition of the poverty level has arisen again. The Census Bureau has experimented with raising the poverty line from $16,600 to $19,500, based on the notion that the requirements for human beings do truly differ from those of a cow. Given that definition of the poverty line, 17 percent rather than 12.3 percent of the U.S. population lives in poverty. But if one sets aside the percentages and considers the people, the number is breathtaking: more than 46 million Americans are poor.

To put the number in perspective, Mexico estimates that it has about 40 million people living in poverty, although about 15 million live in what the Mexicans describe as "extreme poverty." If we define extreme poverty as hunger, the rough estimate for the United States is 9.5 million. There can be no doubt that extreme poverty in Mexico is more than half again as severe as in the United States, although poverty in its slightly less murderous form is a little worse north of the border.

Of course, either country could choose at any time to define itself into moral superiority, by lowering the poverty level. In the Clemente Course we began by using 150 percent of the federal poverty level as our benchmark, but the futility of applying that number to the real people whose hands we have grasped in greeting soon became apparent.

The great complication in arriving at an accurate definition of poverty grows out of the uses of the definition, some of which are counterintuitive. For example, to reduce the size of the middle, making the game more efficient, those in power may lower the official poverty level, knowing that reductions in benefits will follow and the number of losers will be increased. Or by raising questions about values, those in power appear to be trying to improve the lives of the poor, but stigmatizing behavior such as out-of-wedlock births merely improves the efficiency of the game by making all single mothers into losers.

Perhaps the best way to define poverty is to listen to people who consider themselves poor.[8] I asked a group of women from the Young Mothers Program in the South Bronx who agreed to help me with New American Blues. Our first task was to define poverty.

Over time, the aspects of poverty, as the women of the Young Mothers Program described it, fell into two categories. Their definition was not complete, because they were a homogeneous group with a common set of problems and because they had tried for most of their lives to avoid the pain of thinking about their condition. Dur-

---

[8] For the purposes of this book, the poor are those people who have declared themselves poor, which may be done in various ways. The most common is to associate themselves in some fashion with an institution that attends the poor: church programs, the state welfare department, Medicaid or unpaid emergency-room services, low-income housing, low-income community action programs, youth service organizations, settlement houses, legal services for the poor, homeless shelters, battered women's shelters, public or private food distribution organizations, full-time programs for recovering addicts, jails and prisons, minimum-wage or near minimum-wage jobs.

Some people who declare themselves poor by association prefer to say they are not poor, and that is understandable, for poverty is not considered a virtue in America. Others who have no association with any organization or institution connected to the poor may simply say, "I'm poor."

ing our conversations they did not so much define poverty as name some aspects of it, unconsciously following the Marxist notion of quantity becoming quality.

There is some overlapping in the categories they made, for poverty is not as clear as counting:

PRIVATION
1. Lack of money for current needs
2. Lack of capital, both real and intellectual
3. Inadequate housing
4. Insufficient food and fresh water
5. Inadequate clothing
6. Unhealthful living conditions, including lack of heat, hot water, and sanitation
7. No access to medical care
8. Lack of education
9. Unsafe conditions
10. Lack of communication
11. Unsatisfactory social life
12. Dearth of the objects of culture

OPPRESSION
1. Enduring defeat, lifelong and passed on to the next generation
2. Excluded from duties and rewards of citizenship
3. Subject to coercion
4. Without recourse
5. Despised (not hated) by the powerful
6. Death not mourned by the community
7. Limited choice of food, clothing, housing, employment, place of residence, and recreation
8. Reduced to pleasures of the body
9. Responses limited to passivity or violence
10. Prevented from enjoying marriage and family life
11. Excluded from education, schooling limited to training
12. Fungible, in economic terms more like goods than persons

If poverty were one thing, indivisible, with many things growing out of it, a definition both simple and accurate would be possible. But poverty in the modern world is a complex quality, made up of physical deficiencies and many kinds of moral defeat. The women in the South Bronx were correct, and so was Marx: quantity becomes quality. A poverty line, based entirely on income, cannot adequately sort the poor from those who have found a middle life.

The people who lived in the 24th Ward of Chicago in 1936, where I lived the first years of my life, and those who live there now are analogues in many respects, but not in the one that transforms all the others. The blacks are now pitted against the browns, the Jews then were antagonists of the Poles; thugs came from poolrooms, candy stores, and barbershops on Roosevelt Road then, and they still do; racial intolerance wounds more deeply, but religious and ethnic intolerance also hurt; gangsters killed each other then, and their symbolic progeny kill each other now; hardly anyone had long, deep roots in the neighborhood then or now. The critical difference between the 24th Ward today and the ward where my father practiced politics is the kind of poverty suffered there.

During the Depression, the people of the ward thought they lived in absolute poverty. Franklin Delano Roosevelt told them it was the nation's problem, the Communist Party told them it was the system's problem, and Paul Robeson sang to them that it was everyone's problem. When all the people think all the other people are poor, a sadness comes into their lives; it underlies their every action, and in quiet times, as in the moments when sleep refuses to come or rain has ruined the day, the sadness rises to engulf consciousness. But in other times, on other days, at softball games, in barbershops, when baby carriages pass in the street, or children laugh, the sadness can be put away. Absolute poverty functions like a ritual, conjoining the people in their sadness and even when their sadness has temporarily been put away. In the throes of what they understood as absolute poverty, the people did politics.

No one in the 24th Ward accepts the existence of absolute poverty now; even the hungry and the squatters cannot bring themselves to believe they are absolutely poor. Like the women in the South Bronx, they think absolute poverty exists only in foreign countries. No matter where they look, or how they think, or to whom they pray, the residents see only less or more: Wealth is overflowing, spilling out of the fat pockets of everyone else, and in the ward people scramble to pay the rent or the pharmacist's bill and still keep food on the table.

No politics can be done in the 24th Ward now; it is every man for himself. Economics rules. The world is as relative as race, and relative poverty is unendurable, an insult to the modicum of self-regard required to participate in the human community. At the end of the game, when the middle has chosen to ally itself with the winners, thereby defining everyone else as poor, envy comes to the ward. And out of envy: isolation, hatred, and rage.

III.

Born for Each Other

He who considers things in
their first growth and origin,
whether a state or anything
else, will obtain the clearest
view of them.

— ARISTOTLE,
Politics, Bk. I

1

THERE IS A TENNIS COURT in the South Bronx. On some days, after school has let out, a social worker from the Neighborhood Youth and Family Services program takes a group of children to the tennis court. Since there are only two tennis rackets and one tennis court to be shared among the children, they must take turns. The worker begins by giving the rackets to two of the children and asking the others to line up to await their chance to play.

The children form a line, but as soon as the worker tells the players on the court that their time is up, the rest of the children break out of the line and crowd around the players, asking, reaching, demanding, cajoling, desperately wanting to be next to use the rackets.

Each time the rackets are exchanged, the line breaks down, requiring the teacher to sort out the crowd, award the rackets, and restore the line before play can begin again. Much of the afternoon is taken up with the complexities of passing on the rackets to the proper players.

A few miles to the north, at a suburban school, the children are also taken to a tennis court. They, too, must form a line and take their turn at hitting the ball up and back across the net. At the suburban school the children also vie for position, but once they arrange themselves, they maintain their places in line: the rackets are exchanged quickly, and play on the courts is almost continuous.

The children at the suburban school know the rules of political life at their most basic level. They have found the middle road between liberty and order. At the beginning, they are at liberty to find their places; but once they find them, they maintain order. Play proceeds according to the rules defined by the group when forming the line, and it goes along efficiently.

In the South Bronx the group does not govern itself; it chooses liberty over the middle road. In the chaos of liberty, force dominates; the bigger, stronger, or more aggressive students get the rackets every time. The social worker must then intervene to establish order in the group.

The two tennis courts do not serve as perfect analogues of states, but they illustrate an important difference between rich and poor in the United States: The poor children are not political. They cannot find the middle ground between order and liberty. Instead, they attempt to exert what little force they can muster. Much of the time that could be devoted to learning to play tennis is lost in the chaos of force. The poor children do not reflect on their situation at the tennis court, so they cannot recognize the folly of their apolitical behavior. They react, following the rules of force rather than the rules of politics, because force is what they know; it is the world that the world teaches to the poor.

The poor children, who may be equal to or even greater than the rich in natural ability, fall behind in the learning of tennis. In the game of modern society they are beginning to lose.

Many explanations have been offered for the losing behavior of the poor, especially the children. Psychological, social, economic, and racial problems all intervene to wound the lives of the poor. But the rich may also be wounded by psychological problems, as well as social and racial problems. Even economic problems may wound the rich, as in the precipitous fall from affluence following a bad investment or the inability to manage one's life in the wake of social, psychological, or racial problems. All of these may be, as Aristotle said, subsumed under the master art, the one that governs all the others: politics. He did not, however, mean politics as it is discussed in the daily newspaper or the corner tavern.

Politics, the lack in the lives of the poor, has come to be understood in America as electoral politics or shrewd manipulation. Those definitions betoken a healthy mistrust of power, but they do not explain the meaning of politics, the *vita activa* or *bíos politikos* of ancient times.[1] To understand the difference between the behavior of the rich and poor children on their respective tennis courts requires that we heed

---

[1] Language is too important to be tossed around from century to century, continent to continent. Heidegger was correct when he said, "Language is the house of being," putting the burden of consciousness upon the words we use. He insisted that one could understand the Greeks only in the original. It was a good argument, but Heidegger's critics are forever pointing out the errors in his Greek.

There are other models: Petrarch read the Greeks in Latin, although he was not satisfied with the translations. I have relied entirely on standard English translations by sensible and talented men and women (Cornford, Fagles, Fitzgerald, the Jowett I first read as a student, the new Sterling and Scott *Republic,* etc.). When important disagreement among translators exists, I have generally given more than one rendering for the reader to consider. For the exegesis of single words or phrases, I have relied upon the work of experts. Translations of individual words or phrases are from Liddell and Scott, *A Greek-English Lexicon,* 9th edn (New York: Oxford University Press, 1968).

This book is not about the Greek language. Disputes over the understanding of the Greeks here should have to do with ideas rather than renderings. For example, a deep schism exists now between the "liberals," who are interested in Protagoras and the Sophists, as well as Plato, and the "fundamentalists," who follow Plato out the window. The fundamentalists will not be happy with the view taken here, but their displeasure should not arise from questions of translation—Bloom or Cornford or Shorey or Jowett. The issues should have more to do with democracy, elitism, and that ever elusive notion—justice.

the ancient advice to consider things in their first growth or origin to gain a clear view.[2]

2

We followers of Socrates—and in the modern world we are all his intellectual progeny—live with the loss or misrepresentation of much of what he said. Plato and Xenophon claim to have noted his thoughts in dialogues and memoirs, and Aristophanes provides us with the contradiction of satire, but Socrates refrained from writing down a word. He did not write, because he thought the written word was dead; it could not be argued, changed, clarified, improved, or denied. The dialectician believed in the living connection between men; using what he called "maieutic dialogue," the midwifery of the mind, the philosopher led his opponents through the maze of argument to the brilliant aporia, the point at which there could be no escape from truth.

In selecting his method for the Clemente Course rather than the French model, for example, in which the students sit for the lectures

---

[2] The advice is from Aristotle (*Politics,* Bk I, ch. 2). For the reader who holds the view that the politics of Athens have no relevance in modern times, because the Athenians held slaves and did not extend citizenship to women or immigrants, I offer two thoughts from M. I. Finley. The first is that we should not be guilty of anachronism, asking the ancient Greeks to accept our modern morality. The second, from *Democracy Ancient and Modern* (New Brunswick, NJ: Rutgers University Press, 1973), is more subtle: "Before we accept that the elitism of the *demos* renders their experience irrelevant to ours, we must examine more closely the composition of that elite minority, the *demos,* the citizenry." He goes on to describe "a large section of the *demos* . . . the peasants, shopkeepers and craftsmen who were citizens alongside the educated upper classes. The incorporation of such people into the political community as members, an astounding novelty in its time, rarely repeated thereafter, rescues some of the relevance of ancient democracy, so to speak." (p. 16)

Finley is restating the important point made by Pericles, that the democracy includes those who were not members of the aristocracy. Pericles apparently thought them capable of thinking as well as aristocrats, an idea that the Clemente Course in the Humanities (see Chapter XIII) put to the test in New York City in the 1995–96 academic year.

of their professors, we begin the political life of the student, for in his decision not to write Socrates exemplified the political life; he melded thought and action, the marriage of which politics is born. The political life and the life of the mind followed a similar course and used a similar method: politics is always dialogue; it cannot ever be done alone. Like dialogue, politics does not happen within a person, but in the free space between persons, the political space. There cannot ever be a private life of politics, since politics takes place between persons, in a public way, not public in the sense of broadcast or crowds but as the opposite of private.

The Greek word for private, *idios,* stands in opposition to *koinos,* which means in common, public, and the state. *Koinologia* means consultation, discussion, or philosophical dialogue; the foundation for much of the intellectual and interpersonal activity of the Greeks. This intertwining of thought and action describes the core of the world where politics and freedom were born.

Could Socrates have come out of some other tradition? It is unlikely. By the time he put off the armor of a hoplite and settled down "daily to discourse about virtue," the melding of thought and action in public life was common behavior. Politics had long been established in Athens. In about 440 B.C., when Socrates was only thirty years old, Athens was so taken with a political drama, *Antigone,* that its author, Sophocles, was made one of the generals of the city-state. In the play, Antigone violates the ruling of Creon the king by giving a proper burial to her brother, who had been killed while leading a foreign army against the state.[3] The conflict between her duty to family and her duty to the state, the latter eloquently set out by Creon early in the play, leads to the tragic conclusion.[4]

The conflict harkens back to the origins of political life in the reform of Cleisthenes, who broke down the traditional clan structure of

---

[3] See George Steiner's fascinating essay, *Antigones* (New York: Oxford University Press, 1984).

[4] Creon condemns Antigone to be walled up in a cave; she hangs herself; in his grief Creon's son Haemon, who was betrothed to Antigone, falls on his sword; and Eurydice, Creon's wife, commits suicide upon hearing of the death of her son.

the *polis* and reorganized it based on *demes,* which were geographically determined political entities. The proximity of the people within
the *deme* contributed to the making of a public space where the dialogue of political life could take place.

This change from family to political organization, from the privacy
of the clan to the public life of the *deme,* came on the heels of Solon's
reforms at the beginning of the sixth century B.C. Solon, the poet who
became chief magistrate, had not only codified the laws, he had
opened the possibility of the poorest of citizens sharing in the government of the state. Although he had been offered the role of tyrant,
Solon had chosen instead to aid the people in finding the middle
ground between the fiercely limiting order imposed by a tyranny and
the chaotic liberty of people without government. He made self-rule
(*auto nomos*) a reality in law, if not entirely in practice. It was to take
place in the public space between the people.

Every citizen, according to Athenian law, was permitted to participate in the public world of politics. Members of the most important
legislative body, the *boulē,* were chosen by lot—a constant, living
proof to the citizenry of the reality of the democracy and of the melding of thought and action through the medium of language. The
largest legislative body, the *ekkēsia,* comprised about one-fifth of all
the citizens. Together, the election by lot to the *boulē* and the size of
the *ekkēsia* gave the citizens of Athens the sense of legitimate power.

Once the legislative bodies were established, the citizens entered
the circle of power; all belonged to all, but only as long as the power
was active. Power could not be put aside or stored up like grain or the
materials of war; it existed only in practice, in the dialogues among
the thousands who crowded into the Pynx in Athens to debate the actions of the city; it existed only in the quieter deliberations of the
boulē, where the five hundred set the agenda for the great crowd of the
ekkēsia.

Power could be replaced by force in Athens: Thirty tyrants could
take over the rule of the polis. But power and force could not coexist
as equals; force could be a tool of power, but never its mate. Force
could be built up, stored like an army in waiting, but not power, for

power was like Socrates' understanding of language: The moment it stopped—in silence or the immutability of writing—it died.

The political life was properly termed the *vita activa* because it existed only in action, in the constant search for the place between order and liberty, which is politics, and also temperance.[5] The Greek word sophrosyne[6] is generally translated as temperance, but it also describes a moderate form of government and, in a person, self-control, discretion, sanity. Sophrosyne is a description of the state of mind of political life, but it has no place in private life. To achieve sophrosyne, an act that may be translated as "to come to one's senses," requires a plurality of possibilities; a private life offers no alternatives, no other, no possibility, as Aristotle would have it, to find the mean. In a private life there are no boundaries, as in dialogue, to bring the person to his senses.[7]

---

[5] For a discussion of the *vita activa,* see Hannah Arendt, *The Human Condition* (Chicago: University of Chicago Press, 1958).

[6] It is now also an English word. Among many others, I urged the OED to include sophrosyne in its new supplement, giving it equal place with hubris in the English language. On April 16, 1973, R. W. Burchfield was kind enough to write to me that "sophrosyne/sophrosune" would be included, "though our printed evidence is rather thin."

Cynthia Farrar tells us in her illuminating book, *The Origins of Democratic Thinking* (New York and London: Cambridge University Press, 1988), p. 182, that sophrosyne was understood quite differently by the Spartans, who connected self-control to courage.

Thucydides quotes Archidamus, king of the Lacedaemonians (Ch. III), in another connection to temperance: "We are both warlike and wise, and it is our sense of order that makes us so. We are warlike, because self-control contains honor as a chief constituent, and honor bravery. And we are wise, because we are educated with too little learning to despise the laws, and with too severe a self-control to disobey them. . . ."

[7] Cynthia Farrar writes of the role of politics: "Political validity is founded on a decision-making procedure, not on a divinely-ordained truth or order. This is part of the point of politics since . . . the gods may well demand conflicting things. Yet political deliberation cannot in itself *dissolve* a deep and tragic conflict between legitimate claims. . . . The political community must . . . absorb and domesticate conflict. . . ."—*The Origins of Democratic Thinking,* p. 36.

Negotiation over the conduct of the members of the group, the activity of political life, cannot take place in private; in modern societies, it is replaced by reaction, in the form of lethargy or force. In primitive societies, ritual did not permit the political life.

The Greeks often said a life of leisure was necessary to practice politics, but as Sarah Broadie explains in *Ethics with Aristotle*, leisure meant "to escape the pressure of necessity."[8] The concept of necessity meant something quite different to the Greeks than it does in common use today. When Aristotle used the word, he distinguished two kinds of necessity, only one of which did not include violence. Then, as now, to live according to the rule of necessity meant to live by the rule of force. In that situation, according to Aristotle, the political life was not possible.

Not that he thought politics was an easy life or a form of leisure, nor even that it was an end in itself, but the pressure of necessity was such that it pushed a person out of the *vita activa* into a grim existence in which the habits that led to happiness could not be practiced. He compared the life of necessity to slavery.

Perhaps no better definition can be made for poverty in contemporary America than to say it is the life of necessity, with all the violence the Greeks found in that word. To live in poverty, then, is to live according to the rules of force, which push people out of the free space of public life into the private concerns of mere survival.

When necessity rules, there is neither time nor energy to live the political life, to participate in the circle of power, for power, like the philosophy of Socrates, exists only in action; it is the doing of politics, and the moment it ceases it dies.

Long after the fall of Athens, the most political state of the ancient world, perhaps in all of history, came to flower in Rome. It was deeply affected by the Stoic philosophers, who imagined politics spreading beyond the city into a great brotherhood of man, an idea that lies behind Cicero's summation of the political life: "Men are born for each other."

---

[8] (New York: Oxford University Press, 1991), p. 421.

In that plainspoken sentence he tells us that politics is in the nature of human beings, that we are many, not one, public, not private, that we exist in the melding of speech and action, and that we are sufficiently temperate to live together, to absorb conflict through politics. It is his expansion of Aristotle's belief that man is a political animal, but it holds out no promise for those who are born, not for each other, but for the struggle to survive against the force of necessity.

Two thousand years after Cicero, in the richest nation in the history of the world, necessity has been redefined to include color television and hundred-dollar sneakers, but in light of the wealth of the nation, poverty has become as starkly relative as it was in the beginning of the modern world. There are many reasons for the inequality at the conclusion of the game in America, many explanations for the relativity of wealth, but it becomes clear when listening to the poor that politics and poverty do not share the same house.

IV.

The Golden Age of Poverty

AT THE END OF THE eighth century B.C. Hesiod, a wealthy aristocrat, lost his money and position as a result of a revolution in Boetia, and went into exile. Or so it is said; in truth, very little is known about Hesiod. He may not have been an aristocrat, but something happened to him, some fall that led him to invent the devastating notion of a Golden Age. There is evidence of this in his writings, where he rages against poverty, claiming that it "eats the heart out and destroys."

In his epic poem *Works and Days,* Hesiod confirms the notion of the modern world as a game when he speaks of gods and men beginning as equals, and then goes on to make the first clear exposition of the central myth of the poor of his time and ours:

> *And now with art and skill I'll summarize*
> *Another tale, which you should take to heart,*
> *Of how both gods and men began the same.*

The gods, who live on Mount Olympus, first
Fashioned a golden race of mortal men . . .
And like the gods they lived with happy hearts
Untouched by work or sorrow. Vile old age
Never appeared, but always lively-limbed,
Far from all ills, they feasted happily.
Death came to them as sleep, and all good things
Were theirs; ungrudgingly, the fertile land
Gave up her fruits unasked. Happy to be
At peace, they lived with every want supplied.

Then he spoke of "a lesser, silver race of men." And after them a race of bronze, "worse than the silver race." Then came the race of heroes, "the race before our own. Foul wars and dreadful battles ruined some. . . ."

After the race of heroes came "The fifth, who live now on the fertile earth. / I wish I were not of this race, that I / Had died before or had not yet been born." Men are now of the race of iron; they spend their days working and grieving, and at night, "they waste away and die."[1]

The idea of a Golden Age has a celebratory sense when applied to literature or movies, but it has a different meaning when it serves as the central myth of man. Hannah Arendt said that it "implies the rather unpleasant certainty of continuous decline." Hesiod intended a harsher view. He does not say exactly how these ages changed, but he makes it quite clear that man's fall from one age to the next-lower age was not of his own doing. An outside force, nothing less than the gods themselves, caused the fall.

Nearly three thousand years later, the poor in America embrace the same explanation of the world. If it seems an impossible stretch of the imagination to see similarities between Hesiod and an unemployed man in San Francisco or a woman in the South Bronx, listen to this tale of origins by a formerly homeless woman named Hyacinth: "My

---

[1] Hesiod, *Works and Days,* trans. Dorothea Wender (Harmondsworth, UK: Penguin Books, 1973), pp. 62–64.

grandfather bought this land—you'll excuse me—from a white man who thought he was selling him some no good land, but this land turned out to be big, so he lived on it and even had white sharecroppers who worked on it. And my grandfather had so much land even the sheriff had to ask his permission to come on the land. They had everything on the land, even a smokehouse for the pigs they killed, everything. Why, my momma never went into a big grocery store, like a supermarket, until she came up here to New York. Didn't have to. They had everything on the land.

"My momma was one of thirteen children; they all come up here.

"My grandmother could make anything. She could look at a picture of a wedding dress, no pattern, nothing, just a picture, and sew it just like the picture."

She went on to say that the farm was in Alabama, near Mobile. She named all the vegetables that grew on her grandfather's farm, and cotton, too. She said what the sharecroppers grew and picked, and again and again she told of the respect the white sheriff showed.

Yet Hyacinth could not explain why her mother and all her twelve siblings deserted the farm for New York City, or why her mother took to drink. And when I asked her, doing what seems in retrospect a cruelty, why she did not return to her grandfather's farm, she spoke of her mother again, of the clubs in New York City where she was lured by the fast life.

Hyacinth was not simply a liar, nor did she live in addict's dreams. She spoke with a recovering addict's frankness of her own troubles: She told how she had spent a week partying in a motel with a strange man who had a thousand dollars' worth of drugs. "Then he went back to his life," she said, "and left me with this addiction."

Her tale of the farm in Alabama followed the structure of Hesiod's tale of the decline from the Golden Age. Hyacinth's cruel gods were alcohol and crack cocaine. They had brought her down to the Iron Age, when she truly spent her days grieving, often wishing she had not been born.

The bones of Hesiod's tale and Hyacinth's dreamed history occur again and again among the poor. The structure of the myth is always the same: Plenitude—an act of force—poverty. It is not mere nostalgia, but it includes nostalgia; people feel homesick for the Golden Age.

Like Hesiod's tale, stories of a Golden Age need not be true in the sense that facts are true. They are metaphorical explanations of the history of the world as it made the life of the storyteller. The danger of them, as with all imagined truths, is that they are incontrovertible: Who can deny a metaphor? Once the poor accept the mythical explanation of their situation, it becomes the central myth of their lives, and to overcome it may be nearly impossible.

Having such a myth not only explains the world, it comforts in a cruel way by removing the poor from control and thus responsibility for their own lives. Who can overcome the will of the gods? Who can overcome history? It requires an act of hubris that inevitably ends in defeat or destruction, which of course is the notion of classical tragedy.

Among Americans with African ancestry the myth works perfectly to their detriment. Africa was paradise; slavers came and plucked people out of paradise, putting them into the worst of conditions, like Hesiod's men of iron. If there were no Golden Age in Africa, if blacks came up from slavery, the myth would have the same structure, but it would move in the opposite direction. As one would expect, blacks who have succeeded in America speak of coming up from slavery, while the poor, like Marcel Walton, a man in a dirty skullcap at the Pride Day Picnic in the K-Town area of the West Side of Chicago, preach the fall from the Golden Age.

For those who are not poor in a nation of immigrants the same structure serves, but in the opposite direction: They proceed from a difficult life through the force of their own moral will to a better life.[2] Who has not heard of people pulling themselves up by their

---

[2] Assimilation and multiculturalism do not appear to be predictive of wealth or poverty. In general, assimilation opens more opportunities than retention of an old country culture and language, but one may succeed without assimilating, as evidenced most recently by some Cubans, Hasidic Jews, West Indians, Pakistanis, and Russians. Members of these and other groups have established themselves in businesses and professions within a small community, or have limited their private lives to a small homogeneous community, with old country cultural traits, while

bootstraps? What is the story of America but the tale of upward mobility? Even the Pilgrims arrived with so little they had to depend on the largesse of savages to enjoy their first Thanksgiving, so says the myth.

The myths of rich and poor are homologous; one simply has to be turned upside down to show how it resembles the other. The United States may have been founded in a political revolution, but the central myth of America is economic. All Americans, rich and poor alike, subscribe to it. But the poor are ill served by the myth, while the rich are made to feel morally comfortable.

All through history the rich have used myths to control the poor while aggrandizing themselves. Consider the Calvinist notion of "the elect of God." It follows the same structure as Hesiod's tale; Calvin simply turned it upside down. Instead of the gods moving humans into continuously lower forms of life, the one God elects to take them into Heaven, which explains their good fortune on earth: A man becomes rich through God's election. Since such things are in God's hands, the poor may resign themselves to their lot.

This aspect of resignation, based on the comfort of the Golden Age myth, is not mere speculation. In discussing the nature of the American economy with a group of young adults, all of whom live at or near the poverty line, the common response to abject poverty, even slavery, is that some people can be happy under such conditions, but only when they think it is their lot in life; in other words, when they have a Golden Age myth to explain their situation.

Overcoming the myth—making melodrama rather than tragedy of a life, as Aristotle would have described it—demands a different worldview; that is, a new understanding of the central myth.

---

doing business with other Americans outside their communities. The economic danger in multiculturalism, when it leads to ghettos, is that outsiders will come into the cultural ghetto and drain the money from it. Banks, savings and loans, fast-food franchises, retailers of clothing, jewelry, and household goods have been the most frequent venturers into ghetto communities, with the banks causing two kinds of economic harm by taking money out of the ghettos and then redlining them when it comes to making loans to ghetto dwellers for housing or business.

In the past, social revolution has served—theoretically—to turn the myth on its head, the revolution taking the rule of force, and the goal being to turn the game of the modern world into a ritual, with the revolution as the unforgettable equalizing act. In states founded on such revolutions, like Mexico or the former Soviet Union or Cuba, remembrances of the revolution become the ritual.

The problem for the poor in a country where revolution is unlikely, if not impossible, is how to overturn the central myth. If they abandon the Golden Age, they lose the comfort of it, and if they hold on to the myth, they remain poor and in need of the comforting explanation. The effort to rise from multigenerational poverty, to break the double bind of the central myth, requires a heroic risk, one that often results in tragedy, for the courage of the valiant poor may be great, but it is the nature of myths to endure.

V.

The Surround of Force

THE GOLDEN AGE OF POVERTY, the central myth of the multigenerational poor in America, like all myths, has worldly origins. Force, which plays the determining role in the myth, holds the same key position in the daily lives of the poor. But without the revealing clarity of the myth, the role of force can be difficult to recognize:

First, there is not one force, there are many. Twenty-five different forces will be listed and put into context in the following pages, and the list could easily extend to thirty or forty.

Second, the observer's distance from them transfigures the lives of the poor: Their own acts of force become salient, while the forces that act on them fade into the background. It is exactly the reverse of the beautifying effect of distance on New York or Chicago viewed from an airplane at night.

Third, observers look from the wrong direction: the forces that act on the poor often come from the direction of the observer. Attempting to look at the poor in what we think of as objective fashion, i.e., from the wrong direction, requires a certain arrogance and invariably leads to deceptions. In the case of the multigenerational poor, it leads to the appearance of the poor bringing their troubles on themselves.

Fourth, forces do not exist in the abstract. Like transitive verbs, they need objects to make sense; objects are the human context that makes them understandable.

Fifth, recognizing the forces that act on the poor often entails counterintuitive thinking; for example, helpers, social services, marriage, and the law do not usually present themselves as negative forces.

Sixth, it may not be to the advantage of the observer to understand the role of force in the lives of the poor, because it would change his or her understanding of the way the game of inequality is conducted.

Finally, the observer may think that force is something else entirely, because force can have various meanings, ranging from the definition used in the physical sciences to that used by the military and the police. Force is sometimes used as a synonym for power or violence, but that leads to confusion, as in the work of the early twentieth-century Marxist Georges Sorel.[1] In relation to multigenerational poverty, force has a clear and specific meaning, which distinguishes it from violence to a large extent and places it in opposition to power. Moreover, force initiates a predictable and circular pattern of response not unlike the one Michel Foucault describes for prison inmates in Discipline and Punish.[2]

Force is not negotiable, nor can the object of force agree with it; the object can only succumb or react. Although force need not be physical, it produces the same state in the object as physical threats or acts and an equally limited choice of responses. A bureaucracy, which Hannah Arendt calls the "rule of nobody," exemplifies force in modern society. The bureaucracy does not use violence to exert control, but it

---

[1] Isaiah Berlin said of Sorel: "How the use of violence in practice can be distinguished from the use of force is never made clear." *Against the Current* (New York: Viking Press, 1980), p. 322.

[2] (Paris: Gallimard, 1975; first American edn, New York: Pantheon, 1978).

does not permit negotiation. Some bureaucracies have elaborate appeals systems through which they feign negotiation, but everyone who deals with bureaucracies soon learns that the force they exert is non-negotiable.

Force cannot be withdrawn once the act has been done; the arrow cannot be returned to the bow and the word cannot be unspoken. Like the arrow loosed or the word said, force occurs, and everything that follows is contingent.

Unlike argument, which has a dialectical shape, involving thesis and antithesis, and lies at the heart of political life at all levels of society, force closes off dialogue. It is not like the endless rope of social discourse; force presents itself as a wall.[3]

Since force can neither be negotiated nor withdrawn, it cannot occupy a middle ground. In an abusive marriage, for example, the man tells the woman, "You're an ugly whore." He cannot, like a congressman or a corporate officer, say, "I misspoke," nor can the man and woman find a middle ground, such as, "You're ugly, but chaste." Similarly, once it occurs, the experience of eviction cannot be withdrawn, and there is no middle ground between eviction and occupancy; the door is either open or closed.

Isolation, racism, theft, insult, disease, hunger, fear are all forces, and none can be withdrawn after they are loosed. Nor can they be negotiated. Diseases can be cured, but a person either has AIDS or asthma or high blood pressure or he doesn't. Racism is, by definition, immoderate. A television set cannot be more or less stolen. Insults and imprecations do not lend themselves to negotiation (a person cannot be slightly damned), and silence is not an antidote: The wordlessness of isolation, which also leaves no middle ground in which to execute human maneuvers, may be one of the most dreadful of all the many forces people use against each other.

The exertion of force happens so frequently that it might appear to be part of what defines us as human, but that is not the case: various

---

[3] In Chapter VIII it will be shown that the function of this sometimes metaphorical, but often very real, wall is to exclude the poor from the life of the citizen.

species use force as well as violence to maintain their existence. Everyone has seen films of lions and wolves and so on in which they use force, in the form of shaming, isolation, threats of violence, or withholding food, to manage the pride or pack. What distinguishes us from the other species is that we have an alternative to force, not that we so often employ force instead of killing.

1. Force and Violence

When force and violence are confused, as in the work of Georges Sorel, who said that force was used by oppressors and violence by the oppressed, the moral value of the concepts seems to get lost. Sorel argued at one point that violence was everywhere, using the police as an example. But it made no sense within Sorel's larger definition, for the police were employed by the oppressors, who used force; violence belonged to the oppressed, it was their form of resistance.[4] Sorel's confusion of means and motives—giving the same act a different name and moral value according to who committed it—may not have been his only error, but he eventually lost control of his ideas about labor, creativity, and violence, and descended into fascism and anti-Semitism.

The temptation to differentiate force from violence according to an ethical prescription did not die with Georges Sorel. In the movies, television, and the press, violence continues to be associated with the poor while force belongs to the rich; and just as Sorel can be a villain or a hero to those on the left or on the right, the poor appear as violent in *The Nation* and *The National Review* while force belongs to "the establishment" according to both ends of the spectrum.

---

[4] Sorel believed that violence would lead the producers (the oppressed) back to a Golden Age like the one that existed before Plato and Aristotle and all the "corrupt intellectuals" ruined the world of creativity. Although I am not sufficiently conversant with the genesis of Sorel's Golden Age theory to make a judgment, it appears that he adopted the structure common among the multigenerational poor—the oppressed producers, in his view.

A recent case of the confusion of motives with means can be found in the pronouncements of Louis Farrakhan, the leader of the Nation of Islam. Farrakhan deplores racism when blacks are the objects, but adopts racist language and tactics when speaking of Jews. Like Sorel, he wants to believe that the same act is moral in one situation but not in another. Interestingly enough, Farrakhan seems to be following Sorel in his interest in fascism, which may grow out of the same confusion: In 1996 Louis Farrakhan traveled to Africa and the Middle East, visiting, embracing, and soliciting money and moral support from Fascist regimes in Nigeria, Libya, Iraq, and Iran.

Instead of moral origins, which can only lead to confusion, force and violence should be defined as they appear in the world. In other words, if a striking worker shoots a capitalist or a policeman hired by a capitalist shoots a worker, it is an act of violence. On the other hand, if the capitalist locks out the workers or the workers close down the plant with a picket line, it is an act of force. The motive does not define the act and the act does not imply the motive.

Force describes a condition in which a person or group of persons coerces another. In most cases, force is an ongoing relation in which the one who exerts the force compels or obliges the object to behave as the forceful person wishes.

Violence is a kind of force, a subset in the logical sense; it is quick, physical, savage, and of furious intensity. Violence or the threat of violence accompanies virtually every act of force; it is the physical strength that gives force its authority.

Force constrains its object, defining the object and his or her life condition; it creates suffering and pain through demeaning the object, debasing and shaming him. Violence does not constrain or shame its objects, it is not ongoing. Violence strikes; it has echoes but no duration. Murder is an act of violence. Imprisonment is an act of force.

Some acts prove more difficult to define; hunger, for example. It has many of the characteristics of violence, but it does not become violent unless it is an ongoing condition. Missing dinner does not constitute violence; going to bed hungry every night does terrible violence.

Since violence is a subset of force, force and violence must be essentially the same, even if they are formally distinct. Once we know the essence, the two acts become homologous: The one who exerts the force or does the violence is the subject and the other is the object. The subject creates, defines, controls, and the object reacts, accepts, obeys.

Here again distinctions can be troublesome, but not impossible. Who is the subject of ill health? When the cause is malnutrition or toxic waste or unsanitary conditions, the subject is clear. When the amount of salt in the drinking water of the city of Greenville, Mississippi, is five times the national average and the incidence of disease caused by hypertension is greater than the national average, there truly is no subject. The subject/object relation here comes in the nature of health care. The lack of medical insurance is a force, and the subject of that force is not only known, it appears to be proud of its role.[5]

Force seems most often to be the work of institutions and government and violence the work of individuals, but the distinction does not hold in all instances. The rogue cop who kills an innocent child represents a group, as does the rioter who shoots a cop in the street. We may think of one group as heroic and the other as villainous, but no matter which side we choose, it is a side, a group that can be defined and counted.

The moral distinction between force and violence does not hold when Sorel makes it from the left or when Charles Murray and Ken Auletta make it from the right. Violence does not belong to the poor any more than force belongs to the rich. Power is another matter.

---

[5] I refer, of course, to those members of the U.S. Congress and the various state legislatures who want to reduce medical care for people in the bottom economic quintiles, whether they are working or receiving entitlements. Legal immigrants were advised early in 1997 that they were no longer eligible for SSI payments. About 1 million people suddenly found their meager benefits cut to zero.

2. Force and Power

The Pueblos of the American Southwest drew a clear distinction between force and power, according to the historian Ramón A. Gutiérrez.[6] The Inside Chiefs held power in the form of authority granted to them by the gods and the members of the pueblo.[7] Within the pueblo itself, neither acts of violence nor any other acts of force were permitted. A second group lived outside the pueblo. These were the warlike Outside Chiefs and their band of hunter/warriors. Although the Outside Chiefs had the greater physical strength and ability, the Inside Chiefs held the power of the pueblo. They directed the Outside Chiefs to hunt, make war, and defend the pueblo using whatever force was required. The Outside Chiefs could not conduct raids, hunt, or even defend the pueblo without the consent of the Inside Chiefs.

Using this convention, the Pueblos were able literally to maintain a wall between force and power. It was this Pueblo wall that led some early and very romantic anthropologists to think the Pueblos were pacifists when, in fact, they had developed something even more important: the ability to separate force and power.

In modern democratic societies, at least since Periclean Athens, the distinction has been as clear as the Pueblo wall. Force remains an instrument of power, a means. Legitimate power is still an end in itself, a way of living, and force can never be an end, only a means. Force can serve as an instrument of power, as in the case of the Pueblos, but power can never serve force. When there is no legitimate power, however, force fills the vacuum.

Power differs from force in that it is self-contained, both the subject and the object. Force is always lonely, while power never occurs in isolation; one person alone among others cannot have legitimate power. At the extremes, ultimate force is one against all, as in a tyrant

---

[6] *When Jesus Came, the Corn Mothers Went Away* (Stanford, CA: Stanford University Press, 1991).

[7] Cicero described this as "power in the public [or people], authority in the senate."

against the people, while ultimate power is all against one, as in the people against a tyrant.

Force increases by destroying the humanity of its object, but power, having no object or other, can only grow by inclusion. If force and power were turned into simple illustrations, power would appear as a circle and force would be an arrow.

In the abstract, some of the conditions in which the poor live seem pleasant enough. What could be the force in neighbors or luck or law? For the rest of society, pregnancy is a blessing, law is a protection, helpers are appreciated. But in the context of poverty, everything changes.

Twenty-six of the forces that affect the poor are listed below. None of these should be considered alone, for the poor do not often deal with one force or two or half a dozen. They live in a surround of force, which differentiates them from those inside the circle of power and determines the outcome of the game.

Instinctively one thinks of a surround, any enclosure, as forcing people together, binding them, like the casing of a sausage or a belt around a bale of cotton. If that were the case, the surround would be the genesis of political life, a kind of polis created by force in which the poor would live public lives. But the forces of the surround do not affect the poor, they affect poor persons, not even families, but persons, one at a time. Everyone who lives within the surround lives alone. The weight of the forces separates them, splintering the body of the poor like glass underfoot, driving the shards of family, community, society into feckless privacy.

3. The Surround

Force is used not by those who have
become weak under the preponderance
of the strong, but by the strong
who have emasculated them.

—PAOLO FREIRE,
The Pedagogy of the Oppressed

Public Housing   Hunger   Helpers   Luck

Other Men's Eyes: Intellectual Muggings   Feudalism   Law

Guns   Hurrying & Pressure   Isolation

Government   Family Violence

Neighbors   Graffiti

Landlords | THE POOR | Meanness

Drugs   Prison

Criminals   Illness

Other Men's Eyes: Media   Other Men's Eyes: Racism

Police   Selling   Abuse   Ethnic Antagonisms

In America before the Europeans and the Africans came, the natives hunted and made war using the same tactic: the surround. Buffalo, deer, small game, and human enemies could be killed or captured most efficiently within a surround. Isolated, with no place to turn, no place to run, they panicked, and then the killing began. Over the course of history many variations of the surround have been employed in killing. The pincer movement is among the best known of the military tactics, but any plan that prevents the escape of the enemy, or even reduces the enemy's ability to maneuver, is likely to produce a victory.

The Germans nearly changed the course of World War II by using that tactic during the Battle of the Bulge. If Patton's tanks had not arrived or the weather had not cleared, permitting air drops, the German surround would have annihilated an important American military force.

Sometimes a wall, a mountain range, a river, or a cliff will serve as part of a surround: the Jews at Masada and the native people of Illinois at Starved Rock capitulated to cliffs. And not only humans use the surround. Wolf packs kill that way, and so do other predators. The tactic has two advantages: First, of course, it isolates the prey and eliminates the possibility of escape; but perhaps more importantly, it changes the behavior of the animals or humans caught inside the surround. The moment the prey recognizes the surround, it becomes desperately lonely, raging or suicidal, unable to think. With no hope of escape, it succumbs to the notion of fate; the modicum of hubris that enables a person to rebel against the deadly promise of fate dies at the instant of recognition of the surround. Only the heroic do not die, and they are few.

VI.

The Mirror of Force

*. . . this irrepressible violence is
neither sound and fury, nor the
resurrection of savage instincts, nor
even the effect of resentment: it is
man recreating himself.*

—JEAN-PAUL SARTRE,
Preface to Frantz Fanon,
The Wretched of the Earth

1. The Problem of Anomie

WITHIN THE SURROUND OF FORCE, people live in poverty and panic. They scurry, going from place to place, looking for food, a new apartment, medical care for a child. The iron wall of the surround pens them into a limited area, but the panic inside the surround has no limits; they may do nothing and everything, suffering from excesses of both order and liberty.

This state of affairs, in which the rules of life make no sense, currently has no widely accepted name or clear definition. "The underclass" will not do, for it is more pejorative than descriptive. There is a word, however, which has a history, both ancient and modern, and goes a long way toward clarifying what happens within the surround.

A hundred years ago, Emile Durkheim revived a Greek word *anomia,* meaning "lawlessness" or "negation of law."[1] Anomia has a cousin in language, anomiletos, which means "having no connection with others, unsociable." It is also useful to keep in mind the context of this revival: Durkheim's famous study, *Suicide.*

Durkheim said that anomic suicide "results from man's activity's lacking regulation and his consequent sufferings." This happened, he said, during crises, especially economic crises. But he did not limit such crises to declines in a person's fortunes. Sudden improvements could also lead to anomie. It is the disjunction between a person's desires and abilities that brings about the crisis, according to Durkheim: "No living being can be happy or even exist unless his needs are sufficiently apportioned to his means."

It is restraint, regulation, that is lacking in a state of anomie, he declared. Dire poverty does not lead to anomic suicide, because "it is a restraint in itself." Durkheim gave the examples of Ireland, Calabria, and Spain, all very poor areas at the end of the nineteenth century, and concluded, "nothing excites envy if no one has superfluity."[2]

Anomie, the crisis that precipitates suicide, occurred in the case of relative poverty, but not when poverty was absolute. Durkheim's theory proved out in the North Lawndale district of Chicago, which remained tightly organized and political during the Great Depression, but has become a classic case of anomie at the end of the twentieth century when television daily drives home the relative nature of poverty.

Half a century later, Robert Merton revised Durkheim's definition, continuing to understand it as the inability to accommodate desires to the means for satisfying them, but introducing the idea of anomie as the result of failing to conform. Merton showed how peo-

---

[1] *Anomia* translates into the English "anomie" or "anomy"; both spellings are acceptable.

[2] Emile Durkheim, *Suicide* (New York: The Free Press, 1951), pp. 254, 258. The first quotation is correct; the infelicity is the work of the translator.

ple adapt to anomie, however, describing theft, for example, as an innovative way to satisfy a desire by abandoning legitimate means. He also described drug use as a retreat from the desire to achieve goals.

While Merton said anomie was the result of the inability of people to achieve the American dream of success at the end of the 1950s, others were beginning to use the word in conjunction with juvenile delinquency. Anomie was becoming the crisis rather than a reaction to crisis.

In its new incarnation, anomie became a synonym for the underclass and the culture of poverty. In both the underclass and the culture of poverty, the poor, especially the young, did not obey laws or behave according to accepted social norms. The connection of anomie to suicide faded into the background and Merton's innovation—crime—came to the fore.

Life within the surround, however, began to lose its likeness to the world Durkheim or even Merton used as a basis for understanding anomie. The game of modern society continued to produce unequals, but the crisis in many parts of the country had become endemic: The multigenerational poor lost before they could even attempt to compete; for many poor people the crisis was born with them, and ongoing. Still, it differed from life in absolute poverty. In America, every poor person knew he or she was poor in comparison to Bill Cosby or Donald Trump, the corporate executive Michael Jordan or the basketball player of the same name; every poor person knew that somebody could buy new sneakers or an automobile or a house in the country—in fact, according to television programs and advertisements, practically everyone but the real losers could afford such things.

This kind of ongoing crisis had less connection to the rest of America than to the colonies of the Third World, those places where relative poverty is expressed in the relation of natives to settlers (or conquerors) rather than to each other. In 1961, a young psychiatrist from the island of Martinique, Frantz Fanon, published his view of life within the surround of force as it was lived in Algeria under French colonial rule, *The Wretched of the Earth*. A preface to Fanon's book, written by Jean-Paul Sartre, elaborated on some of Fanon's observations about the character of life within the colonial surround. Addressing Fanon, he wrote, "You said they understand nothing but violence? Of course; first, the only violence is the settler's; but soon they will make it their own; that is to say, the same violence is thrown back upon us as when our reflection comes forward to meet us when we go toward a mirror."[3]

Sartre had found the beginning of an endless series of reflections: the mirror of force. The response to force, as Sartre read it in Fanon, was exactly as Hannah Arendt and others understood it: "If he shows fight, the soldiers fire and he's a dead man; if he gives in, he degrades himself and he is no longer a man at all; shame and fear will split up his character and make his inmost self fall to pieces."[4]

The third option, to use greater force to overcome the oppressor, is the advice of Fanon and Sartre to colonialized peoples. Fanon the psychiatrist argued from this third alternative that man re-creates himself through violence, adding yet one more to the standard list of such re-creations: Christians hold that man re-creates himself through the love of God; Hegel thought it happens through the power of mind; Marx said labor was the way. The Greek concept of autonomy may also be considered a means for man to re-create himself.

Fanon spoke of violence as a unifying force on the national level and "At the level of individuals . . . a cleansing force. It frees the native from his inferiority complex and from his despair and inaction; it makes him fearless and restores his self-respect."[5]

In his comments on Fanon, Sartre recognized one other aspect of violence: "If this suppressed fury fails to find an outlet, it turns in a vacuum and devastates the oppressed creatures themselves. In order to free themselves they even massacre each other. The different tribes fight against themselves since they cannot find the real enemy. . . ."[6] In the United States, this is the only possible response for the poor. They cannot mirror force with overwhelming force. Even if Sartre's no-

---

[3] Frantz Fanon, *The Wretched of the Earth* (Paris: François Maspero, 1961), Preface by Jean-Paul Sartre, p. 17.

[4] Ibid., p. 15.

[5] Ibid., p. 94.

[6] Ibid., p. 18.

tion of man re-creating himself through violence in a colonial situation was reasonable, it would not apply in the United States. Even if the poor are considered an internal colony, they cannot re-create themselves through feeble acts of violence against their powerful oppressors; they can only turn the violence against each other and themselves, isolating themselves from each other and the world, inviting a lonely death.

A structure of force begins to emerge:

In a society that operates like a game, turning equals into unequals, the crisis of change produces a state of anomie where the rules fail to hold.

The poor, those who lose in the game of modern society, are thrust into a surround of force. Inside the surround, they experience anomie: panic is limitless action within a surround, but the surround ruthlessly limits the freedom of its objects by enclosing them. In other words, there are no constants within the surround, no reason, no stability, and no rules; there is only force.

The one who experiences force within the surround mirrors it; that is, the object of force reacts instantly, at the speed of light, if you will, like an image in a mirror. And there can be virtually no end to these reactions. As in any set of facing mirrors, the images bounce up and back to infinity.

When those inside the surround cannot effectively mirror the force exerted on them, they turn it on themselves; they become the object of their own rage: Durkheim's anomic suicide, Merton's innovation (theft) or retreat (drugs), and Sartre's devastation of the oppressed. Of these, drug addiction, which has lately been described as "self-medication," comes closest to a pure act of suicide. Drug addiction generally includes both the death of the conscious rational person that occurs following the administration of the drug, and immersion in a drug culture, which may lead to actual death resulting from a drug overdose, disease, violent confrontation, or a dealer/customer relationship more like indentured servitude than a business exchange.

Since the poor are rarely able to turn the tables on their antagonists in America, to mirror force with force, the keystone of the structure is the act of suicide, which takes many forms: drug addiction, alcoholism, poor-on-poor crime, or withdrawal from society into slavery, gangs, cults, homelessness, hypersexuality, violence, or depression.

The alternative to life within the structure is to create a new structure—one that interferes with the mirror of force at its inception. It too begins with reflection, but of a very different kind, one that leads to the light of political life rather than the darkness of self-destruction. Man, who enters the world alone, more fearful than any other creature, has but this one opportunity to re-create himself in the modern, secular world; that is, to go among men, which the Romans thought of as a description of life itself. It is this going among men, this profound step out of the private world into the public space in which politics occurs that enables the lonely organism to re-create itself as political man, the one who participates in governing himself.

2. The Example of the Prison

The surround of force appears in a highly evolved miniature in the prison. It begins at the outer boundary of the institution with the wall, which may be made of stone or concrete, rising to the height of the rooftops and beyond, or constructed of chain-link fence and razor wire. The force represented by the wall is enhanced by the guard towers and the men who stand watch with weapons loaded and ready, threatening the prisoners with the violence of the rifles and automatic weapons while constantly exerting the force of surveillance.[7]

---

[7] During the 1995–96 academic year, I spent some hours in the Bedford Hills Correctional Facility in Bedford Hills, Westchester, N.Y., teaching a course in the humanities. Bedford Hills is a maximum-security prison for women. It is a model institution, run by Elaine Lord, one of the most enlightened prison superintendents in the United States. An extraordinarily intelligent woman now serving a life sentence there said, "If I have to be in the joint, this is where I want to be." Nevertheless, Bedford Hills is a prison. Many of the redbrick buildings are very old, some of them built in the nineteenth century. The heat is poor in many of the units. Ice forms on the walls of some of the cells in winter.

Some of the ironies of prison life, even in this prison, are nearly unbearable.

Prison operates as the purest surround of force. Inside the prison every inmate lives in panic, unable to discover a single face to present to the world. The prisoner who turns force against force at one moment, acts as a supplicant the next; growling and making a show of teeth in the morning, and in the afternoon peeping in a mendicant's voice and humbled stance. The demeanor of the prisoner, the set of his shoulders, the timbre of his voice, betrays the shift from one reaction to the other. And the reaction is always quick, almost instantaneous: suicide or murder; submit and be destroyed, attack and be destroyed.

Within such an anti-political world, the solution suggested by Fanon and Sartre makes sense to the prisoner. Even the confused terms and definitions of Sorel come to have a certain clarity. Violence seems the only rational as well as the only emotional response appropriate to the situation. Anything else requires a surrender to fatalism or an otherworldly martyrdom.

No prisoner dares to trust another, even if they are of the same "family" or they are long-term sexual partners; the only relation is to those who are in control, the hierarchy of force. And in such circumstances, the prisoner may only resist and be punished or submit to the ongoing punishment. Deceit would appear, at first, to offer a way out of the dilemma, but it is merely a form of submission.

All the prisoner sees is hierarchical, force responding to greater

---

Judith Clark wrote of one such irony in a prize-winning poem describing the construction of death row on top of the nursery where the children of inmates are raised until they are eighteen months old.

Women's prisons are far less violent than the prisons for men, but the separation of women from their small children is in itself an ongoing act of terrible force. Women are less likely than men to force each other to endure sexual acts, but the rape of female prisoners by male guards is a commonplace. In an extraordinary case at the Bedford Hills prison in Westchester, a woman who was forced to perform fellatio on a guard held his semen in her mouth until she could spit it out into a cup and bring it to the guard's superiors as incontrovertible evidence of the act and the identity of the attacker.

force. In a prison setting legitimate power does not exist, since power must be given willingly by those within the circle, and there is no circle, only a rigid hierarchy of force. There can be no public life in a prison, only the privacy of isolation within the surround of force. No model of the *vita activa* exists within the prison.

The person who leaves the prison knows less about politics, if that is possible, than he or she did upon being forced inside the wall. When the prisoner finally goes outside the wall, the experience of prison has sealed him inside the surround. He is poor, an ex-prisoner, and inexperienced in the art of politics, condemned to loneliness and the bitter speed of the reactive life. By destroying their political life, the prison farms the poor, raising its own crop of prisoners through recidivism and infection.

The prison world not only mirrors the world of the poor, there is a constant exchange of persons, language, and style between the prison and the poor. Among non-whites—and to a lesser extent among whites—the prison system, which extends out into the community through the probation and parole officers, the courts, the police, and the criminals, exerts force against every person, beginning with young children.[8]

When a person enters a prison, the sudden fall, the situation Durkheim said would produce anomie, takes place. In terms of relative poverty, nothing drives the point home more effectively than the restriction of the prison. Inside the walls, prisoners speak of "the free world" that is denied them. To counter the anomic state of the prisoner, the prison exerts terrible and constant force through surveillance and punishments; the suicides of prisoners take place in symbolic fashion, in the form of drug use or depression.

When a person leaves a prison, the sudden rise creates another spawning place for anomie, and in the world outside the prison nothing can counter the anomic urge so well as politics, for politics is the

---

[8] As it moves deeper into American society, the prison system seems to me to be an increasingly important aspect of racism.

polar opposite of anomie. But the prisoner comes out of the prison with no sense of politics, a creature of isolation, jobless, penniless, confused by the sudden shift in the kinds of force that form the surround. It would be difficult to imagine a more perfectly anomic situation. In effect, the prison system has exported anomie to the outside world, seeded it again among the poor, whom it farms to produce more clients.

VII.

The Fallacy of Work

WORK! The word has a good, solid, Old English sound. It is as blunt as the Protestant Ethic, as stern as a strap, as good as gruel on an icy morning. Work! Verb or noun, it grunts the old values, before Marx and FDR, before babies having babies and rock 'n' roll. Work is what good people do. And its opposite is sin: Sloth! Idle hands . . . Welfare queens.

Work is not only good for the pocketbook, it soothes the soul and brings order to the mind. "Work itself," said Mickey Kaus, not money, but work itself will cure the poor of their moral ailments and rid the nation of the last vestiges of the welfare system. Work itself, the slogan of the Protestant Ethic, has caught the imagination of Americans. Everyone in power in America has heard the message. The President of the United States wanted to "end welfare as we know it." Since Mr. Clinton signed the Welfare Reform Bill, vast numbers of people have left the system. Some have simply been lost to the view of the investigators. Others have gone from welfare to work and become even poorer.

The numbers of people who were getting poorer because of being denied welfare so that they might work had begun to be documented by late 1999. According to the House Ways and Means Committee, the poorest families headed by single mothers had been losing money by going to work. Quoted in the *New York Times* of August 25, 1999, Ron Haskins, the staff director, said that on average the poorest 20 percent lost $577 a year and the poorest 10 percent lost $814 a year. The victims of welfare reform who suffer most are, of course, the poorest children in the country. The number of people receiving food stamps declined from 88 percent in 1995 to 55.9 in 1998. Many have been dropped from the welfare rolls, but when the truly draconian time limit of five years is applied in 2001, the number of children who will go hungry, without proper clothing or shelter or medical care, will tax the imagination. The moral issue raised here is whether the hunger of children or the idleness of single mothers is the greater affront to man and God.

All other moral questions seem to disappear before the work ethic. The chain gang, that sermon in the southern sun, has come back.[1] Women on workfare in New York City have reported being denied bathroom privileges for as long as eight hours. The governor of Wisconsin has experimented with forcing people to work by making the alternative unbearable; other governors have instituted similar plans. Workfare is a national craze, like the mambo or the macarena. At the end of the twentieth century, work is the popular response of God and man to both the bleating and the rage of the poor.

But what of a family like the Weedens of Greenville, Mississippi? By working nights on a gambling boat anchored off Greenville, Mississippi, Robert Weeden earns a little over the minimum wage. His wife works, too, in a fast-food restaurant. And they have devised a schedule that spares them the cost of child care. Yet they are deep in poverty. How is it that they have been so badly beaten in the game of American life? What moral flaw has thrown them into the surround of force?

---

[1] Alabama, the first state to use the chain gang again, stopped the practice in June 1996.

Work does not guarantee the Weedens even a steady diet of rice and beans augmented with pork fat and bread. The problem for them, like most of the working poor, is that there are many hungers. After the Weedens pool their wages, they simply do not have enough to live on. Take the rent, the electric bill, his child support payment, the mandatory school uniforms, gasoline, shoes, soap, toothpaste, medicine, socks, and underwear out of Robert and Barbara Weeden's $1,100 monthly net income, and what is left for food? A hundred dollars a week to feed six people? They have never had that much.[2]

A budget so divided makes the final hunger a controlling force, not only on the day when the last item in the pantry has been eaten, but on all the other days leading up to the crisis. A budget attempts to reduce the pain by spreading it out over all the days. In that way, hunger takes only a little from the plate every day, but hunger takes it every day, even the day when the restaurant or the clothing factory or the fish-processing plant or the lady of the house passes out the checks.

The work ethic belongs in the realm of theory; it proposes that the world conform to an abstraction: work for its own sake. The theoreticians of the work ethic claim this abstraction has divine inspiration and high moral purpose, but in reality it is a strategy for playing

---

[2] Their annual net income of $13,200 (their earnings minus Social Security, Workmens Comprehensive Insurance, child support, etc.) left the Weedens well below the federal poverty line, which was $15,600 for a family of four in 1996. The increase in the minimum wage passed in 1966 would not be sufficient to bring the Weedens out of poverty.

A response to this problem of the working poor has begun on the local level. In Baltimore, Milwaukee, Santa Clara County in California, and other local jurisdictions, a "living-wage movement" has led to raised minimum wages for a small number of employees of city or county contractors to $6 an hour and up, according to the *New York Times* (April 9, 1996). In most instances, so far, the minimums apply only to direct contractors, not to their suppliers. In one city, the minimums are in effect only for contractors to the school district.

The living-wage movement was spurred by the Industrial Areas Foundation (IAF) and churches affiliated with it. The IAF, begun by Saul Alinsky, is a politically liberal, often socially conservative, organization, operating in both urban and rural areas throughout the United States.

the game of modern society. Whatever its genesis, moral or economic, the work ethic is intended to modify the behavior of those who have fallen from equality and to increase the gap between winners and losers.

In order to put the theory of the work ethic into practice, its champions have been forced by the secular nature of America at the end of the century to abandon much of the argument of divine inspiration that was so useful in earlier centuries, and turn instead to self-interest and common sense. The common-sense argument for work is that it will provide an adequate economic and social life for a person and his or her family. But in many cases it does not.

Since the theory of the work ethic has such currency again in America, especially as a cure-all for the problems of the poor, it is imperative that the social, economic, and moral character of work be considered from the point of view of the poor rather than from the God's-eye view of the makers of theory. It may be that "work itself" does not solve the problem of poverty when the rules of the game are so well known as in contemporary America. Work itself may not offer a way out of the surround or the means to survive within it. Perhaps the poor are unable to work or do not know how to work; life in the surround may teach habits of reaction to force that put the political world of work beyond the reach of the poor.

Economic questions about work are not new. Karl Marx wrote about the value of labor and who got to enjoy it, and labor unions organized workers by teaching politics and economics to people whose jobs were still conducted according to the ancient rule of capitalism, which was to pay the workers only as much as was necessary to keep them alive so they could continue to work.

Marx's labor theory of value does not explain much in a world of global outsourcing of labor and other kinds of international competition, but the effect of unions on the lives of working people may be an important clue to the failure of work itself to solve the problems of poverty. A union is first a political, then an economic organization; without its political basis, a union could not conduct collective bargaining. Although it is almost always an economic issue that opens people to the process of political organizing, collective bargaining cannot begin without a collective.

The lives of the working poor raise several questions about the work ethic in contemporary America: Who is served by the work ethic? Does work performed for other people, even if the work is not done alone, constitute a political life? Or is work, in the case of the poor, those at the bottom of the dual labor market, another force in the enclosing surround? Current theories of the value of "work itself" impose work on the poor; these theories assume that the imposition of work will be an act of force, necessary for an unruly mob of poor people. Can people who already live according to the rules of force accept work under such conditions as anything other than more force, adding to a vicious circle—force, reaction, force, reaction, force—in which the moral character of satisfying work can have no role?

For a long time it was thought that the problem of poverty was mainly structural; i.e., as soon as there were enough jobs for everyone, the number of people living in poverty would decline. But the unemployment rate at the end of the twentieth century was barely more than 4 percent, the economists worried about the low rate of unemployment bringing about inflation, and there were still 34 million Americans living in poverty (using the low threshold income—47 million at the new number suggested by the National Academy of Science and being considered by the Census Bureau) all year round and perhaps an equal number who moved in and out of poverty during the year.

Work does not appear to be the structural solution to poverty, particularly multigenerational poverty, and it has not been entirely successful as the alternative to hunger and homelessness for those who are cut from the welfare rolls. What is to be done?

As the new threshold income figure recognizes, children need shoes and doctors and the ability now and then to satisfy the insistence of the salespeople who control their dreams. And everyone must eat. Some way must also be found to combat the loneliness of life within the surround of force, to ease the panic that makes society impossible. Work itself cannot solve such problems; at less than a living wage, work is no antidote to force, it is merely force in the form most useful to those with power.

Work itself has no moral influence. Acquiescence to superior force is not what Aristotle meant by a good habit; ethics does not mean defeat.

The problem with work, as viewed by the world of thoughtful people, comes as much in the definition of the word as in the set of tasks itself. Work has come to mean, even to those with the best intentions and the largest, most competent staffs of researchers and analysts, work like the work they do. It follows logically to them that such work will produce lives like the lives they live. But there is no reason to expect that life within a surround of force will ever be like that of the world of the university or the foundation or the House of Representatives.

Those who want to solve the problem of poverty through work will have to take a different view of the lives of the poor—black, white, brown, and Asian—if they want to use a just alternative to "end welfare as we know it." Work must, of course, be the greatest part of the antidote to poverty, but work within the surround of poverty is disorderly. The force of such work produces force in response, increasing the panic of the poor within the surround; the worker is not rebellious, merely unruly. The result of the panic cannot be moral, for the frame of mind of morality begins from temperance and panic is not a temperate state.

This does not mean that poverty is permanent, as in a culture of poverty. The role of force in the life of the poor points to a different antidote—one that includes work, but is not so limited or so wishful on the surface and exploitive at the core as "work itself." The poor do not suffer from sloth or indolence, but from force. If the antidote to force can be found, work will follow, if there is work to be done.

VIII.

Citizenship by Exclusion

*Hence it is evident that the state is a creation of
nature, and that man is by nature a political
animal. And he who by nature and not by mere
accident is without a state, is either a bad man or
above humanity; he is like the "Tribeless, lawless,
heartless one" whom Homer denounces—the
natural outcast is forthwith a lover of war; he
may be compared to an isolated piece at draughts.*

— ARISTOTLE,
Politics, Bk. I

1

THE WATTS RIOT was the first of a series of explosions of the
poor in the last third of the century—Chicago, Detroit, Atlanta. At
first, most of the rioters were black, but as the century neared its end,
a different pattern emerged: In the riots that broke out in response to
the verdict in the trial of the white police officers who beat Rodney

King, as many as half or even more of the rioters were not black. Most of the others were Latinos, but apparently some whites and Asians also participated in the burning and looting. The riots spread out of south-central Los Angeles County into the heavily Latino sections of the central city and on to the less affluent commercial streets in Hollywood. What had appeared at first to be a pattern of rioting based on race had changed into the rioting of poor people of many races—mostly blacks and Latinos, still almost exclusively non-white, but no longer defined by African origins and a history of American enslavement.

This time the wealthier sections of the county of Los Angeles were not out of reach of the rioters. It was not necessary to "keep your rage up through three transfers," but the destruction was still confined mainly to the neighborhoods where the rioters lived and often worked.

In all the writing and talking that followed the riots, very little was made of the location of the looting and burning, and it was only months later that the media recognized the multiracial makeup of the rioters. The destruction of their own neighborhoods by the rioters, now the non-white poor, had in the past been attributed to rage, shrugged off as striking out at the things closest to hand. But this matter of destroying their own place, in large ways or small, has been an aspect of the behavior of the poor in America for a long time.

Whether the poor actually destroy neighborhoods or are prohibited from living in anything but run-down areas is one of those chicken or egg arguments, answered only by stipulating that the poor generally move into neighborhoods that have been abandoned by richer people, and then make them worse. This kind of behavior has been ascribed to a culture of poverty. If that were so, however, it would be among the few human cultures, if not the only one, that purposefully destroys its immediate surroundings.[1]

---

[1] Ecologists will be quick to point out that humans have been destroying the land, sea, and air around them since the demise of Neolithic societies and their cultural view of living in harmony with nature. The ecologists are correct, but I am speaking here of knowing destruction, a form of war on one's own place and kind.

A culture of self-destruction does not fit with any known patterns of human behavior, and if such a culture did exist, it would be very short-lived. The obvious fact of culture is that it arises to preserve the species rather than to destroy it. Cultures have to do with continuity, as we know from the monuments and other records left behind by cultures that died out as a result of war or climatic change. The idea of a culture of poverty devoted to the destruction of its habitat and eventually of itself is every bit as crazy as it sounds. The riots must have some other explanation.

Had the rioters been citizens of the place in which they lived, their interest would have been in the preservation of the place rather than the destruction of it. Citizens have always been the defenders of the polis, the nation, the state. The tie of the citizen to place was one of the ways in which Solon's reforms constructed the Athenian polis: They broke down the power of the clans, redirecting it to the geographically defined *demes,* setting the stage for the political reforms of Cleisthenes.

The defense of the polis as the responsibility of the citizen goes back to the arguments of Archidamus and the Funeral Oration of Pericles, spoken over the graves of the first Athenians who fell in the Peloponnesian War. According to Thucydides, Pericles said:

> . . . there is justice in the claim that steadfastness in his country's battles should be as a cloak to cover a man's other imperfections; since the good action has blotted out the bad, and his merit as a citizen more than outweighed his demerits as an individual. But none of these allowed either wealth with its prospect of future enjoyment to unnerve his spirit, or poverty with its hope of a day of freedom and riches to tempt him to shrink from danger. No, holding that vengeance upon their enemies was more to be desired than any personal blessings, and reckoning this to be the most glorious of hazards, they joyfully determined to accept the risk. . . . So died these men as became Athenians.[2]

---

[2] *The Complete Writings of Thucydides,* trans. R. Crawley (New York: The Modern Library, 1934), pp. 106–107.

All through history the character of the citizen has been loyalty to the polis. The Greek word for citizen comes from *polis;* the Latin word for citizen, *civis,* joins with the word for home to work its way through the French *cité* to become our English word "city." The city is home, home is the city. When the citizen destroys the city, it can only be madness or some strategy to save the polis in time of war, as in the destruction of foodstuffs and shelter to make it impossible for an invader to live off the land.

A person who abandons the polis by leaving it or turning against it cannot be a citizen. That person is excluded from citizenship, made a part of the vast world outside the polis, an internal or external exile; in the Athenian view, like a dead person. When the poor riot in the streets or in other ways destroy the places in which they live and work, it is not an act of madness, but a result of their exclusion from citizenship, which means they have no place, no home.

In the United States, we say that a citizen is a person who was born here or born overseas to parents who were U.S. citizens. We also accept small numbers of people into citizenship every year by asking them to swear loyalty to the state, to obey its laws, and so on. Because the Constitution describes rights in terms of persons rather than citizens, the citizen has little more than the non-citizen in that way, except the right to vote. And even that distinction has been eliminated in some jurisdictions, where non-citizens may vote in local elections.

Citizenship no longer follows the rigid rules of ancient Greece, where women and slaves and foreigners were not citizens, and prior to Solon's reforms, only landholding citizens could vote. At the founding of the United States, citizenship rules, in the sense of how widely citizenship was to be conferred, followed closely on the Athenian model before Solon. Only very slowly did the Roman view, based on the Stoic notion of the brotherhood of all men, come into favor, expanding the category of citizen. Even so, the *Dred Scott* decision held, in 1857, that people of African descent were not citizens; women's suffrage came only in the twentieth century; and the poll tax, which effectively limited voting rights to property owners, was not completely abolished until the second half of the twentieth century. Through one means or another, the poor have been excluded from full citizenship for most of the history of the United States.[3]

Voting rights issues still come before the courts. Joaquin G. Avila, formerly president and general counsel of the Mexican-American Legal Defense and Education Fund, tried a voting rights case before the U.S. Supreme Court in 1996. Nevertheless, the legal prohibition from citizenship has largely disappeared for native-born Americans. How, then, is it possible to argue that the rioters of Los Angeles and Chicago and millions of other poor people in the United States are not citizens?

Why does contemporary America have more fiercely exclusionary

---

[3] Garry Wills drew a distinction between ancient and American views of rights and the state in *Inventing America* (New York: Doubleday, 1978): In classical and medieval thought, the "rights" of the individual were not a topic of conventional discourse; there, the citizen did not rule but was ruled. Of course every man had certain things owed to him by divine and human law—his *dike* or *jus.* But these were not pregovernmental "rights" in the modern sense. They could not be. A man received political status by initiation into a tribe or people, by vows to a liege lord or suzerain. These gave each member privileges *of the body.*

The idea of an original "rule" over oneself, partly surrendered to another power (aliened), arose as a corollary to fully articulated social-contract theory in the seventeenth century (pp. 214–215).

Whether or not citizens have rights under the social contract to equal nutrition, housing, education, health care, and so on is the critical political question in the United States. It is also the critical moral question, for the moral stance of the founders was deeply influenced by the seventeenth-century Scottish philosopher Francis Hutcheson's notion of moral goodness as the promotion of the happiness of others.

The only way in which a state founded on a social contract, which assumes the right to the decent minimums of life required for the "pursuit of happiness," can avoid the contractual question of large-scale multigenerational poverty is by removing the poor from consideration as citizens. Of course, even this maneuver cannot release the state from its moral obligations to human beings within its boundaries, unless they are declared enemies of the state.

economic criteria than ancient Athens, where Pericles said poverty was no bar to citizenship? He sought a kind of equal opportunity of service to the polis, quite different from the equal opportunity to make money that we fight for in the United States. But his ambition for the Athenians stands to reason, for they revered political and cultural life, and he wished the citizens nothing more than to enjoy their citizenship, in the public life:

> If we look to the laws, they afford equal justice to all in their private differences; if to social standing, advancement in public life falls to reputation for capacity, class considerations not being allowed to interfere with merit; nor again does poverty bar the way if a man is able to serve the state, he is not hindered by the obscurity of his condition.[4]

There is some truth in what Pericles said about the condition of Athenian citizens, but a closer look at the reality of citizenship in Athens, where it began, and in the United States, where it enjoyed a rebirth at the end of the eighteenth century, will show that even in Athens, where no more than forty thousand men enjoyed the possibilities of citizenship, there were few citizens.

Citizens are not merely residents; Pericles very pointedly asked more than mere residency of citizens. Those who were not legally excluded had to pass through another set of exclusionary tests. "Our public men," he said,

> have, besides politics, their private affairs to attend to, and our ordinary citizens, though occupied with the pursuits of industry, are still fair judges of public matters; for, unlike any other nation, regarding him who takes no part in these duties not as unambitious but as useless, we Athenians are able to judge at all events if we cannot originate, and instead of looking on discussion as a stumbling-block in the way of action, we think it an indispensable preliminary to any wise action at all. Again, in our enterprises we present the singular spectacle of

---

[4] Thucydides, *The Complete Works,* p. 104.

daring and deliberation, each carried to its highest point, and both united in the same persons; although usually decision is the fruit of ignorance, hesitation of reflexion.[5]

Idios and *koinos,* private and public, set up another binary system. Citizenship excluded private persons, for even "ordinary citizens" were "fair judges of public matters. . . ." Those who lived a private life were excluded, for they were passive persons, the subjects of the citizenry. The process of exclusion defined the circle in which legitimate power was held. To open this circle to men other than aristocrats, Pericles began the system of payment for public service. His goal was to give the values of the aristocrats, by whom he meant the public men, to the rest of the citizenry.

Although it may be anachronistic to ascribe modern political and social sensibilities to such an act, it seems likely that he wanted the poor among the citizenry to understand themselves as citizens, which meant living the public life, the *vita activa.* For citizens did not truly feel loyal to the clan or phratry, but to the *vita activa,* which was the life of action, the Athens that existed in the doing of politics or philosophy or the making of art. There was little else to attract them. Fecundity and ease could not have been the allure of the polis; Athens itself was merely another city in a poor country, where the land was worn out. Herodotus said that Greece and poverty had always been bedfellows. Homer thought Ithaca was "a rugged place."

The wonder of the polis, as Protagoras and Socrates and the great discussants knew, lay in dialogue, the active life, which was always a public life, for the obvious reason that men who talk to themselves are more often loony than wise. Political life was the real life of the polis; there was no other worth considering. But political life in Athens had certain requirements, among them leisure.

In considering this aspect of political life, it is important again to avoid anachronism. "Leisure" did not hold the same meaning for the ancient Greeks that it does for us. There were no labor-saving de-

[5] Ibid., p. 105.

vices; slaves, women, most of the alien residents, the metics, and the poor among the citizenry worked long, exhausting hours, leaving little, if any, time to rest their bones, let alone to enjoy what Aristotle called the *summum bonum*, the contemplative life. Even in the democracy, politics, the *vita activa*, belonged to those with the leisure to live it.

Solon and after him Pericles attempted to draw those citizens who had no leisure out of the isolation of tedious labor into the public life. In that way, the Athenians attempted to solve the political problem of the game of modern society in which the losers are not citizens. The primary act was payment for service in the legislature, leisure provided by the state, the active life subsidized, citizenship granted to the citizens.

The freedom of Athenian citizens was entirely public; it differentiated them from the excluded, especially the slaves, who (except for those who toiled in the mines) looked very much like the citizens. In fact, the Athenians were criticized by other states because it was difficult to tell, by their dress and demeanor, the less affluent citizens from the slaves.

In contemporary America, no such confusion exists. The discerning can easily separate the rich from the poor, and no one is more discerning than the poor themselves. The poor understand that they have been excluded from the circle of power; that is, from citizenship. They cannot deceive themselves about who operates the government, for they are administered to by the government. Nothing indicates this more clearly than the language of the allies of the poor, the people who speak constantly of "empowering" their clients.

The deceit that resides in the word "empower" has yet to be discovered by most poor people; to them, the thought of being empowered carries some hope. In practice, however, "empowerment" has come to mean learning to deal with power, much like the psychotherapeutic concept of "adjustment."

Critics of the philosophy of adjustment have often asked why one should adjust to a bad life. Empowerment deserves similar scrutiny. When women are empowered to deal with the welfare department, they learn to accommodate their behavior to the rules, however arcane and unfair, of the system. Power, on the other hand, means taking con-

trol of the welfare department through legitimate means. Empowerment grows out of the passive role of the non-citizen, the one who has
accepted exclusion from the circle of power. Power results from the
vita activa, the citizen's public life; power is the *vita activa.* There can
be no legitimate power except in the doing; it cannot, as Hannah
Arendt said, be stored up. Power dies the moment action ceases.

However, this action of a citizen must fall within the agreed-upon
limits of the circle of power; political life is not anomic. When the residents of Watts or Detroit riot in their own neighborhoods, it is because
they are not citizens of Watts or Detroit or the United States of America. There is no polis they can call their own; they have been excluded
and dishonored, condemned to privacy. In the private panic of the surround, people become enemies of each other, even of themselves. Of all
the effects of living in a surround of force, the most profound is the isolation of people, one from the other, the absolute prohibition of power.
Cicero's idea of men being "born for each other" has no place inside the
surround, where men are set against each other. Politics for the poor is
difficult. Citizenship, the *vita activa,* is virtually impossible.

2

If the chief reward of the public life is inclusion in the circle of legitimate power, a secondary, but not inconsiderable, reward comes in the
honor of citizenship. We can read it in the speech of Archidamus and
again in the words of Pericles. "Honor" held one meaning for Sparta,
where it was opposed to shame, and another for Athens, where it
meant devotion to the polis life. In Rome, Cicero declared honor was
the citizen's reward. In each instance, honor required citizenship, inclusion in the Greek polis or the Roman state.

There were no levels of citizenship, but there were levels of honor.
Greece and Rome were modern societies, constantly sorting the winners and losers. Everyone entered contests: playwrights, javelin throw-
ers, philosophers, and boxers. Playwrights who were enormously
successful, like Sophocles, were elevated to the highest positions.
Roman honors included elevation to the position of Caesar.

The *vita activa,* worldly, public, yet reflective, produced citizens who were both artists and military leaders, poets and senators, philosophers and consuls.[6] Honors often came in more than one field of endeavor to those who were included in the circle of power.

In the United States, some groups of the excluded have managed to live the *vita activa* by creating a virtual polis, making citizens of themselves, collecting honors, living a public life, while holding no power in the general society. These citizens of the virtual polis, some of them poor by economic measures, have been able to escape the panic and isolation of the surround of force, even though they live partly within it.

Inside the virtual polis, it has been possible for those who were excluded from the actual polis to live a political life. The best known virtual polis in America was, until it was disrupted by racial integration in the 1960s, the sphere of influence of the black churches, particularly in the South. Within the virtual polis centered on the church, southern blacks were able to live in virtual, if not actual, autonomy. Honors were accorded the citizens who served the polis best in social, political, artistic, and economic functions.

A less successful virtual polis existed in the hills of Appalachia—one so separated from the larger state that many members of the virtual polis did not ever in all their lives mingle with the citizens of the larger state, the one from which they were effectively excluded.

Latinos, Jews, Swedes, Chinese, Japanese, and a host of religions, from the Mormons to sects having only a few members, constructed the same kind of virtual state in which their members could live the political life. Although the virtual polis began with poor people in almost every instance, the citizens did not remain in that condition for long. The rule of the political life, reflection instead of reaction, power instead of force, leads to success in many areas of life, including economics.

Blacks, who suffered the greatest force and were the poorest, having come up from slavery, built businesses, colleges, and professional

---

[6] In the *Nicomachean Ethics,* Aristotle's notion of the highest form of the *vita activa* is the *vita contemplativa,* which is arrived at through action.

schools. An aristocracy of the educated, most of them teachers, grew up in the South. Like Pericles, these aristocrats attempted to spread the values of the aristocracy to all the citizens, and many were successful at their work.

When the civil rights laws of the 1960s opened the doors of the virtual polis onto the wider horizons of the entire nation, those who had practiced the public life within the virtual polis rushed out into the real state prepared to be citizens, and were immediately successful. Teachers in segregated schools, graduates of segregated colleges, practically everyone connected to the black churches, and the owners of funeral homes and other businesses that the whites left to the blacks suddenly leaped into the economic mainstream. But more important, their children and grandchildren quickly became government employees, corporate managers, and entrepreneurs.

The practice of creating a virtual polis continues among many excluded groups. Among Latinos, Asians, some recent Russian immigrants, and others, such devices for the creation and maintenance of the virtual polis as bilingualism are being used to good effect. More than anything else, even more than skin color, language enables the creation of a separate state, although it is only a state of mind. A distinct language, along with other cultural attributes, enhances the autonomous character of the virtual polis. A body that governs itself in Farsi, Hindustani, Russian, one of the languages or its dialects spoken in China, Spanish, or any of the languages native to America, can be more easily self-governing than one that speaks English, for the simple reason that its speakers can be public persons within their own community even though limited to private life in the actual polis.

In time, members of the virtual polis, prepared by virtual citizenship to live the *vita activa,* use their political skills to move into the actual polis, where they quickly find themselves at ease and able to negotiate their way past the surround of force.

Sometimes the virtual polis pleases everyone who observes it. Many people who are not African American make donations to the United Negro College Fund; no one can fail to be charmed by a first-rate bilingual education class in Miami or San Francisco; and the style and sound of the black churches have been widely noted as one of the glories of American culture. But it is not quite the same when one hears Louis Farrakhan ranting his anti-white, anti-Semitic, anti-American line, or when a Muslim religious leader urges his followers to blow up the World Trade Center, or radical right-wing groups destroy a federal building in Oklahoma or declare themselves a separate nation-state in Montana.

The distinction between autonomy and anomie applies to the virtual polis as well as to the general society. Anomie is never a training ground for politics; it is a prescription for tragedy.

3

Until the last half of the twentieth century, the poor had been separated from the rest of society, but not from each other. Dogpatch and Catfish Row, like most myths, had some grounding in reality. The society portrayed in the myth was premodern, made of people who were more or less equal, maintained in their equality by the ritualistic life of Dogpatch or Catfish Row. The characters in *The Grapes of Wrath* fit into a similar pattern: Within the community of migrants, there was equality, ritualized in the act of migration.[7] Isolated as groups, they maintained a political life, joining unions, supporting various reform candidates, and so on. Even blacks and Latinos, although far fewer in number than the poor whites and suffering from much more virulent prejudice, were able to live a nascent political life within their own communities.

Political loneliness has two sources: hatred of others, who are not good enough to be friends or allies, and hatred of oneself, who is not good enough to have friends or allies.

The trend away from community has found its way into the language in this century. At one time, the phrase "kith and kin" referred

---

[7] The political naivete of Steinbeck's novel is not widely recognized. His white migrants displaced the Mexican-American laborers who had worked the farms in California, cutting their incomes, putting many of them out of work, and eventually supporting the government when it deported huge numbers of American citizens of Mexican descent for the avowed purpose of giving their jobs to the white migrants.

to two distinct groups: "kin" referred to blood relations; "kith" first meant knowledge, then the rules of behavior, the place of residence, and then for the longest time it described one's friends, acquaintances, neighbors, and countrymen. But "kith" has lost its meaning now, becoming nothing more than a synonym for "kin." The phrase "kith and kin," which once described a person's world in its social and political entirety, has become a common example of pleonasm, the useless repetition of words.

Perhaps the loss of meaning of a single word cannot describe the end of political life, but there is some history to be considered: It was the great reform of Cleisthenes that separated kith from kin in ancient Athens, ending the role of kinship alliances in the ruling of the polis and replacing them with the new power of the deme, the kith of Athens.

While the notion of kith has fled from every economic level, the loss has been most devastating to the poor, for "kith" had meaning beyond mere locality, it included behavior and knowledge, the common world of political animals, the public world. Among kin, one set of rules existed, dominated by culture; among one's kith, another set of rules existed, influenced by culture but not dominated by it. The world of kith could include people from distant places, other cultures, come together to live in the brilliant place between the chaos of absolute liberty and the rigid order of intransigent culture—the political world. The rich of the modern world transformed their kith into an economic polis, politics of the pocketbook, the suburb, exurb, management, unions, ownership. The poor were left with loneliness and kin.

IX.

Across Cultures

IN AMERICA THE WAR of cultures did not begin in earnest until the middle of the twentieth century. There had always been wars between the dominant culture and the others, but cultural differences had been no more than an excuse to take another person's land, force people into slavery, replace slavery with cheap labor; it had been a reason to despise the poor and so to make the use of them more comfortable for the rich. Culture itself had been of little interest; the framers of the Constitution had not even bothered to make English the official language of the new country. They were concerned with politics. The United States of America was the most political creation in the history of states: There were no economists, few churchmen, and not a single anthropologist present at its birth.

No culture but Western culture was in the minds of the colonists, and for all but a few of the very rich there was precious little of that.[1] As for blacks and Native Americans, they were thought of more as members of a different species than people of other cultures.

Questions of culture did not even arise with the emancipation of blacks; it was assumed that blacks would choose to become like their former masters. Otherwise, white citizens of the time reasoned, why would they want to be freed? At the time of emancipation, Native Americans were still a military problem; the whites, with the help of many black troops, were interested in eliminating them by any means possible—slaughter, disease, starvation, alcohol, or schoolbooks and beans; the choice, such as it was, belonged to the Indians. In that case, as with blacks, culture was not an issue, for the whites placed no value at all on their cultures. The sentiment was returned by Native Americans who had to pay attention to the military prowess of the Europeans, but had no regard at all for their culture. The natives thought of the invaders as avaricious individualists who smelled bad; the word for a white in the Lakota language, for example, means greedy (literally, he-who-eats-the-fat).

During the great waves of immigration at the end of the nineteenth century and the beginning of the twentieth, culture did not become a major issue because it was assumed that immigrants would first adapt to the established culture, then adopt it. And for the most part, the immigrants did just that. They settled in the ghettos of the great cities, and worked their way out. Some Germans had their own

---

[1] Ethnocentrism was not, as some have argued, a European invention. Most of the cultures native to the Americas named themselves "the People," as if no others could even be described as human beings. The practice was not limited to any language group—the Siouan-speaking Lakota of the Great Plains as well as the Ute-Aztecan speakers of the Southwest gave themselves such names. We know them, of course, by the names given them by their adversaries. The Lakotas, Dakotas, and Nakotas are known to us as "Sioux," a word their neighbors to the east used for them; it means "snake" or "enemy." Similarly, the word "Apache" or "Apache de Nabajo," used to describe the Diné of Arizona and New Mexico by the Pueblos to the east and south of them, meant "enemy," while the word the Apaches, including the Navaho branch, used for themselves, "Diné," means "the People."

schools for a time, as did some Jews, Chinese, Swedes, and so on, but immigration had been a way to come to America, not to retain old country values. For these people there was one culture, American culture; they jumped into the melting pot, and were glad to be there.

The melting pot did not welcome everyone, however; blacks, Latinos, Native Americans, a good number of Southeast Asians, some Southern Italians and Eastern Europeans, and others, did not fit comfortably into the pot. The discomfort of these people, many of them non-white, led to the view that it was not merely the prejudice of the dominant culture but their lack of love and understanding of their own cultures that caused their suffering.[2] Multiculturalism was born as a response to the purported problem. Americans began to dress themselves in masks of lost cultures, a papier-mâché of inconceivable values, irretrievable times; they did not learn their antecedents, they attempted to become their antecedents.

An undisciplined discipline was invented: multiculturalism, which should have been taught by historians and anthropologists, became the province of multiculturalists. Each culture thought itself superior to all the others. "Black is beautiful" soon came to mean black is most beautiful. At the same time, Oscar Lewis's "culture of poverty" was revised by Ken Auletta to mean the "underclass," which was exclusively brown and black. The lines were drawn.

The battle was joined on one side by such social and political conservatives as the late Allan Bloom, who wrote a prissy diatribe, *The Closing of the American Mind,* in which he said, "Culture is a cave," referring to Plato's Allegory of the Cave.[3] Bloom's ethnocentrism was so

[2] This lack of appreciation of their own cultures is blamed entirely on the dominant culture, the historical process of assimilation, the demand of the dominant culture for conformity, and so on. The argument is well known. The question here is not about the value of cultures, since a pluralistic view is assumed all through this book, but about the effect of culture on poverty in the United States.

[3] (New York: Simon & Schuster, 1987). Bloom's idea of "culture as a cave" implies the existence of an excluded middle. He claims a place for philosophy outside the cave. But philosophy was a part of Athenian culture, so it must have been both within Bloom's cave of culture and outside it.

all-consuming that he considered Western civilization beyond mere culture as it was lived by all other peoples. On the other side, Orlando Patterson wrote *Freedom*,[4] in which he redefined the word into a "triad" of personal, sovereignal, and civic freedoms, giving the West credit for the invention of personal freedom, although only as a response to slavery, and showing that other cultures did not need the West's notion of personal freedom because they offered their people sovereignal and civic freedom:

"I have suggested that freedom as a value was generated by, and socially constructed out of, the interaction among master, slave, and native nonslaves. Elsewhere, I have demonstrated that slavery was a nearly universal institution. It should follow that the value of freedom was constructed everywhere. Yet, we know that this was not so. Indeed, one of the major objectives of this work is to show that freedom was a peculiarly Western value and ideal. How is the discrepancy explained?

"Simply, by noting that while the idea of freedom was certainly engendered wherever slavery existed, it never came to term. . . . Resisting the promotion of freedom as value was the natural thing to do for

---

[4] (New York: Basic Books, 1991). Patterson and Bloom both offer views of the ancient world to explain the contemporary world. Patterson's concept of a chordal triad of freedom may not survive the test of time, and a few of his ideas fail my admittedly Western idea of the test of reason, but there can be little doubt that slavery played an important role in permitting, if not causing, the Athenian democracy, the practice of philosophy, and so on. If nothing else, slavery gave the Athenians the leisure Aristotle said was absolutely vital to the practice of politics.

Bloom, who translated *The Republic,* seems not to have read it. He credits Plato with what he was not (an advocate of the liberal arts, which include the humanities) and neglects Plato's anti-democratic views. But the worst part of Bloom's work is that his Greeks are all dead, even in their own time. The intellectual excitement that is the true enduring gift of Greece appears nowhere in Bloom's work. He apparently did not understand the role of Protagoras, for neither Protagoras nor the Sophists even merit listing in the index of his book. It is difficult to imagine a man who spent much of his life with the classics, even teaching dialectic as method, yet did not understand that the glory of unjust, imperfect, reflective, disputatious, democratic Greece was not the answers but the questions.

most human societies. . . . What is unusual is the institutionalization and idealization of this value, given its degraded, servile source. It is the ancient West that needs explanation. Because we are of the West and share its central value, we have turned the history of human societies around, and ethnocentrically assumed that it is the rest of humankind, in its failure to embrace freedom, that needs explaining." (p. 20)

At one time I had theorized that each culture produced a different response to force, conforming to the rule of the war of cultures, which is that America has no common culture, but a collection of mutually exclusive cultures, each of which determines other aspects of life for those born into that culture.[5] Even the politics of this book—and *New American Blues* before it—could be argued according to the rules of the war of cultures, using as a basis both Herder's idea of a culture as a person's one and only home and Hegel's belief that "Freedom is to be at home."

The trouble with trying to make a structure out of what already exists, however, is that the collection of bric-à-brac we call the world does not always lend itself to the expectations the writer brings with him to his labors. The idea that poverty is generated by culture would not even make a wall; no matter how the pieces were twisted and turned, the structure would not stand. But another structure, unlike culture, asserted itself.

Listening to the poor, taking what they said and showed as the only world to be considered, led to the understanding that culture affected American economic life, but did not alone determine it. A taste for

[5] In the war of cultures in the United States, cultures are often conflated into larger categories identified as races. Of course, Latinos "may be of any race," which is the most obvious breakdown of the racial categories.

In April 1996, *Harper's* magazine published a conversation in which I served as moderator while Professors Cornel West of Harvard and Jorge Klor de Alva of U.C. Berkeley discussed the question of race. Both men said race was "a social construct," but West was unwilling to give up the idea of race, while Klor de Alva argued that it was an unreasonable and damaging concept and should be gotten rid of as soon as possible.

certain foods, a set of gestures, choices of clothing, child-rearing practices, skin color, even language could not overcome the fact of living within a surround of force in a society so determinedly political that it subsumed everything else under the idea of legitimate power.

It might be argued that those who came from or ally themselves with a non-Western culture do not participate in the exercise of legitimate power because the idea is too foreign to them, but the nature of immigration is the search for a new social contract, inclusion, citizenship. Immigration is perhaps the only possible revolution in the twentieth century. And for those who were born in the United States, the idea of legitimate power is home.[6]

The American state, for all its flaws, permits and even encourages diversity of opinion and the possibility of legitimate power for people descended from any and all cultures; it offers a home in politics to all of its citizens. Politics is transcendent in America. In every descendant culture it determines who will long suffer poverty and who will not.[7] Any American, any person, may be strengthened by taking pride and pleasure in the knowledge of the culture of his or her forebears, but an old culture cannot make a new life.

Culture plays a powerful role in the lives of Americans no matter what culture lies in their past. When they are poor, they almost always have only three attributes in common: All of them live in the United States; all of them suffer the surround of force; and none of them will have discovered how to live the political life at any level of social organization, from the family to the polis. Reflective thinking plays lit-

---

[6] Compare this to Herder's notion of a culture as a person's one and only home.

[7] I have used the adjective "descendant" to describe cultural groups within the United States because there are few, if any, unbroken cultures. Every group has been affected greatly by the dominant culture as well as by other descendant cultures. I have eaten tacos with Chinese Americans and joined a group of Mexican Americans for lunch in a Japanese restaurant. An Irish American recently sent me a note in which he used the Yiddish word *gelt*. America is not a melting pot, but neither is it Paris, Bombay, or Tenochtitlán. Contemporary cultures cannot be transplanted whole to new nations and Neolithic cultures cannot survive unchanged when the chiefs operate casinos and preach computer literacy to the young braves.

tle or no role in the lives of such families, although some of them may have had a political moment or at the very least, a moment of false politics. Yet there is no American descendant culture I know of that prohibits reflection. And there is a simple proof of political thinking by most people in every culture in the United States: They are not poor.[8]

---

[8] For a description of the special situation of Indians and Alaska Natives see, among others: Shorris, *The Death of the Great Spirit: An Elegy for the American Indian*, New York: Simon and Schuster, 1970.

X.

Political Inventions

WITHIN THE WORLD OF relative poverty, which comprises most of the nations of the earth, and especially the United States, neither nature nor culture keeps people poor. In the modern world, it is never easy to escape from poverty and never impossible. The problem, of course, is that the nature of the modern world is as nearly intractable as the nature of the sub-Saharan desert. Modern society is built upon the concept of inequality, and even though inequality does not require that anyone be poor, in the sense of suffering physical want, it has always worked out that way.

In contemporary America, the poor must overcome the panicked reaction of people who live in a surround of force in order to escape from poverty; that is, they must learn to think reflectively and act politically. Tens of millions of people have done so. Since the early part of the nineteenth century, social mobility has been the hallmark of American society. Tocqueville foresaw the great leveling of America into a single class, a single culture, a desperately powerful majority.

Blacks, Latinos, and Native Americans did not have a place in this great, overbearing majority, but for everyone else an almost primitive equality seemed possible.

The early years of the twentieth century saw a new kind of social mobility as the waves of immigrants came, but their change in status, from poor Polish or Southern Italian greenhorn to middle-class white was not cultural or even economical at its core. The successful immigrants were the beneficiaries of a political epiphany. To emigrate was to revolt against the past and to immigrate was to strike a new social contract that permitted, among other things, inclusion in the circle of power. The dames of Fifth Avenue, Back Bay, and Newport may not have invited the Irish and the Italians and the Jews into any parts of their lives other than the kitchens and the counting houses, but they did permit them into their political parties.

Three-quarters of a century later, in Texas, Willie Velasquez founded the Southwest Voter Registration and Education Program.[1] His grasp of the issues of immigration and poverty was extraordinary. During the height of the Brown Beret radical movement, Velasquez often invited the radicals to barbecues in the backyard of his house, where he advised them to put aside their copies of Marx and Mao and read Aristotle. It was, as I have noted elsewhere, his attempt to make Mexicans into ancient Athenians or Englishmen, not culturally—Velasquez was pleased to be Chicano—but politically. He had learned how immigrants succeeded and what had to take place before the poor could bring themselves up out of poverty.

Velasquez was not the only leader of poor people to register voters. At about the time he first became a political activist, voter registration drives among poor blacks, especially in the South, were recruit-

---

[1] More about the late Willie Velasquez, the Mexican-American Legal Defense and Education Fund lawyer Joaquin G. Avila, and Vilma Martinez, then executive director of MALDEF, can be found in Earl Shorris, *Latinos: A Biography of the People* (New York: W. W. Norton, 1992). Velasquez's understanding of immigration, poverty, the inclusive aspect of political power, and the origins of political thinking were an important influence on this book.

ing tens of thousands of people in every state. Not every person who registered voters shared Velasquez's sophistication. Fannie Lou Hamer and the Mississippi Freedom Democratic Party had a somewhat less philosophical approach, which in no way detracts from her courage or goodwill or her role in history, but may have contributed to the failure of some registered voters to become political persons. The Reverend Martin Luther King, Jr., preached a far more political view, although he couched his politics in a code of ethics grounded in the teachings of the church.

The wisdom of Dr. King in connecting politics to the black church simply cannot be overestimated. Unlike the whites who controlled the War on Poverty, Dr. King knew something about the behavior of black people in circumstances that permitted, even in a limited way, reflective thinking and the *vita activa*. After all, he was himself the beneficiary of this limited public life. He did not understand black people, or any poor people for that matter, as deficient. To Dr. King it was the larger society, not the poor, who were at fault. Perhaps that is what so interested J. Edgar Hoover.

The Reverend Martin Luther King understood full well that when poor people, including blacks, were able to evade the panic of the surround of force, they could think reflectively, behave politically, and succeed economically, even in the face of racism. He knew, too, that the only place where autonomy could be practiced by the poor was the church, for whites did not attend black churches, enabling the blacks to manage their own affairs, to establish circles of power within the world permitted them. The development of the black leadership, I believe, grows directly out of the syncretism of Dr. King's movement.

On the other hand, poor whites were often unwelcome in their churches, although the exclusion was politically less important because the white churches were not separated from the general life of the city in the same way as the black churches; autonomy could not be enjoyed in the same way, for the circles of power in the white community overlapped. Dr. King was surely aware of this aspect of the lives of poor whites, for the oppressed are invariably the best students of the character of the oppressor. And he put his knowledge to use. Whether it was for moral or political reasons or a felicitous combination of both, Dr. King made a church of his movement, granting a sense of autonomy to the poor within the confines of his Southern Christian organization that would not have been possible in a purely secular organization. The inclusion of the white poor culminated in the Poor People's March on Washington (1963), and died with the murder of Martin Luther King and the ensuing separation of the races.

Since the death of Dr. King and the dual effects of the dispiriting attitude of the "culture of poverty" theorists in the War on Poverty and the dismantling of many federal programs to assist the poor, the problem of relative poverty in the United States has consistently worsened. Changes in federal programs to assist the poor, proposed by the Congress and approved by President Clinton in 1996, will make life more difficult for millions of Americans, many of them children, in the future.

Long before the Welfare Reform Act, people moved out of poverty. The reasons for this movement, particularly off the welfare rolls, have been quantified a thousand times over. Single mothers on welfare get married, and live better, at least for a while. People find jobs that pay enough money to move them out of the federally defined slough of poverty. Since the implementation of welfare reform, statistics point to the draconian nature of the policy more than to the behavior of the poor. Figures from earlier periods are more illuminating. The number of people moving out of poverty between 1967 and 1979 was 35.5 percent, but the number who moved out between 1980 and 1991 was only 30.4 percent, a decline of 14.3 percent in the rate of moving up. Meanwhile, the increase in the number of people moving down into poverty rose from 6.2 percent to 8.5 percent in the same periods, an increase of 37.1 percent in the rate of fall. There can be no doubt that getting out of poverty had become more difficult, while the slide into poverty had become far easier.

Looking at poverty by race confuses the issue even further. Far more black single mothers work than either whites or Latinas, but fewer blacks live in complete families, although the number of white single mothers is increasing far more rapidly than the number of black.[2] The racial breakout of single mothers indicates that a new kind of family unit is being defined by the American culture: it includes a mother and children, but no father. Black women, perhaps because they have more experience with the new family unit, appear to be adapting better to the circumstance.

Nonetheless, the experience of the Clemente Course over its first four years indicates that the problems of single parents—Asian, black, brown, or white—are sometimes simply insurmountable. They are often connected to health issues, but other calamities, such as eviction from an apartment, loss of a job, and so on, can disrupt any family, but especially the single-parent family, where the fact of only one parent makes the situation more precarious.

Government policies, however, fail to recognize the new cultural definition of the family, and continue to punish these families, particularly the children, when a more rational view would attempt to adjust the government to this increasing number of its constituents, enabling the number of people who move out of poverty to increase while at the same time slowing the rate of fall into poverty.

---

[2] The increase in the number of children born out of wedlock may be deceptive, since it is almost always expressed as a percentage of all children born during the specified period. If the total number of births falls, largely because married couples are having fewer children, while the number of births among unmarried women remains stable, it will appear that the number of out-of-wedlock births has risen.

Nevertheless, the single-parent family has become a part of modern American society, regardless of the economic condition of the parent, and should be considered a legitimate family, with the efforts of the general society revised to support the new family rather than wounding it with specious arguments about illegitimacy and lack of family values. Such arguments and the policies that flow from them cannot help but wound great numbers of American families economically as well as morally.

The consistent attacks on single parents, all but a tiny percentage of whom are women, by people who support "family values" may be the cruelest irony of our time. The idea, consistent among social conservatives over generations, that a widow with children is a family while an unmarried woman with children is not, makes clear the sexual origin of the problem that leads social conservatives to hurt those they claim to love. The problem for thoughtful people, those who value the family in all of its expressions, is how to teach ethics to social conservatives.

The punishing character of government and society makes it far more difficult for people to follow what appears to be the path out of long-term poverty, but still not impossible. This path, curiously enough, follows the rules Tolstoy set for happy and unhappy families. While families in poverty seem to be apolitical each in their individual ways, those that escape are much more alike: political. Moreover, they become political in similar ways.

The role of the family in the establishment of a political life continues to follow a pattern established during the very invention of politics. The barrier to political life in that time came in the extended family, which Fustel de Coulanges defined as people who had a common ancestor; followed by the *phratry,* in which one extended family joined with another that followed the same god; and finally, the tribe, which was made up of several phratrys.[3] Among the differences between these familial groupings and the geographically defined demes, according to Fustel, was the capacity of the deme to participate in change, "to be flexible and variable"; that is, to govern itself rather than to be governed by the absolutism of religion and ritual. Autonomy was not only uncommon in the extended family; it was expressly forbidden. Members of the extended family could not worship strange gods or disobey the rulings of the patriarch.

Extended families in the ancient city were based on ancestor worship (a practice that operates in a more subtle way in extended families today), and though there may be economic aspects to kinship structures, there is nothing political about them: they are not flexible or variable; a cousin cannot become a brother and an uncle cannot become a sister-in-law. Kinship rules have always been stable, more than stable, immutable: incest, for both genetic and economic reasons, is taboo, everyone must marry out; on the other hand, in many societies a man with a wife and children is obliged to marry the widow of a dead brother to maintain the stability of the extended family.[4]

---

[3] See Fustel de Coulanges, *The Ancient City* (New York: Doubleday Anchor, 1955).

[4] This was a custom among the Lakota of the Great Plains, who accepted polygamy in that situation, but it also happened in my wife's family, where a widower married his brother's widow.

Within the nuclear family, however, relations change constantly. The unit forms out of the union of a man and woman; the birth of a child revises the unit; the departure of either the male or female adult revises the unit again, as does the birth of more children. Perhaps even more importantly, the unit is constantly revised by the change in status of the children, from infant to adult, and all the stages along the way. Kinship rules, such as the prohibition against incest, apply within the nuclear unit, but the general stability of the extended family cannot apply to the dynamic nuclear family. The nuclear family changes, and in worldly ways, chooses its alliances outside the unit. In the extended family, alliances are defined by the rules of kinship.

Extended families can, of course, include many nuclear families. The distinction I want to make—one that has been drawn many times before—is between the nuclear family and the family that functions only in its extended form. It is these two kinds of families that can be likened to the distinction Fustel made between the forms of organization in his Ancient City.

Given its propensity for change, the nuclear family adapts much more easily to political life. One of the expectations of the nuclear family is that the children will achieve a certain degree of autonomy as part of the process of maturation. In the extended family, however, the relationships remain the same throughout the lifetime of all the members, with the exception of the new patriarch, who inherits the position according to the rules of kinship rather than through the free choosing of the members of the extended family.

In the United States, as many anthropologists and sociologists, including Oscar Lewis, have noted, the long-term poor tend to live in extended families—an arrangement which I believe affords them a certain amount of stability but inhibits political life. Within the nuclear family, however, which is naturally unstable, the flexibility and variability that Fustel related to the establishment of political life happens quite easily.

Of the many instances of families moving out of poverty, almost every one I encountered followed the same pattern of flexibility within the nuclear family and distance or even separation from the extended family. This may be construed to mean that the separated unit was forced to be autonomous without the economic and emotional support of the extended family, but I do not think so. The details of the rise from poverty indicate otherwise.

Although instances of the rise out of poverty of nuclear families are common and similar, I do not know of a single instance of the rise of an entire extended family, with the exception of immigrants, from poverty to a more comfortable and secure economic situation; nor do I know of an instance where an entire extended family of poor people began to think reflectively and to live a political life.[5]

The pattern of the escape from multigenerational or long-term poverty repeats itself with little variation. In every instance that I found, family members avoided the envy that drives people away from politics into anomie.

Mrs. Irene Guster of Greenville, Mississippi, who grew up picking cotton on a plantation and now lives in a fine house, with generations of successful children around her, thought for a very long time before she could say exactly what had changed in her family, how they had learned something that brought them up out of poverty. She did not minimize the fact that she had been born under the yoke of servitude almost indistinguishable from slavery. She gave much credit to the church and the study of the Bible, which had made a cultured woman of her and professionals and intellectuals of her seven children; but when she thought about the difference between her family and so many others, she recalled a lesson her father had taught his children.

He sat under a tree with his six children gathered around him and taught them a lesson with a piece of string and six sticks. He tied the string around the sticks and showed the children how the six together

[5] Such occurrences among extended families are not impossible, although they are not likely. During the 1960s, when the civil rights movement opened the doors of the ghetto for many black families, the economic status of these families changed. But to say that these families were poor and apolitical prior to the civil rights movement would be incorrect, a misunderstanding of the autonomous aspects of black community life prior to integration.

could stand. He demonstrated the strength of them. Then he untied the sticks, and let them fall.

It was not a lesson in family, she said, for people are born into a family. It was his lesson in how to live. Politics.

His lesson did not raise the pay they collected for chopping cotton. The earth still steamed in August when little Irene Guster and her brothers and sisters bent to their work. People still fell breathless in the fields.

The surround of force existed for those who got out of poverty just as it did for those who remained behind, but they overcame the panic that limits the surrounded to a desperate life of reaction. In all those I have met who moved out of poverty there is also a sense of creative opposition, a positive response to the surround of force, which bears more relation to the development of freedom in opposition to fate than to the concept of class struggle.

When nuclear families move out of poverty, and they do so one-at-a-time, not as part of extended families or clans, the first step is always the end of isolation not from the wider world but from the nuclear family itself. The members of the nuclear unit begin to understand their survival and success as the survival and success of the unit, but they do not do this according to ritual or even culture. The first norm they learn is the norm of the unit, and they establish this miniature polis consciously; they understand that they are each other's "hostages to fortune." The screaming silence of private life comes to a close, the endless dialogue begins, they are reborn for each other, and within the tiny polis the surround of force is broken.

In Dallas, Texas, Mrs. Frances Rizo said that when her husband left her and four children with little money and no prospects, the family changed:

"In our family everybody had input, everybody had part of the decision-making process, but when we got to where we wanted something we couldn't afford or something illogical, I could step in with my authority.

"All the children had to carry their own load. The boys learned early how to wash their own clothes. We had a family conference when the kids started fudging on their chores. I asked them for a solution. We used to change assignments every day, but then we turned to having the same assignment all week long. When I had a problem I couldn't solve, generally with money, I would sit down with the kids and explain it, and they would come up with a solution. We called it 'our little democracy.' "

XI.

A Prison Epiphany

"Slaves," so ran a Greek proverb,
"have no leisure"—it was a definition.

— BERNARD KNOX

IN RETROSPECT, IT SHOULD HAVE been no surprise that the idea came from a woman who had been in a maximum-security prison for more than eight years, because prison lies at the extreme end of the continuum of society, where a cold-eyed view of all the rest of the world may come more readily, if the prisoner can see at all. Prison shares very little with what the prisoners call "the free world," for the first rule of prison life is the denial of autonomy. That is the function of the rolls of razor wire, the guard towers, the weapons aimed at the prisoners, the cell doors, the constant searches and counts, and the punishments: isolation, transfer, and withdrawal of the few amenities permitted prisoners. Prison is worse than slavery in many respects, worse than long-term relative poverty in others.

What better place than prison to think about how to avoid poverty or escape from it? Inside those prisons still concerned with rehabilitation as well as punishment, the staff[1] and the prisoners attempt to use the metaphor of the prison to understand the real world. Much of this is futile stuff, amateur psychotherapy, a way to pass the time without having to break rocks or wash dishes, but some programs work.

At the Bedford Hills Correctional Facility, the maximum-security prison and intake and processing center about fifty miles north of New York City, the Family Violence Program, designed largely by Sharon Smolick and managed now by Terri McNair, encourages prisoners to explore damaging aspects of family life through the invention of revealing dramas.

These dramas show that those who live within a surround of force either sink into passivity or react to force with force. Nothing of the ideas of Sartre and Fanon, in which man recreates himself through violence, succeeds, according to the dramas; man cannot recreate himself that way. The practice of viewing the world through the clarifying filter of these dramas has taught some of the women in the program to use a cold eye to view other situations. And no one has learned it better than Viniece Walker.[2]

She came to Bedford when she was nineteen years old, a high school dropout who read at the level of a college sophomore, a graduate of crack houses, the streets of Harlem, and a long alliance with a brutal man.[3] On the surface, Viniece has remained as tough as she had been on the streets of Harlem. She speaks bluntly, and even though the AIDS infection has progressed during her time in prison, she still swaggers as she walks down the long prison corridors. While in Bedford Hills, she completed her high school requirements and pursued

---

[1] Psychologists, social workers, teachers, and medical practitioners, as distinct from the guards.

[2] Viniece "Niecie" Walker and I have known each other for several years. We started out as acquaintances, then became allies, and finally friends. It has also been my good fortune to know the women of Bedford Hills who have produced a major book on women and AIDS and a volume of poems.

[3] It is considered bad form in prison to discuss a person's crime. I will follow that rule here.

a college degree, with a concentration in philosophy. She became a counselor to women with a history of family violence and a comforter of other women who suffered the debility and certain fate of AIDS.

Only the deaths of other women cause her to stumble in the midst of her swaggering step, to spend days alone with the remorse that drives her to seek redemption. She goes through life as if she had been imagined by Dostoyevsky, but even more complex than his fictions, alive, a person, fair-skinned and freckled, and in prison. It was she who responded to the sudden question, Why do you think people are poor?

We had never met before. The conversation around us focused on the abuse of women. Niecie's eyes were perfectly opaque, hostile, prison eyes. Her mouth was set in the beginning of a sneer.

"You got to begin with the children," she said, speaking rapidly, clipping out the street sounds, southern sounds, as they came into her speech, in the way Norman Mailer bowdlerizes his own speech by editing out the Yiddish past.

She paused long enough to let the change of direction take effect, then resumed the rapid, rhythmless speech. "You've got to teach the moral life of downtown to the children. And the way you do that, Earl, is by taking them downtown to plays, museums, concerts, lectures, where they can learn the moral life of downtown."

I smiled at her, misunderstanding, thinking I was indulging her. "And then they won't be poor anymore."

She read every nuance of my response, and answered angrily, "And they won't be poor *no more.*"

"What you mean is . . . "

"What I mean is what I said, a moral alternative to the street."

She did not speak of jobs or money, not then or ever during the years we have talked about poverty in America. From her vantage within the prison, a place in which spies and informers rob people of their very thoughts, putting them, as Tacitus said, into a life worse than slavery, she had discovered something about reality. And it was not an aberration, something grown up in Harlem and nurtured in the bitter soil of prison. She did not speak of God or church or the bosom of family. She had a cold eye. In a glance, passing, like the horseman of the Yeats poem, she saw what others had said, and went on.

Of all those I had listened to, the poor and yesterday's poor as well, none had spoken of jobs or money. They thanked God, but they did so rich or poor, the poor more than the formerly poor, because their fear was greater. No one spoke of God the employment agent or God the paymaster. They thanked God, but not for the business of life.

It was not release from poverty that interested Niecie; she had been in prison long enough to know that release had nothing to do with autonomy: A prisoner cannot release herself, she can only be released from prison. The moral life does not consist in being acted upon, but in acting. Autonomous persons act.

But what of politics? Had she skipped a step or failed to take a step?

"The moral life of downtown?" What kind of moral life does music teach?

How can a museum push poverty away? Who can dress in statues or eat the past?

The answer was politics, not "the moral life of downtown." Only politics could overcome the tutelage of force. But to enter the public world, to practice the political life, the poor had first to learn to reflect. That was what she meant by "the moral life of downtown." She did not know downtown, she could not even imagine the moral life of Wall Street or Fifth Avenue. She lived in prison, in a cloud of Dostoyevskian remorse, amid dreams of redemption. The moral life was the political life in her mind; she did not make the error of divorcing ethics from politics. Niecie had simply said, in a kind of shorthand, that no one could step out of the surround of force directly into the public world.

There are many paths out of poverty. Those who know poverty least concentrate on jobs and money, as if poverty was merely quantitative and labor was God's own panacea. The formerly poor, and those who live in the distance of metaphor, know that the game of the modern world can be overcome; that politics, unlike economics or the strutting of status, is not a contest but a public accomplishment of power.[4]

---

[4] This kind of change has happened before. Josiah Ober described one instance in *Mass and Elite in Democratic Athens* (Princeton, NJ: Princeton University Press, 1989):

No one can release the poor from poverty, no one can accomplish power for them. Efforts to mobilize the poor, as exemplified in the history of the National Welfare Rights Organization, have always failed. In 1971, Frances Fox Piven and Richard Cloward, in *Regulating the Poor,* described the movement as "burgeoning." Six years later, in *Poor People's Movements,* they tried to explain why the mobilization had failed.[5] It did not occur to them that they, the political people, had attempted to release the poor from poverty.

In her answer to the question about poverty, Niecie had assumed that the poor could not be mobilized or otherwise released from poverty. She knew they would have to act as autonomous persons; what she meant by "the moral life of downtown" was something that had happened to her. She did not describe what had happened; perhaps she was not even entirely aware of it. But she knew that because of her education a radical transformation had occurred: She had discovered the extent of her own humanness.

The radical solution to the plight of the poor did not await them on the right, with its plan of deprivation and coercion; the poor knew full well that jobs and money were ancillary aspects of getting out of poverty, outcomes rather than process. And the other side had no solution to offer at all; liberals and leftists simply stood by, tongue-tied

---

"The bonds of mutual interdependence between citizens were now based on an assumption of political equality. This assumption tended to weaken the old bonds of deference which had been based on class and status inequality, because the new ties cut across the horizontal strata of birth and wealth." Ober went on to compare many of the aspects of this kind of decision making in ancient Greece after Cleisthenes instituted the system of *demes* to that of Massachusetts towns at the end of the seventeenth century (pp. 70–71).

Resistance to the change in Greek social and political organization was apparently minimal. In the United States, where the rules of the game have become a bulwark against the leveling character of fairness, such change would most likely encounter strong resistance.

[5] *Poor People's Movements* (New York: Pantheon, 1978). The extent of the failure of the organization they founded with George Wiley was described by Michael Harrington, who wrote that Wiley was able to enroll only 22,000 people out of a potential membership of "around 9 million."

and bankrupt, remembering Roosevelt and relying on the sputter of compassion in the twilight hours of Daniel Patrick Moynihan, while more people descended into poverty, and the lives of the poor, especially the children, worsened year after year.

Niecie Walker had followed the same path that led to the invention of politics in ancient Greece. She had learned to reflect. In further conversation it became clear that when she spoke of "the moral life of downtown," she meant the humanities, which had been the source of reflection for the secular world since the Greeks first stepped back from nature to experience wonder at what they beheld.

If the political life was the way out of poverty, the humanities provided an entrance to reflection and the political life: the poor did not need anyone to release them; an escape route existed. But to open this avenue to reflection and politics, a major distinction between the preparation for life of the rich and poor has to be eliminated. The game of modern society, as it has been practiced in America since the founding, will have to be reinvented, with a new set of rules promoting fairness and a commitment to the dialogue of equals. To do so will require revisions and reforms not only in the lives of the poor but in the entire society.

XII.

Radical Humanism

Man is the measure of all things.

—PROTAGORAS

Wildflower

THE WOMAN SAT HUNCHED over a metal and wood veneer table in the intake section of the clinic. It was the beginning of winter in New York, the season of darkening days and influenza. She wore two knit caps, one atop the other, both of them pulled down over her temples. Her body was thin, curled like a bent wire inside her pale, almost white raincoat. She wore the coat buttoned to her chin and belted tightly at the waist, even though she was indoors in a heated room. Her name was Silveria, which means "of the woods," like a wildflower.

In profile, she appeared to be drawn down, curled over her woes. All the forms of her were curled in the same way, as if she had been painted by an artist overly concerned with repetitions. Even her hands were curled, half-closed, resting tensely upon the table.

The girls, her daughters, were also bent over the table. They had not curled up like their mother, but their eyes were downcast, and their elegant, equine faces were impassive. The mother and the girls sat alone, shut off from the rest of the room. The psychologist in charge of the session whispered that they lived in a shelter for battered women and they were very depressed.

During the intake session the woman and her daughters said little. They filled out the forms provided to them by the psychologist. The mother did not remove her coat or her caps. The faces of the girls remained stony, a practiced gray.

When some workmen came to repair a wall in the intake room, the session was moved into another, smaller room. The mother, who had curled up in the new place to fill out the intake forms, wanted to know the meaning of a word as it was used in one of the questions and how it could apply to a person's mental state.

I responded as best I could. She accepted the answer and went on filling out the form. The girls finished their forms first, and sat still and silent in their chairs, gray stone horses. I asked one of the girls if she went to school.

She said she was a high school student, but that she was not happy in her school.

"Are you a good student?"

"Yes, I get only A's."

"And what is your favorite subject?"

"I like to read books."

"Do you have a favorite author?" I asked.

"Yes, Gabriel García Márquez."

We began to talk about García Márquez, about this story and that. About *One Hundred Years of Solitude,* which we spoke of as *Cien Años de Soledad.* In a matter of moments, the two girls and I were in deep discussion about our favorite Latin American writers. Then the mother joined in. "Neruda," the girls said. The mother reminded us of the value of the Cuban, Carpentier. Did I know that it was Carpentier who had first written of a rain of butterflies? I asked if they knew the Dominican poet, Chiqui Vicioso.

We talked about the Mexicans: Carlos Fuentes and Sor Juana. Octavio Paz was still too difficult for the girls. They were interested in Elena Poniatowska, but they had not read her. They did not like Isabel Allende very much.

The mother uncurled, opening like a fern. The equine girls laughed. They told their favorite stories from literature, they talked about the Cuban movies made from the García Márquez stories: *The Handsomest Drowned Man in the World, Innocent Erendira, A Very Old Gentleman with Some Enormous Wings.*

Soon, the young psychologist joined in. One of the girls recited a poem she had written. Everyone in the room listened. The mother told a joke, pausing twice in the middle to cough. A Puerto Rican woman on the other side of the small room told the names of her favorite stories. Before long, the curled-up woman and her equine daughters and all the other people in the room, including the psychologist and the writer, had created a public world. The room of depression became a community of equals. The battered woman, who had no work, no place to call home but a secret shelter far from any place she had ever known, shared in the power of the public place. She removed her caps and let her hair fall loose, and when she smiled everyone could see that she was the source of the elegance of her daughters.

1

There are many routes to the political life, but it is a long journey up from loneliness, and very difficult, perhaps the most radical act in human history. Nothing quite compares to it. To expect the multigenerational poor, who live within the surround of force, in panic, to accomplish so radical a dream would seem to demand too much of them. But it happens. Human beings re-create themselves; by one method or another, by instinct or instruction, they prepare themselves for politics.

These are some of the ways in which the long-term poor become political:

1. Immigration can lead people into politics, if they understand the process. However, for those who feel unwelcome in the new country, as they did not feel at home in the old country, immigration is often not a way of recreating themselves, but only the transporting of their loneliness and suffering from one place to another. Immigration, of course, is not an option for people born in the United States.

2. Doing politics can make people political, but only when they *choose* to do politics; when people are mobilized, as so often happens to the poor, they do not experience autonomy. Choosing to do politics occurs when people join together in the public world to fend off criminals or protect their environment. The Mothers of East L.A. is an example of this learning of politics through doing politics.

3. Unions and other forms of cooperative endeavor, from tenant organizations to sweat equity housing to the PTA, bring people into the public world and in many instances enable them to do politics. Even corrupt unions may do this for their members, because of the sense of autonomy of the union. Unions fail to bring people into the public world when the membership does not understand what they are doing; that is, when union membership is like mobilization.

   Historically, progressive labor organizations have used education, including literature, history, politics, and economics, to bring their members to politics. Corrupt unions do not usually make such efforts.

4. Some churches create a public world for their members. The church itself may be an autonomous or semi-autonomous organization in which politics and worship support each other, but the most important function of the church in making the poor political grows out of the teaching of the humanities.

   Black churches in the South have had this effect. Through the charismatic movement and practices brought to the United States by priests who had worked in the *comunidades de base* in Latin America, the Roman Catholic Church is attempting to change its practices to accommodate this need for the parishoners to practice exegesis by reading directly from Scripture and to organize more along the lines of small Protestant churches.

Some churches hold the practice of politicizing their members as a goal nearly equal to that of believing in the tenets of the religion. The small church in Sun River Terrace, Illinois, a black community near Kankakee, has taken the creation of a public life for its members as a vital part of its work. Among those who preach to the membership, which includes some ex-convicts and recovering addicts, is Robert Ervin, a former Chicago police officer. Ervin understands the dual function of the church, and preaches accordingly.

5. Families devise strategies for survival that require a public life within the family unit that then extends to the larger community. In many instances these strategies are worked out in conjunction with church or legal rights organizations.

The surprise comes in the similarity of the method, which has continued over centuries and across cultures: Human beings become political by cultivating their inborn humanity. They follow the pattern established at the beginning. They embrace the humanities in one way or another; most often religion leads to reflection, but the law or organizational theory or political philosophy can have the same effect. They must do so, however, with little help from those who claim to care either for the poor or for the humanities.

To call for the study of the humanities now as an answer to the problem of poverty in the United States contravenes the views of both the left and the right. The left has abandoned the study of the humanities as the cultural imperialism of dead white European males, giving it over to the conservatives, who have claimed it as their own. In fact, the humanities should belong to the left, for the study of the humanities by large numbers of people, especially the poor, is in itself a redistribution of the wealth. The right, on the other hand, has had no use for the living humanities since Plato banned poets from *The Republic*.

Objection by the left to the study of the humanities can be dealt with quickly: The division should come between market-driven culture and the humanities, not between the beauty of an Asian poem and a European poem. When Petrarch called for a return to the classics, meaning the work of Greece and Rome, he knew no other. His notion of civic humanism would not include the study of bricklaying or popular culture now as it did not then. Nor would the humanities comprise the manufacture, programming, or repair of computers. But I think Petrarch would make world literature his text and find art influenced by Africa, Asia, and the Americas as interesting as the sculptures of Greece or the architecture of Rome. History, of course, has no limits and logic no substitute. The answers arrived at by philosophers differ from time to time and place to place, but the questions, as Kant set them out, have always been the same: What can I know? How shall I live? What may I hope? And what is man?

The humanities will always be heavily influenced by the work of the dead white men of Europe, for they have been history's troublemakers, the fomenters of revolutions and inventions, the impetus of change, the implacable enemies of the silence in which humanity perishes.[1] No other great body of work invites criticism or denies loneliness to the same extent, and no other body of work in all the history of the world led to politics, with its still astonishing notion of autonomy. The left abandons the humanities at its peril, for without the humanities for a gadfly, the left sits idly, contented by memories of distant thoughts and small victories, and dies.

Conservatism presents a more complex problem, because conservatives have attempted to seize the university, especially those aspects of education dealing with Western civilization, as their own. The most widely read exponent of this view, the late Allan Bloom, a member of the Committee on Social Thought at the University of Chicago, advised readers of his *Closing of the American Mind* of the kind of students included in his "sample" (his quote marks):

> It consists of thousands of students of comparatively high intelligence, materially and spiritually free to do pretty much what they want with

---

[1] Even when studying American cultures in the original languages, the impetus to organize the courses and to understand their value as precursors of the political life comes from ancient Athens, which bolsters the variety of cultures with the notion of empathy from Socrates and the interest in other ways of thinking from Herodotus. Later, of course, the influence of Herder came to bear on the idea of the uniqueness of cultures.

the few years of college they are privileged to have—in short, the kind of young persons who populate the twenty or thirty best universities. There are other kinds of students whom circumstances of one sort or another prevent from having the freedom required to pursue a liberal education. They have their own needs and may very well have different characters from those I describe here.

Lest there be any mistake about those he considers proper students of the liberal arts, Bloom quotes himself from an unidentified source in 1965:

I am referring to . . . those to whom a liberal education is primarily directed and who are the objects of a training which presupposes the best possible material. These young people have never experienced the anxieties about simple physical well-being that their parents experienced during the depression. They have been raised in comfort and with the expectation of ever increasing comfort.

To Professor Bloom, "these students are a kind of democratic version of an aristocracy." And these are the only students he deems fit for a liberal education.[2]

---

[2] *The Closing of the American Mind* (New York: Simon & Schuster, 1987), pp. 22, 49. Professor Bloom and I both came under the influence of the University of Chicago during the Hutchins era when the entire four-year curriculum of The College, based largely on the Great Books, was composed of fourteen required courses in the liberal arts and two elective courses. Some of the students entered The College after two years of high school by taking a long and quite rigorous entrance examination, made longer and far more rigorous for those who applied for scholarships.

The Hutchins Plan, as it was known, was flawed, but it was in my opinion the best education available in America. Some years later, after he had left the university, I talked with Hutchins about it. He spoke matter-of-factly about his years at Chicago, wondering aloud, in the chill, ironic fashion he reserved for people he did not know well, especially former students, why anyone would be interested in his experiment.

I do not know how Hutchins would have responded to Bloom's book. I suspect that parts of it would have made him laugh, but that Bloom's antipathy to freedom and fairness would have disgusted him. Perhaps not. When I met Hutchins, he was

As he goes on, however, it becomes more and more difficult to associate Bloom's ideas with an education in the humanities. He cites Plato's *Republic* as the great work on education, taking comfort in Plato's anti-democratic sorting, which underlies Bloom's own ideas about society and the university. He begins with a *fundamentalist* reading of the Allegory of the Cave, writing of Plato's intent: "Nature should be the standard by which we judge our own lives and the lives of peoples. That is why philosophy, not anthropology or history, is the most important human science."[3]

Bloom has put his foot down: Man is not the measure of all things! With a couple of sentences, he dismisses Protagoras and the Sophists.[4]

---

already exhausted, a *Wunderkind* in late middle age. He had been both more forgiving and sharper in his youth.

Bloom does not mention Hutchins or the Hutchins Plan in his book, although he does talk about the university during the 1950s, which leads me to think that we may have read Plato for the first time in the same surroundings, two bright young Jews, confounded and excited by the same lectures, the same examinations.

My interest in Professor Bloom's personal life does not go beyond this coincidence. To avoid the temptation to argue *ad hominem,* I have refrained from saying any more about him; his "friend" Saul Bellow has said more than any antagonist would dare. Our divergence on the value of the humanities and the importance of freedom may have personal or intellectual sources or both. For my part, the experience of The College of the University of Chicago was difficult and formative. I still have the newspaper clipping headlined, "Boy, 13, Wins Scholarship to U. of Chicago." The humanities helped to raise me; Plato also had his chance at parenting.

All of this may have something to do with the idea of radical humanism as an answer to long-term poverty: a rebellion against the politics of Plato's *Republic,* the sense of one's own insignificance beside the Great Books, nostalgia, etc. I would like to think not. Leo Strauss led Professor Bloom to the right, the world led me to the left; it is as clear as that.

[3] Ibid., p. 38. My choice of the word "fundamentalist" is used here with only a little irony. Bloom claims in the preface to his version of *The Republic* to have done a perfectly literal translation. He devotes the rest of the preface to an attempt to bury the lively, readable Cornford translation under pages of scorn and abuse.

[4] A distinction should be drawn between sophistry and the Sophists. Plato, who was a rival of the Sophists, used them as foils in several of his dialogues, and he did it so effectively that we now understand "sophistry" to mean a false or misleading argument, deceit.

His caricature of sophistic argument comes close to what we now understand as subtlely deceptive selling or advertising; that is, it appears to be true, but isn't. Protagoras was reputed to have been able to argue either side of a question (probably in the practice of eristic, a form of debate), like a modern salesman, who can champion one product or its competitor, or a political consultant, who can work for George Bush in one election and Bill Clinton the next. They will never merit mention in his book on education. Unlike Plato or Aristophanes, Bloom doesn't even bother to have some fun with his opponents. He goes glumly about his business of saving democracy from itself, with elitism for his sword and tradition his shield.

For Bloom, the fundamentalist, the idea of man as the measure of all things leads to relativism, and nothing else. He will take nothing from it in the way of praise for the works of man, including politics and the humanities, for Plato has said no to Protagoras. When the Sophist says that the discussion of poetry is the most important part of a man's education, the fundamentalist cannot even hear him, for Plato has banned the poets from his ideal republic. The idea of Protagoras as a teacher of the humanities, using critique as an avenue to the consideration of ethical questions, including politics, must be rejected by the fundamentalist, because Plato has labeled the poets subversive.[5]

---

[5] Bloom's insistence upon students who were born to the comforts of wealth may have some relation to Plato's arguments against poets. Bloom, like Plato, is interested in happiness and not in catastrophes or suffering. His view of the rock 'n' roll sixties is Plato's view in Book IX of *The Republic* of the man who is commanded by the lowest part of the psyche.

Stripped of its references to the world of philosophers after Plato, Bloom's book is a repetition of Plato's exposition of the "long-standing quarrel between poetry and philosophy," and might be summed up by these lines, from Book X, ". . . when you encounter admirers of Homer who say that this poet is the tutor of Greece, that to study him is to refine human conduct and culture, and that we should order our entire lives in accordance with his precepts, you must welcome them and love them as people who are doing the best they can. You can certainly agree that Homer is the greatest of poets and first among tragedians. But you must hold firm to the position that our city will admit no poetry except hymns to the gods and fair words about good

Protagoras confirms the assertion that he intends to teach the art of politics and to make men good citizens—an intention one would expect the right, with all their professed patriotism, to cherish, but it is not so. Protagoras is a subversive among the good citizens of Plato's idea of a republic, a democrat; he was chosen by Pericles to help write the constitution for a state based on the idea of participation by autonomous persons. The connection between this first critic and professor of the humanities and the codification of democracy makes clear that the Greeks understood the relation of critical thinking inspired by the humanities and the ongoing dialogue of which political power is made.

On the other hand, Plato, the arch conservative, and Bloom, his fundamentalist follower, have opted for the state as "the man writ large," an immutable organization prescribed by nature, and ruled by a philosopher-king. Poetry will confuse this perfect state, corrupt it. The study of the humanities makes poor men disputatious, unruly, a sickness in the state. The nightmare on the right is today, as it has always been, the humanity of the poor. They "have their own needs," according to Bloom and the fundamentalists, which are not the same as the needs of those who "have been raised in comfort."

The conservatives permit the humanities only under special terms, on the recommendation of Plato. Certain things must not be permitted, especially for the poor who do not know better (by virtue of their poverty perhaps?) than to think they can also live the public life, outside the domination of violent necessity.

---

men. Once entry is permitted to the honey-tongued Muse, whether in lyric or epic form, pleasure and pain will become kings of the city, law will be displaced, and so will that governing reason which time and opinion have approved"—trans. Richard W. Sterling and William C. Scott (New York: W. W. Norton, 1985). Francis Cornford ends the paragraph in a more straightforward political fashion: " . . . pleasure and pain will usurp the sovereignty of law and of the principles always recognized by common consent as the best."

Thomas Gould has devoted an interesting and enlightening book to *The Ancient Quarrel Between Poetry and Philosophy* (Princeton, NJ: Princeton University Press, 1990).

Allan Bloom has identified a view of literature, philosophy, history, and art which is to him the canon. Like Plato in Book III of *The Republic,* he will permit the citizens to read only those works he deems good for them (Alas, poor Socrates, who hoped he might meet Homer if after sleeping he did, indeed, awaken!). Furthermore, the canon is not just the work, but the official, acceptable interpretation of the work. Therein lies the greatest distinction between the liberals and the fundamentalists: The humanities, as Protagoras taught, live; the dialogue never ends, the works never die. Like Socrates, who objected to the death of dialogue caused by writing, Protagoras chooses the life-giving character of the changing world. His humanities are the preparation for politics.

It is not merely the reaction to slavery, but the struggle against fate that gives rise to the idea of freedom. The essence of tragedy comes of man's will to be free, independent of his fate, whether it is determined by gods or government. That is the great lesson of the humanities and the reason why Plato found the humanities intolerable in his state.

Following Plato, the right has laid claim to education, while opposing the very idea of the humanities. In his detestation of Cornford's sense of the living humanities, Bloom sets down the canon of the right: No word will be changed, no debate permitted. For him, no one could have been more in error than Socrates: Everything should be written, cast in stone; the humanities must die. But the world has not yet come to an end; the problem for the rich remains how to keep the world from changing, while the poor must find a way to reverse the damage. That is the argument between Protagoras and Plato, between the humanities and the sepulchral business the conservatives would use as a replacement, between inclusion and exclusion, power and force, democracy and our last breath.

2

The living humanities still have the same possibilities that produced the marvel of politics in Athens, only now in a radical way as an instrument of justice for the poor. Unfortunately, we have been so conditioned to understand the humanities as the province of the rich that the idea of teaching the humanities to the poor seems preposterous, a prisoner's fantasy, a joke told by Aristophanes.

The rest of this book is about the Clemente Course, an experiment—perhaps not so experimental any more—in pedagogy, but there was an experiment with a far larger sample in the black communities of the American South. The political life and the rise from poverty of Americans descended from slaves was engendered by the study of the humanities. Even before manumission, the study of the humanities went on in the slave quarters. There was one text, but there were many different courses, ontology, ethics, literature, rhetoric, and epistemology among them. The text, of course, was the King James Version of the Bible.[6]

Despite the horrors of life after Africa, including a broken culture and generations of chattel slavery, the blacks developed communities and practiced politics. As Dr. Goldie Wells, president of Saints Academy in Lexington, Mississippi, and others remembered, the black churches revered reading, loved the language and the cadences of their text, put their text to music and sang it (imagine the consternation of Plato!), and discussed every chapter, every verse in church meetings and at home. Black preachers delivered sermons that were more often than not exercises in exegesis. With nothing more than the King James Bible and the powers of the human mind, the descendants of slaves reinvented themselves through the humanities, preparing themselves for the political life.

A political world populated by people of African descent, educated to autonomy through the humanities, grew up under the low ceiling

---

[6] It is important here to draw a distinction between superstition and religion. Millennialists and premillennialists, all those who know with certainty what is to come, practice superstition. Superstition cannot be questioned; shamans, santeros, faith healers, snake handlers, swamis, and religious revivalists do not debate cures or causes with their patients. Superstition belongs to the explained world of the Neolithic mind. It is literal, fixed; if the circle is broken and the world changes, everything falls apart. But in the collapse of superstition, politics and freedom become possible.

of white hegemony. Not all blacks found a home in the humanities and not all of those who did became educated to politics. The surround of force in which blacks were forced to live made the leisure to learn the humanities all but impossible, yet the study went on.

3

Blacks differed from most Americans in that slavery barred them from the immigrant experience, which has been the primary education for politics over the last two hundred years. Immigrants, who came largely for economic reasons, did not understand freedom in contrast to slavery but as the alternative to fate, which had been the condition of their lives. They did not study the humanities, but in the overcoming of their fate or at least in the expectation of it, they became the material of the humanities; they undertook to live the political life in many instances without even knowing what it was. They experienced democracy without experiencing its underpinning in the humanities, which is what Tocqueville saw when he visited America in the nineteenth century. Market democracy, that is, democracy in its unreflective form, grew out of this.

Immigration still teaches politics, when immigrants can expect inclusion in the circle of power, if not immediately, then in the next generation. But the exclusion of immigrants from the possibility of power leaves them permanently in the surround of force, with no alternatives. These immigrants without politics fall into the category of the poor; all the rest have committed themselves to the struggle against fate. The action of the humanities takes place within them, as it always has.

This is not to suggest some irremediable difference in the character of blacks and whites, but to describe at least one more common path to the political life. The end is always fragile, no matter how one comes to it. The political life has always been beset by enemies: those that Plato and Aristotle imagined, and more. Sophrosyne has a brief season, and then something less human, sameness or rage, attempts to take its place.

4

Although the idea of the humanities as the original precursor to politics rarely meets with objection, very little has been written specifically about the process, mainly because, as M. I. Finley said, the Greeks had no theory of politics.[7] Bernard Knox assures us that it happened, but he does not describe the process. Jean-Pierre Vernant is more specific in his belief that politics and thought were intimately connected in ancient Greece. For him, public life in the polis served as the origin of rational thought. Cynthia Farrar, who wrote about "Athenian political theory," places the origin of politics in reflection, but for her, tragic drama provided a concrete example of the theory and "promoted exploration of the questions raised by . . . democratic politics. . . ."[8]

Farrar sees the sense of autonomy in Greece arising from the ability of men to separate themselves from the control of the gods, to take personal responsibility for their actions. Homer may have provided another impetus to political thinking, surely to reflection, in his portrayal of the battle for Troy. Never before had there been an "objective" telling of a story, until Homer gave his readers the chance to consider two sides of an argument. Before that, the point of view had always rested with the storyteller.

After Homer, the listener or reader had to consider more than one possibility, which may be as good a definition as any of the practice of reflection. The audience for *Antigone* could debate forever the political implications of the play. The only certainty one could take away from it was that Creon and Antigone could not do politics; each held on to a single idea, preferring death or destruction to mediation. With the prize-winning play of Sophocles to inspire them, ordinary people

---

[7] He suggests, in *Democracy Ancient and Modern,* that Protagoras may have had such a theory, which led Plato to spend so much time and effort mocking him. But it is only speculation; Finley concedes that no concrete evidence has survived (p. 28).

[8] Farrar, *The Origins of Democratic Thinking,* p. 30.

reflected on the polarities of social life: order and liberty. They invented politics, they took control of themselves.

This self-control, or *sophrosyne,* was also a synonym for politics. Thucydides used the word to mean a "moderate form of government." Violent behavior, like that of the suitors in Aeschylus' *The Suppliants,* transgressed the idea of sophrosyne.

There may have been many instances when the humanities, reflection, and politics united in a single concept, but none contains them all so well as sophrosyne, which denoted the temper of the world of public persons. In the idea of sophrosyne, the history of politics can be traced from its inception in the distancing of men from fate to the implementation of autonomy. Sophrosyne contains the road traversed by the humanities, the calm, contemplative path through the undeniable oppositions of human life; it is a defense against force, a definition of power, humanness.

5

The case for the humanities as a radical antidote to long-term poverty rests finally on the question of who is born human and to what extent a person is capable of enjoying his or her humanity. Pericles faced the question as it applied to the citizens of Athens, and he responded that all citizens were capable of noble deeds, "nor does poverty bar the way; if a man is able to serve the state, he is not hindered by the obscurity of his condition."

Elitism in the United States, in this manifestation the withholding of excellent education from the poor, as suggested by Allan Bloom, has its analogue in the Greek view of slaves. Aristotle thought they were slaves by nature; the education of them for politics was therefore out of consideration. Bloom, Charles Murray, et al. take this view toward the poor, particularly blacks and Latinos.

There is, however, no reason to think the multigenerational poor any less capable than the rich of the study of the humanities. The *a priori* assertions of the elitists have been accepted without ever being put to the test. On their advice the poor have been denied access to the humanities, and therefore to one path to politics. The evidence, however, points to the unfairness of the elitist position. Even within the surround of force that existed under chattel slavery and the systematic oppression that followed on it, American blacks found a way to study the humanities, develop a political life, and burst out of their bonds in a noble movement for civil rights. Through the humanities, they had become more human than their oppressors.

Before he was murdered, Dr. King sought to extend this state of enhanced humanness to the poor of all races. Though we cannot know whether his national pulpit could have replaced generations of exegesis and art, it is undeniable that the humanities, presented in the full flower of freedom, can be as effective for the poor as for the rich. Neither wealth nor poverty bars the way to enjoying a more human life; the economic situation of the student is irrelevant. Sentience and intelligence are all that matter.

The rightists are not fools in the defense of their own interests, however; they take Plato's warning with utmost seriousness. And from their point of view correctly so, for the study of the humanities is a radical act on the part of the poor, almost certain to educate them to the political life and catapult them into the public world, where power resides.

Reflection and the publicking of life benefit the poor more than the rich, because the winners in the game and even those in the middle have other means to power: They are included at birth, the favored of the game, without the tutelage of force to impede them.

The radicalism of the humanities in America is the denial of this essential distinction between rich and poor: the birthright of power. Once this happens, freedom is possible in the minds of the poor, and Plato's republic falls before the onslaught of poets, the parents of politics.

Those who appreciate ancient history understand the radical character of the humanities, for they know that politics did not begin in a perfect world, but in a society even more flawed than ours—one that embraced slavery, denied the rights of women, accepted a form of homosexuality that verged on pedophilia, and endured the intrigues and corruption of its leaders. The genius of that society originated in man's re-creation of himself through the recognition of his humanness in the expression of it by art, literature, rhetoric, philosophy, and the unique notion of freedom. At that moment, the isolation of the private life ended, and politics began.

Why not let it happen again now? Why should the poor be excluded, made to live out their lives in a surround of force? Robert Maynard Hutchins and Viniece Walker have the same prescription for America: radical humanism. As Hutchins said, "The best education for the best is the best education for all."

XIII.

The Clemente Experiment
Begins

After the final no there comes a yes
And on that yes the future world depends.
No was the night. Yes is this present sun.

. . .

It can never be satisfied, the mind, never.

— WALLACE STEVENS,

"The Well Dressed Man with a Beard"

The first year of the Clemente Course produced many errors, but also set the pattern for teaching the humanities to the poor. Although the course continues to be refined, there has been no basic change. The end remains to bring the students into the public world, to take them from the isolation of poverty to the political life of citizens. The means is still to use the Socratic method to teach the humanities at the university level in a form that integrates the disciplines.

Because the course has not undergone major changes, the experience of the first year remains as relevant as that of the fifth year and may be as useful to anyone thinking about the life of the poor and the value of an education in the humanities.

1

BY SPRING OF 1995 a theory had appeared, and the mere suggestion of a theory implies a will to change the world. At the same time a theory demands some form of proof or else it will have no weight, and float away on the next hypothetical breeze. Among the inescapable questions posed by the theory were these:

A. Can a method be found and institutionalized to help poor people become political?
B. Will the humanities lead poor people to reflection, which is a necessary stage on the way to political life?
C. If the first two questions can be answered with a yes, does it strongly suggest that the long-term poor are human, equal, and capable, and imply that there is neither an underclass nor a culture of poverty?
D. Since there are other ways for poor people to become political, is teaching the humanities a relatively effective and efficient way to bring the poor to the public world? Or would teaching the humanities merely repeat something learned long ago in a psychological experiment: If we pay attention to people, they will behave differently?

My mentors—Petrarch, Hutchins, and Viniece Walker—could not help. Two were dead and the third was in prison. The choice was to find some way to test the theory or simply to assert it, as Allan Bloom had done with the idea that the poor were unfit for a liberal education.

A study of students who came from poverty, entered prestigious universities, and succeeded in the world would leave two unanswered questions: Did they study the humanities? And were they exceptions to the rule? To the first, few universities offer an education in the humanities and few students choose such an education when it is available.[1] To the second, such students were by definition exceptional, and if the humanities affected only exceptional people, the elitist argument would be proved.

A search of existing data for the effect of the humanities on the poor was not possible, because the conservative argument against teaching the humanities to the poor had been put into practice with very close

---

[1] The Great Books curriculum at St. John's is perhaps the only exception, although a core curriculum has become more important at many universities during this decade.

to complete effectiveness in the United States. The data would have to be generated from something new. Three things were required: students, faculty, and facilities. Quantitative measures would have to be developed, but with only a small sample, anecdotal information would also be useful.

Finally, the ethics of the experiment had to be considered. Experiments involving human beings usually find a moral stance in the notion of the greatest good for the greatest number: a hundred people get the pill that can save their lives and a hundred get a placebo. The test works perfectly: a hundred live and a hundred die. For an experiment in the humanities no such choice was necessary: the control group was vast, and growing. This experiment could follow a different rule: First, do no harm. Using that rule, the experiment would not have a "sink or swim" character; it could aim to keep as many afloat as possible.

When the idea for an experimental course became clear in my mind, I discussed it with Dr. Jaime Inclán. If anyone was prepared by experience and character to consider such an idea, it was Dr. Inclán. He had no fear of new ideas about institutions; he had founded the Roberto Clemente Family Guidance Center in New York City to provide counseling to poor people, mainly Latinos, in their own language in their own community. His writings on psychotherapy were interesting, often daring. And behind the apple cheeks and the twinkling eyes, the sympathetic therapist's face, was a sharp, highly trained intellect. I had seen him at work among his peers; he did not hesitate to point out errors.

It was with some trepidation that I revealed the idea to him. We had talked often about questions of force and power, reflection versus reaction, the political life, but we had only touched on the idea of the humanities as a precursor to politics, mainly as it had affected the abused and depressed Silveria and her daughters (see Chapter XII). He listened attentively, without comment, while I set out the theory of the humanities as an education for politics and my intention to test the thesis through an experimental course.

I said that I wanted to pattern much of the course around The College of the University of Chicago during the Hutchins era: Two sessions a week, each lasting ninety minutes; the Socratic method, with students seated around a boat-shaped table; one comprehensive exam at the end of the year; and a sense of freedom in a formal setting.

Only then did he respond. The healer's smile broke across his face: "I'll give you the walls!"

"We'll call it the Clemente Course in the Humanities."

"That's good," he said. "The people in the community will be comfortable with the name."

The walls would be the conference room of the Center. In place of the finely made boat-shaped table of a University of Chicago classroom we would have three metal tables and one wooden table placed end to end and surrounded by two different kinds of metal and fabric armchairs. In the back corner of the room, we would set out fresh coffee and cookies on a card table. The front wall was covered by a floor-to-ceiling blackboard, and from time to time we were to make use of every inch of it.

2

The Clemente Course lacked only students and teachers. With no funds and a budget that grew every time a new idea for the course crossed my mind, I would have to ask the faculty to donate their time and effort. Moreover, when Hutchins said, "The best education for the best is the best education for all," he meant it. He insisted that full professors teach discussion sections in The College. The Clemente Course had to follow the same pattern. It required a faculty with the knowledge and prestige students might encounter in their first year at Harvard, Oxford, or Chicago. Ideally, they would be people of some accomplishment.

I turned first to the novelist Charles Simmons. We had been friends for many years, and I knew him to be a man of goodwill and a true literary man. He had been assistant editor of the *New York Times Book Review,* taught at Columbia University, and had written criticism, editorials, and stories, but I admired him most for his novels, especially *Wrinkles,* which I had turned to many times for the lucidity of the prose and the author's masterful engagement of life and mind.

"I'll teach poetry," he said. And then, without hesitation, not even a pause to indicate a new paragraph, "I'll begin with simple poems, Housman, and end with Latin poetry. We won't have a textbook; I'll teach exactly as I was taught by Raymond Weaver at Columbia. At the beginning of the class I'll give them a copy of a poem. We'll read it and discuss it."

Grace Glueck, whose art news and criticism has long been one of the cultural lights of the *New York Times,* said, "Oh, my dear, I don't know if I'm up to it. I'll have to prepare. I'll get the slides from the Met—they have a wonderful collection, and you can borrow them, you know.

"And we'll have to make field trips to the museums. When I was a little girl. . . ." All this in Grace's Seven Sisters vowels and neatly formed consonants, stylish, charming, but never flighty. She was one of the women who had fought the management of the *New York Times* over the hiring and promotion of women reporters and editors, and won. The fashionable woman was also a woman of politics.

"Sir, I should be delighted," said Timothy Koranda in his rotund, slightly ironic manner. "Before devising a curriculum, however, we shall have to ascertain whether any of them have had logic before." It had been twenty years since Tim had published his journal articles on mathematical logic. After MIT, where he had done his graduate work in logic at the end of a joint program with Cornell, Tim had paused to become fluent in Chinese and earn an MBA before building a career as a speechwriter. He had traveled, as he might have put it, from logic to rhetoric, but logic had been his first love, and I think he was genuinely pleased at the thought of coming back to it.

Thomas Wallace, a historian by training and an editor by profession, taught the first few classes in American history, but then withdrew for personal reasons.[2] For my part, I began putting together a syllabus to teach moral philosophy. Some help in that endeavor would come later, from an unexpected source.

---

[2] It is not very courageous to attempt to assemble a faculty from one's friends, but I am lucky to have friends of such character and accomplishment.

Since I was a naif in this endeavor, it did not immediately occur to me that recruiting students would present a problem. I did not even know how many students I needed. All I had were the criteria for selection:

Age: 18–35;
   Household Income: Less than 150 percent of the federal poverty level (although this was to change slightly);
   Educational level: Ability to read a tabloid newspaper;
   Educational goals: An expression of intent to complete the course.

Dr. Inclán and I talked about where to find such students and how many we would need to form a class. He put together a group of people who worked with the poor and were interested in the possibilities of an experimental course in the humanities. A week later, the group met in the conference room at the Robert Clemente Center. Of a dozen people he invited to the meeting, four showed up:

Lynette Lauretig, director of Educational Services at The Door, a large and extremely successful program that provided health care, counseling, instruction in English, GED preparation, painting and sculpture classes, even dinner and carfare to young people from around the city;

Saul Nieves, the community coordinator for U.S. Representative Nydia Velásquez, who also represented his wife, Susan Matloff, director of Youth Services at the Forest Hills Community House;

Rafael Pizarro, contract coordinator for Hospital Workers Local 1199;

and Angel Roman, of the Grand Street Settlement House.

After I made a brief presentation, there was a silence that extended into two or three minutes as people drank coffee and considered the idea. I felt no enthusiasm in the room, no willingness. The silence went on. The presentation had been too brief, the idea of teaching the humanities at that level to people who lived in poverty was apparently too radical.

Before the course died in the silence, Rafael Pizarro spoke. "I know what the humanities can mean to a person," he began, leaning forward in his chair, his shoulders rolled forward, too, and his hands in motion, Nuyorican, a man sparring with the world. He told the story of the brothers Pizarro. They had been close, two boys growing up together in the barrios of New York. One, Rafael, had developed an interest in the humanities early in life. He loved opera, read Dante and Sophocles. His brother loved the "fast life" of the streets. One night, Rafael remembers, his brother telephoned to tell their mother that he had killed a man. "It was only a Cuban," the brother said.

Rafael's brother went to prison. Rafael went to Sarah Lawrence College. He concluded his story by saying that the only difference between him and his brother had been the humanities, and that was why the course made sense to him.

Pizarro's story transformed the meeting: The question of whether to hold such a course was behind us. The conversation turned immediately to the details. The hours changed, as did the schedule. Nieves was adamant about the need to offer college credit. Pizarro said that the humanities were reward enough, but he, too, believed that an offer of college credit would help to retain students.

The course had to provide bus and subway tokens, because fares ranged between $3 and $6 per class per student, and the students could not afford $60 or even $30 a month for transportation.[3] We had to offer dinner or a snack, because the classes were to be held from 6:00 to 7:30 p.m. And we needed a television camera and a camera operator to experiment with providing a mix of personal teaching and videotape to Viniece Walker and the other women who attended the course at the Bedford Hills prison.

---

[3] Some students needed both bus and subway tokens, because transfers from subway to ground transportation are still not always available in New York City and many people live too far from a subway station to walk, especially at night in winter. Three students did not live on a bus line, and traveled to the subway by jitney at a cost of $3 each way, a total cost of $9 for every class they attended.

During the first few classes, I stopped at a subway station and bought packets of tokens, doling them out very carefully to the students. After a while, I asked the students to sign up for as many tokens as they needed, and just take them out of the pile my wife, Sylvia, or I put on the table at the end of each class.

3

The first recruiting session came only a few days later. With the help of Nancy Mamis-King, executive director of the Bronx Neighborhood Youth and Family Services program, some prospective students were identified in the South Bronx. Through one of the programs she supervised, about twenty clients and their supervisors were assembled in a circle of chairs in a conference room. Everyone in the room was black or Latino, with the exception of one social worker and me.

After I explained the idea of the course, the white social worker was the first to ask a question: "Are you going to teach African history?"

"No. We'll be teaching a section on American history, based on documents, as I said. We want to teach the ideas of history so that . . . "

"You have to teach African history."

"This is America, so we'll teach American history. If we were in Africa, I would teach African history, and if we were in China, I would teach Chinese history."

"You're indoctrinating people in Western culture."

I tried to get beyond her. "We'll study African art," I said, "as it affects art in America. We'll study American history and literature; you can't do that without studying African-American culture, because culturally all Americans are black as well as white, Native American, Asian, and so on."

It was no use. The social worker convinced her clients that no education was better than an education in the humanities; not one of them applied for admission to the course.

Following my defeat by the white multiculturalist, I walked across Tremont Avenue to the Young Mothers Program, where I asked four of the women if they were interested in a course in the humanities. Two declined and two asked for application forms.

I was pleased to have two prospective students, but I did not know what to expect of them. Carmen Quiñones had not yet overcome her ten years in prison and there was still a question about her ability to control her addiction. Carmen had been on the street, slept in parks and shelters, and the state had taken her children from her. She said that her hatred of men had made her gay. I had never met such a tough-talking woman. On winter evenings she had walked to the bus with me, dressed in her black leather biker's jacket, fearless in the dark in the South Bronx. Yet she had the sweetest face, round and wide-eyed, a grown-up version of the face painted on dolls. Either she was mad—a disjunction of mind and body—or the little girl was still trying to figure out how to stay alive. I liked Carmen, but she would be a very difficult test for my thesis.

"If you'll fill out the application form," I told her, "I think you can do this work."

"Okay, Earl," she said. "I'll give it a try."

The other woman, whose name was Bernadette, was to die before the end of the year.

Lynette Lauretig arranged a meeting with some of her staff at The Door. It was a heated and interesting discussion, one that would be repeated with many people over the next few years. How rigorous should the course be? We argued for nearly two hours. Although I could not change their views, they agreed to assemble a group of Door members who might be interested in the humanities. The pedagogical argument had ended in a draw; the goal had never been in dispute. The Door would soon become one of the closest allies of the Clemente Course, a source of innovation as well as support.

A few days later, in the early evening, about twenty prospective students were scheduled to meet in a classroom at The Door. Most of them came late. Those who arrived first slumped in their chairs, staring at the floor or greeting me with sullen glances. A few ate candy or what appeared to be the remnants of a meal. The students were mostly black and Latino, one was Asian, a few were white, although all but one of the whites were immigrants who had severe problems with English. When I introduced myself, several of the students would not shake my hand, two or three refused even to look at me, one girl giggled, and the last person to volunteer his name, a young man dressed in a Tommy Hilfiger sweatshirt and wearing a cap turned sideways, drawled, "Henry Jones, but they call me Sleepy, because I got these sleepy eyes."

"In our class, we'll call you Mister Jones."

He smiled, and slid down in his chair so that his back was parallel to the floor. One eyelid remained closed to a slit, giving him the appearance of a drug addict or a drunk.

Before I finished attempting to shake hands with the prospective students, a waiflike Asian girl with her mouth half full of cake said, "Can we get on with it? I'm bored."

I could not imagine a better group. I liked them immediately.

Having failed in the South Bronx, I resolved to approach these prospective students differently. "You've been cheated," I said. "Rich people learn the humanities; you didn't. The humanities are a foundation for getting along in the world, for thinking, for learning to reflect on the world instead of just reacting to whatever force is turned against you. I think the humanities are one of the ways to become political, and I don't mean political in the sense of voting in an election, but political in the broad sense: The way Pericles, a man who lived in ancient Athens, used the word 'politics' to mean activity with other people at every level, from the family to the neighborhood to the broader community to the city/state in which he lived.

"Rich people know politics in that sense. They know how to negotiate instead of using force. They know how to use politics to get along, to get power. It doesn't mean rich people are good and poor people are bad. It simply means that rich people know a more effective method for living in this society.

"Do all rich people or people who are in the middle know the humanities? Not a chance. But some do. And it helps. It helps to live better and enjoy life more. Will the humanities make you rich? Yes, absolutely. But not in terms of money. In terms of life.

"Rich people learn the humanities in private schools and expensive universities. And that's one of the ways in which they learn the political life. At every level. I think that is the real difference between the haves and have-nots in this country. If you want real power, legitimate power, the kind that comes from the people and belongs to the people, you must understand politics; the humanities will help.

"Here's how it works. We'll pay your subway fare; take care of your children, if you have them; give you a snack or a sandwich; provide your books and any other materials you need. But we'll make you think harder, use your mind more fully than you ever have before. You'll have to read and think about the same kinds of ideas you would encounter in a first-year course at Harvard or Yale or Oxford.

"You'll have to come to class in the snow and the rain and the cold and the dark. No one will coddle you, no one will slow down for you. There will be tests to take, papers to write. And I can't promise you anything but a certificate of completion at the end of the course. I'll be talking to colleges about giving credit for the course, but I can't promise anything. If you come to the Clemente Course, you must do it because you want to study the humanities, because you want a certain kind of life, a richness of mind and spirit. That's all I offer you: philosophy, poetry, art history, logic, rhetoric, and American history.

"Your teachers will all be people of accomplishment in their own fields," I added, and spoke a little about each of them. "That's the course. October through May, with a two-week break at Christmas. Why are we doing it? This is a demonstration project. It is generally accepted in America that the liberal arts and the humanities in particular belong to the elite. I think you're the elite."

The young Asian woman said, "What are you getting out of this?"

"This is a demonstration project. I'm writing a book. This will be proof, I hope, of my idea about the humanities. Whether it succeeds or fails will be up to the teachers and you."

It worked. All but one of the prospective students applied for admission to the course.

I repeated the new presentation at the Grand Street Settlement House and at other places around the city. There were about fifty candidates for the thirty positions in the course. Personal interviews began in late September 1995.

Meanwhile, almost all of my attempts to raise money had failed. Only Starling Lawrence, the AKC Foundation, and W. W. Norton supported the experiment (and they have continued to do so every year). We were far short of our budgeted expenses, but my wife, Sylvia, and I agreed that the cost was still very low, and we decided to go ahead.[4]

4

Of the fifty prospective students who showed up at the Clemente Center for personal interviews, a few were too rich (a postal supervisor's son; a fellow who claimed his father owned a factory in Nigeria that employed sixty people), and more than a few could not read. Two home-care workers from Local 1199 could not arrange their hours to enable them to take the course. Some of the applicants were too young: a thirteen-year-old, and two who had just turned sixteen.

Mrs. Medina, a woman with five children who had once answered the door at the single-room occupancy hotel with a butcher knife in her hand, was the oldest person accepted into the course. Carmen Quiñones was the next eldest. Both were in their early thirties.

The interviews went on for days.

Abel Lomas shared an apartment and worked part-time wrapping packages at Macy's. His father had abandoned the family when Abel was born. His mother was murdered by his stepfather when Abel was thirteen years old. With no one to turn to and no place to stay, he lived on the streets, first in Florida, then back up to New York City. He used the tiny stipend from his mother's Social Security to keep himself alive.

All I knew about Abel came from a conversation held in my car on the way uptown from the recruiting session at The Door. As I drove up Sixth Avenue from Canal Street, Abel talked about ethics. He had a street tough's delivery, spitting out his ideas in crudely formed sentences of four, five, eight words, strings of blunt declarations, with

---

[4] We cut the budget where we could. One of the cuts was a part-time administrator/bookkeeper, so we have only a vague idea of what it cost to hold the course. The course as administered by Bard College now costs $40,000–$45,000, with $25,000 to faculty and site director, and the rest to day care, books, carfare, copying, supplies, and administration.

never a dependent clause to qualify his thoughts. He did not clear his throat with badinage, as timidity teaches us to do, nor did he waste his breath in tact. If it is true that the style is the man, I had never encountered a man like Abel.

"What do you think about drugs?" he asked, the blunt, strangely breathless delivery further coarsened by his Dominican accent. "My cousin is a dealer."

"I've seen a lot of people hurt by drugs."

"Your family has nothing to eat. You sell drugs. What's worse? Let your family starve. Or sell drugs?"

"Starvation and drug addiction are both bad, aren't they?"

"Yes," he said, not yeah or uh-huh, but a precise, almost formal "Yes."

"So it's a question of the worse of two evils? How shall we decide?"

The question came up near 34th Street, where Sixth Avenue remains a hellish place well into the night. Horns honked, people flooded into the street against the advice of the stoplight. Buses and trucks and taxicabs threatened their way from one lane to the next as the overcrowded avenue split into two even more overcrowded streets. When we were through Herald Square and making our way north again, I said, "There are a couple of ways to look at it. One comes from Immanuel Kant, who said that you should not do anything unless you want it to become a maxim for the general will; that is, unless you think it's what everybody should do. So Kant wouldn't agree to selling drugs or letting your family starve."

Again, he answered with a formal "Yes."

"There's another way to look at it, which is to ask, what is the greatest good for the greatest number? In this case, keeping your family from starvation, or keeping tens, perhaps hundreds of people from losing their lives to drugs. So which is the greatest good for the greatest number?"

"That's what I think," he said.

"What?"

"You shouldn't sell drugs. You can always get food to eat. Welfare. Something."

"You're a Kantian."

"Yes."

"You know who Kant is?"

"I think so."

We had arrived at 77th Street, where he got out to catch the subway before I turned east. I looked at him more carefully now as he opened the car door and the light came on. The almost military neatness of him struck me. He had the newly cropped hair of a cadet. His clothes were clean, without a wrinkle. He was an orphan, a street kid, an immaculate urchin. Within a few weeks he would be nineteen years old, the Social Security payments would end, and he would have to move into a shelter.

Some of those who came for interviews were too poor. I did not think that was possible when we began, and I would like not to believe it now, but it was true. There is a point at which the forces that surround the poor become insurmountable, when there is no time or energy left to be anything but poor. Lydia, who was twenty, marked by a strawberry patch the size of a hand on her face, lived in the back of the basement of a building in Brooklyn. She ate and slept there, in the same room, among sickly children and a hapless mother, living without daylight. And in the middle of the year they were evicted from that place, because they could not pay the rent, and they moved to even worse housing somewhere in the Bronx. She came to class only twice, both times with a small child who sat on her lap and ate cookies, but she telephoned now and then to speak of her woes, to ask if I could help her to find work, housing, help of any kind. But when I made suggestions, she could not act on them.

Near the end of the year, she appeared in the waiting room of the Clemente Center. She looked haggard, as if she had been ill. "I'm glad you came to class," I said.

"I can't stay."

"Do you need help? This is a family guidance center, you know."

"I lost some of the books and papers when we moved."

"I'll see if I can find another set for you."

"Can I have tokens? I don't have money to get home."

"We always give out tokens at the end of class."

"I can't stay," she said.

I gave her a handful of tokens.

She hefted the tokens in her palm, weighing them, counting the number by their weight. We looked at each other for a long time. I felt the winter of her loneliness.

"Do you live near any of the other students? Can they help you?"

"No," she said.

Over the days of interviewing, a class was slowly assembled. I could not then imagine who would last the year and who would not. One young woman submitted a neatly typed essay that said:

> I was homeless once, then I lived for some time in a shelter. Right now, I have got my own space granted by the Partnership for the Homeless.
>
> My great-grandmother was very poor to the point that she could not afford to have running water into her place, nor electricity. She raised me partly. My grandmother was poor and could not make ends meet. My mother has been on public assistance with my brother.
>
> Right now, I am living alone, with very limited means. Financially I am overwhelmed by debts. I can not afford all the food I need and all the supplies and books for the school. Even transportation can be an issue at some point. . . .

In the next-to-last paragraph she wrote: "A friend helped me work out this essay."

A brother and sister from Tashkent came to the little interviewing room. I had not planned to accept immigrants, for I thought immigration was a separate issue, but these were refugees; they had been driven out of their homes after the breakup of the Soviet Union. "We are Joosh peeple," the boy began. "When Musselmen. . . ." He and his sister had a tiny English vocabulary and an emerging sense of English syntax. When I asked questions, they spoke to each other in Russian, then one or the other tried to answer. As best I could understand, the Muslims had made life in Tashkent impossible for ethnic Russians and Jews. The brother and sister now lived with their parents in the farthest reaches of the borough of Queens, in some place far beyond the end of the subway line. Their parents were both ill, they had no money, and they had been refused admission by every college to which they had applied.

They gave their surnames as Iskhakov and Iskhakova, son and daughter, Russians, refugees, the new poor of New York City. I accepted them because I liked them and because I did not want the class to comprise only people of color; there would have been a misleading message in that. For the same reason I accepted a young Albanian who lived in a room without a telephone and survived by working part-time jobs making pizzas and washing dishes.

Laura,* the fourth white person who applied to the course, was a tall, slim girl with dyed blond hair and sickly pale skin. She wrote on her application, "I am nineteen years old. I'm originally from Dallas, Texas. I have spent the past five months in city shelters." She told me she had been abused by her father and stepmother and that she had run away from home to live with street people in Dallas. A girl she met there urged Laura to come up to New York, where they could live with the girl's mother.

It had not worked out. The girl's mother was schizophrenic, according to Laura, impossible to live with. Although she had no job and no money, Laura moved out. She went from shelter to shelter, finally ending up in a place in Harlem. The problem there was that when the police saw a young blond woman on the streets of Harlem at night, they assumed she was a "working girl," and arrested her.

"They took me to the station house and started slapping me around," Laura said, "so I hit them back. And they charged me with resisting arrest or something, and I have a fifty-dollar fine, and if I don't pay it, they're going to send me to Riker's Island. So if they don't send me to jail, I can come to the course."

"Will your shelter put up the money for the fine?"

"I don't think so," she said, her vowels growing broader, more southern. "I asked them, and they said no." Then, as an afterthought, "If I don't go to jail and come to the course, can I bring my friend?"

---

* Not her real name.

"If he applies and is accepted."

"Not he, my girlfriend."

"Same rules apply."

"You know how my stepmother and my father abused me? They went into my room and took all my dolls and all my things off the wall, the pictures and everything, and all my pretty clothes . . . and burned them. That's when I left home."

I told her she would get a letter within ten days if she was accepted for the course. And I asked her to telephone me if she could not raise the money to pay the ticket. After she left, I went to Jaime Inclán's office to ask his opinion about Laura. After describing her and my doubts about the fine and the beating, I said, "I think she's going to make trouble. Or she's in trouble. Something's wrong. I don't know if I should accept her."

He said, "Earl, I think you are prejudiced against white people." We laughed. And of course I accepted her. She turned out to be smart, attentive, and gifted with a mordant sense of humor that all of the teachers and few of the students appreciated. For a long time I thought Jaime had been correct about Laura. Perhaps I was prejudiced against white people. I did not think so, but it was possible.

Hector Anderson, a tall, slim, supercooled fellow, with a pianist's slender fingers and a classic Brooklyn accent, said he had been to several high schools. "In my last semester I got a safety transfer," he said.

"What's that?" I asked.

"They gave me a safety transfer, because I got into a lot of fights."

"Did you win?"

He shook his head, "No, I lost, that's why they had to give me a transfer, for my safety." We had a great laugh together. He turned out to be one of the brightest students in the course. On the final exam he not only answered every question correctly, he wrote a charming parody of a Philip Larkin poem.

There were lies and confessions, crimes, pregnancies, and always loneliness. I argued with them about their possibilities, I sold them hope. They taught me to revise my definition of poverty. The federal guidelines were meaningless. People were poor who connected themselves to institutions that serve the poor: settlement houses, social welfare agencies, shelters, free clinics, gangs, minimum-wage jobs, drug programs, food pantries, soup kitchens. People are poor when they concede that they are poor, when there is no saving politics in their lives. That became the criterion for selection.

As I listened to them, I wondered what effect the course would have. They had no public life, no place; they lived within the surround of force, moving as fast as they could, without a moment to reflect. Why should they care about fourteenth-century Italian painting or truth tables or the death of Socrates?

"I'm pregnant," one young woman said. "And I ain't getting no abortion. I don't believe in that's the right thing."

"Will your parents help you?"

"They are the lowest of the low, way down here, my parents. When I was sixteen, they sold me to a man to have a baby for him."

"What will you do?"

"I gotta move out. I'm sharing a space. I gotta get my own space."

She wept. And then as the pregnancy progressed, she learned to swagger, carrying a beeper and banging the heels of her heavy shoes on the classroom floor. She wore too much lipstick and she spoke of having to be "strapped" when she left the "L-E-S," the Lower East Side, where she lived. A few months into the year she could no longer tolerate the isolation. She disappeared, leaving word that she had gone "upstate."

5

Between the end of recruiting and the orientation session that would open the course, I made a visit to Bedford Hills to talk with Niecie Walker and to be certain everything was ready for the course to be held in the prison. Niecie and Sharon Smolick, who ran the Family Violence Program, and I met in a small office.

It was hot, and the drive up from the city had been unpleasant. I did not yet know Niecie very well. She did not trust me, and I did not know what to make of her. While we talked, she held a huge white pill in her hand. "For AIDS," she said.

"Are you sick?"

"My T-cell count is down. But that's neither here nor there. Tell me about the course, Earl. What are you going to teach?"

"Moral philosophy."

"And what does that include?"

She had turned the visit into an interrogation. I did not mind. At the end of the conversation I would be going out into "the free world"; if she wanted it to be an interrogation, I was not about to argue. I said, "We'll begin with Plato. The *Apology.* A little of the *Crito.* A few pages of the *Phaedo,* so they know what happened to Socrates. Then we'll read the *Nicomachean Ethics.* I want them to read Pericles' Funeral Oration to make the connection between ethics and politics, to lead them in the direction I hope the course will take them. Then we'll end with *Antigone,* but read as moral and political philosophy as well as drama."

"There's something missing," she said, leaning back in her chair, taking on an air of superiority.

The drive had been long, the day was hot, the air in the room was dead and damp. "Oh, yeah," I said, "and what's that?"

"The Allegory of the Cave. How can you teach philosophy to poor people without the Allegory of the Cave? The ghetto is the cave. Education is the light. Poor people can understand that."

6

A few days before the course was to begin, Leon Botstein, president of Bard College, an excellent liberal arts college about two hours north of New York City, offered to place the course under the academic aegis of Bard. After ascertaining that Bard would incur no costs, he said, "Good! We'll get the publicity, and you'll get the credit before God." Of course, there were eventually significant costs to Bard, in terms of both money and time. I did not realize it then, but Leon had a very good idea about what he was getting into. As it turned out, he was willing to give a great deal to the course, more than I could possibly have expected.

A week later, a letter arrived from Dr. Robert Martin, associate dean of the college and dean of the Graduate Center. He promised that

Bard would provide a certificate of accomplishment to those who completed the course, but reserved any decision on course credit until the faculty executive committee could evaluate the curriculum, the faculty, and the progress of the students.

A copy of his letter was included in the packet of materials handed out to the thirty-one students who came to the orientation meeting on October 12, 1995. There were no secrets; the students knew as much about the issue of college credit as I did.

At the beginning of the orientation, Rafael Pizarro told the class about the effect of the humanities on his life. Then each of the teachers spoke for a minute or two. Dr. Inclán administered the questionnaire that he and Ramon Maisonet had devised, using various standardized scales to measure, as best we could, the role of force and the amount of reflection in the lives of our students.

When they had completed the questionnaires, I explained to them that the sections of the course would be given in rotating sequence, beginning with Philosophy, then Art, Logic, Poetry, and History, and starting the sequence again with Philosophy. I said the purpose was to integrate the disciplines, but I did not tell them the other advantage of the rotation. Since poor people suffer more health and personal problems than the rest of the population, I expected their attendance to be spotty. With the five-course rotation and two sessions a week, a student could be out for as long as two and a half weeks and still miss only one class in each subject. The alternative was to teach the sections one at a time, which meant that a two-week absence would almost certainly lead to an incomplete.

At the end of the orientation I gave them their first assignment: "In preparation for our next meeting, I would like you to read a brief selection from Plato's *Republic:* The Allegory of the Cave."

The first class started badly. The young fellow who had volunteered to videotape the sessions (with an eye to making a "brilliant" documentary) telephoned to say he was going to be late, because he was on his way down from Martha's Vineyard where he had been visiting dear friends whom he had not seen for the longest time. I fired him.

Following the orientation meeting, I tired to guess how many of the students would return for the first class. I hoped for twenty, expected fifteen, and feared ten. Sylvia had agreed to share the administrative tasks of the course, and she and I prepared coffee and cookies for twenty-five. We had a plastic container filled with tokens. Thanks to Starling Lawrence, we had thirty copies of Bernard Knox's *Norton Book of Classical Literature,* which contained all of the texts for the Philosophy section except *The Republic* and the *Nicomachean Ethics.*

At six o'clock there were only ten students seated around the long table, but by six-fifteen the number had doubled, and a few minutes later two more straggled in out of the dusk. I had written a timeline on the blackboard, showing them the temporal progress of thinking, from the role of myth in Neolithic societies to *Gilgamesh* and forward to the Bible, the Greeks, Confucius, the New Testament, the Koran, the *Epic of Son-Jara,* and ending with Nahua and Maya poems, which took us up to the contact between Europe and America, where the history course began. It served as context, geography and time, inclusively: no race, no major culture was ignored. "Let's agree," I told them, "that we are all human, whatever our origins. And now let's go into Plato's Cave."

I told them there would be no lectures in the philosophy section of the course; we would use the Socratic method, which is called *maieutic* dialogue. "*Maieutic* comes from the Greek word for midwifery. I'll take the role of midwife in our dialogue. Now, what do I mean by that? What does a midwife do?"

It was the beginning of a love affair, the first moment of their infatuation with Socrates. If it is true that he was the first one to bring philosophy down to earth, it is also true that he was the first one to raise these students up to seriousness. Once he told them that the answer, the truth, was inside them and had only to be brought forth through dialogue, they were never again to see themselves in the same way. The humanities became a mirror in which they saw their human worth, and, like all lovers, they were transformed by love.

Later, Abel Lomas would characterize that moment in his no-nonsense fashion, saying that it was the first time anyone had ever paid attention to their opinions. Keeping to the metaphor Socrates preferred, they were born.

7

What is the life of man? A thing not fixed
For good or evil, fashioned for praise or blame.

—SOPHOCLES, *Antigone*

The first meeting at Bedford Hills went almost as well. About forty women gathered in one of the largest classrooms at the prison. They were older than the students in the city, a complexity of skeptics and innocents, women who had acquiesced to the dark green uniform of the prison and others who wore only the one required piece of the uniform, and completed their attire with sweaters, blouses, fashionable shoes, the symbols of the "free world." Yet others, who had adopted the masculine role in their prison relations, cut their hair short and turned their prison uniforms into military-style fatigues, sharply creased, with the trousers bloused over jump boots. A roomful of accommodations gathered there, awaiting, perhaps with trepidation, another view of life.

My wife and Tom Wallace came to that first meeting in the prison. It was the only time either of them would go to Bedford Hills. I had described the prison to Sylvia, but nothing written, said, or pictured can reproduce the oppressive atmosphere of a maximum-security prison. It is not the clang of gates or the weapons trained on the prisoners, but the weight of remorse and the grieving of women separated from their children that is unbearable. Sharon Smolick characterized it in a single image: "The sound of a women's prison at night is of weeping."

When they found out that I could not guarantee college credit, the Bedford Hills women made a devastating response: Twenty-five of them dropped the course. There were two stages in winning over the small number who remained. The first was intellectual: *The Consolation of Philosophy.* Boethius is hardly a thinker to place alongside Plato or Aristotle, but the idea of Philosophy personified, the nurse of his childhood, coming to visit Boethius in his cell opened a discussion about freedom, pagan and Christian, before and after St. Paul.

Boethius, whose thought lives somewhere in the middle between the pagan and Christian ideas, was the best example, for to one side were the Greeks and to the other the martyrs of Christianity. I do not know whether Philosophy was a consolation to the women in Bedford Hills, but they considered it, for one woman, Ada Velásquez, said in response to Boethius that in the night, after lockdown, she lay awake in her room to think of what she had done with her life. "We did crimes," she said, "but we're still human." She did not say whether she expected Philosophy to visit her cell.

The second part was more difficult. Terri McNair, who worked as a counselor to the women, said that I would have to tell them about myself, convince them that I was not merely a condescending rich white man.

"You mean a confession?"

"Yes."

On the way up to Bedford Hills to teach the next class, I decided to chance it, to tell the students of my mother's addiction to barbiturates and morphine, and of my own troubles in school and in the military. I did not lie to them: I said that for a while, when I was very young, a friend and I had imported marijuana through New Mexico and sold it in East St. Louis, Illinois.

"You don't look like a drug dealer," one woman said. And another called out, "Where you gold chains?"

Terri had been correct. After the laughter faded, the course began. The humanities had moved from the ivory tower to the world. In the end, however, it was not enough. Only a few women completed the course and only a handful earned college credit. And one of those women, Judy Clark, already held a master's degree and did not need the credit. She and I had both been undergraduates at the University of Chicago—although not at the same time; she is much younger than I—and we had both had our troubles there. It helped to have her and Niecie in the class, for there was never that deadly silence when the teacher must supply the answer, never a time when one of them did not break the silence with the next line in the dialogue.

Now and then the world was too much with us in the prison. Near the end of the year, I met with the women to review what they had seen on the videotapes and discussed in class. When we came to *Antigone,* I gave them the assignment for the final paper, which was to be about the play, using what they knew of Socrates, Sojourner Truth, Henry David Thoreau, and the poetry they had read (Charles Simmons did not go to the prison to teach) to reflect on it, and then offer their own opinion of Antigone's decision.

One of the older women in the class spoke about the conflict in the play between family and state. She said she had experienced the same conflict. "You see," she said, rocking back and forth in her chair, "I had that situation with my daughter. I had to turn my daughter in to the FBI."

Her face swelled with tears and her voice died away, although she continued to speak. Something in the "situation" with her daughter had brought her to this place, but I could not imagine what it had been, and the etiquette of prison does not permit asking questions about a person's crime. All I could do was ask, "Can you write about it? You know more about Antigone than any of the rest of us can ever hope to know. You can teach us. Will you do that?"

"Oh, I don't know if I could," she said very softly.

"Will you try? Never mind the rest of the final assignment. Just write about Antigone as you understand her. Or just write about your own decision. Do that. Teach us. Teach me about Antigone."

She said she would. She is a shy, sweet, soft woman, whose skin is gray beneath the brown, as if she had been underpainted with sorrow or with age. She told me later that she had tried to write the essay, and then she lowered her eyes and collapsed inside herself.

8

Grace Glueck began in a darkened room, leading them across the centuries into the caves of Lascaux to imagine early men in firelight, dressed in animal skins, drawing out their dreams or hungry hopes on the vast subterranean walls. And then she took them out again to Egypt—first to the sun, then to the netherworld where the painted figures waited to arise again, whole and happy, perfect in every line. They stayed long in Egypt, not so much to look at the antiquities as to imagine them, to talk about them. Seeing this, Grace arranged for them to visit the Metropolitan Museum of Art, where Felicia Blum led them first to the Temple of Dendur, and then through the Egyptian Collection.

The students arrived at the museum on a Friday evening. Darlene Codd brought her two-year-old son, Yaro. Pearl Lau was late, as usual. One of the students, who had told me how much he was looking forward to the museum visit, did not show up, which surprised me. Later, I learned that he had been arrested for jumping a turnstile in a subway station on his way to the museum, and was being held in a prison cell under the Brooklyn Courthouse.

Had he come to the museum, he might have been in the thrall of the Egyptians, but it was not his luck. It was Samantha Smoot who was transformed by the humanities that night. And it happened while she was standing in the Temple of Dendur.

She is alternately possessed by fear or wishing; at times as carefree and stylish as the images mannikins project, and the next day old bones and chopped-off hair. I have seen her dreaming. One night, after I had taken a group of students to an Italian restaurant in Greenwich Village, Samantha was the last to leave. She walked up a few steps to the door, then turned back to the dining room with a regal air and waved to the eaters, as if they had looked up from their piccata or primavera to adore the young woman who told them of her importance by the deep dimples that graced her smile. "My fans," she said, and with a sweeping gesture of celebrity, turned and went out the door to where her classmates waited, shivering, inadequately dressed for the winter night.

"Did you finish high school?" I had asked in the initial interview. She said she had not, because she "fell in with the wrong crowd."

"Do you live at home?"

"Yes."

"With your parents?"

"My father's not in the picture."

"Brothers or sisters?"

"My brother is upstate."

"For a long time?"

"Yes."

It was she who had said, announced, burst out with the news, in one of the first sessions of the course, that people in her neighborhood believed it "wasn't no use goin to school, because the white man wouldn't let you up no matter what."

She could read, but she could not write. The first paper she turned in was almost incomprehensible. Patricia Chui, a young editorial assistant on her way to becoming an editor at W. W. Norton, had offered to tutor someone in the course. I sent Samantha to her, and they worked together all through the rest of the year: The daughter of a physician, educated at the University of California at Berkeley, and the fearful dreamer from Brooklyn found common ground in the English language. They met twice a week, once in the offices of W. W. Norton and once in a coffee shop in Greenwich Village, to discuss grammar, syntax, and the organization of the mind on paper. At the end of the course, Samantha was not yet ready for publication, but the young editor had made a success of her work, for Samantha's final paper would have earned a decent grade at any college.

Perhaps it was the influence of Patricia Chui or the visits to the offices of the publishing house or the humanities entering into her life, but I think that all of this came together for Samantha in ancient Egypt. In the Temple of Dendur it was she who asked the questions of Felicia Blum, and when they went on to a hall where the statuary was of half-human, half-animal female figures, it was Samantha who asked what the glyphs meant. As Felicia Blum read them, translating the incised stone into English words, Samantha dreamed a dream of Africa. This was her ancient mirror, not forests or savanna, but the splendor along the Nile.

Toward the end of the evening, Grace took over the tour, leading the students out of the halls of antiquities into the Rockefeller Wing, where she told them of the connections of culture and art in Mali, Benin, the Pacific Islands. At the end of the tour the students collected their coats and stood together near the entrance to the museum, preparing to leave. All but Samantha, who stood apart from us, posed in loftly serenity. We left her there—a tall, slim young woman, only a few days older than a girl, dressed in a deerstalker cap and a dark blue peacoat. She smiled at us, dimples of innocence and joy, made an exaggerated wave of farewell, and returned to ancient Egypt whence she had come.

Bernadette telephoned from the hospital the first time she missed a class. I could hardly make out what she was saying. She had no breath with which to make the sounds. A few weeks later she was back, weak and distracted, glassy-eyed. It was not my night to teach; she gave me her three-year-old daughter to hold. The child was as beautiful as Bernadette had been the first time I met her. The girl's skin was not so dark, it lacked the velvety perfection, but she was as delicate, as defined, as her mother.

The lustre had gone from Bernadette's hair, the bite had fled from her conversation, only the hard New York accent remained, now in narrower voice. I walked the halls with the child. I took her to play with the other children, but there was no consoling her, as if she knew. I stood at the side of the classroom, holding her so that she could see her mother, and for a while she was content. In the end, she sat on her mother's lap for the last part of the class. I wondered if the girl, too, was sick, if Bernadette had passed the virus on to her at birth.

We gave a special certificate of accomplishment to Bernadette. Carmen brought it to the apartment where Bernadette languished, in the care of the family of the man who had put her out on the street. Before Bernadette died, her daughter was tested for HIV infection and pronounced free of the virus. Carmen brought that news along with the news of Bernadette's death.

9

Charles Simmons began the poetry class with poems as puzzles and laughs, tiny poems, jokes in form or language, puns. His plan was to surprise the class, and he did, again and again throughout the year. At first he read the poems aloud to them, interrupting himself with foot-notes to bring them along. He showed them poems of love, seduction, commentaries on poems they read in the form of satire by later poets. "Let us read," the students demanded. And he refused.

A tug-of-war began between Simmons and the students, particu-larly Laura and Carmen. He withheld the reading from them, tanta-lizing them with the opportunity to say the poems aloud. In his third class, the students were arguing over a D. H. Lawrence poem about America when Henry Jones rose from his chair, pointed his finger at Laura, who sat across the table from him, and said, in an accusing tone, "Define your terms!"

The gate to poetry was finally opened not by Simmons directly but by Hector Anderson. When Simmons asked if anyone in the class wrote poetry, Hector raised his hand. "Can you recite one of your poems for us?"

Until that moment, Hector had never volunteered a comment, al-though he had spoken well and intelligently when asked. He pre-ferred to slouch in his chair, dressed in full camouflage gear, wearing a nylon stocking over his hair, and eating slices of fresh cantaloupe or honeydew melon.

In response to Simmons's question, Hector slid back up to a sitting position. "If you turn that camera off," he said. "I don't want anybody using my lyrics." When he was sure the red light on the camera was off, Hector stood up and recited verse after verse of a poem that be-longed somewhere in the triangle formed by Ginsberg's *Howl,* the Book of Lamentations, and hip-hop. Simmons was delighted. Later he told me, "That kid is the real thing." In the classroom, he joined in the applause. When the room finally grew quiet, Simmons and the students asked Hector to say the poem again, and he did it gladly.

Like some ancient poet, exalted by his art, Hector Anderson as-cended to a new place in the class. His discomfort with Sylvia and me turned to ease. He came to our house. We spoke on the telephone. As a student, he began quietly, almost secretly, to surpass many of his classmates. But it was always at poetry that he excelled, asking Charles

Simmons writerly questions about a poet's choice of alliteration or sudden rhyme. He wanted to know the surface as well as the sinew of poetry. Anderson and Simmons stood at opposite ends of a long table of age and ethnicity, but they engaged nevertheless, in the way that artists can.

The first questions about Laura arose in the poetry class. She asked to read a Langston Hughes poem in which he describes a park in Harlem, announcing at the start her familiarity with the park, which was across the street from the shelter where she lived. She read well, and Simmons was impressed, but there was grumbling in the room.

Laura asked again for permission to bring her girlfriend to class. I said no visitors were permitted in the classroom. "I have turned away the ABC Television network and the *New York Times,* as well as many curiosity seekers, Laura. The only people who audit our course are the women in Bedford Hills."

At the beginning of the next class, a young black woman sat in a chair against the wall. She wore her hair in cornrows pulled so tight that streams of shining scalp showed between. The skin of her face was tighter still, stretched across her bones, revealing in embarrassing intimacy the details of her skull. "This is my friend," Laura said.

The girl and I shook hands. I told her she could stay this time, but that she could not come again. She smiled, but she made sure I understood the unpleasantness she intended.

Laura missed the next few classes. When next I spoke to her, she said there had been a problem in the shelter; someone had set her room on fire.

One poem affected and interested the students more than any other. At Bedford Hills, Niecie Walker and Aisha Elliott argued about it night after night. In the classroom, the students understood it perfectly, including the ambiguity, which they found intriguing. More than Maya Angelou or even Lawrence and Housman, whose work came so easily to them; more than anything they responded to this poem by William Blake.

The Little Black Boy
My mother bore me in the southern wild,
And I am black, but O! my soul is white;
White as an angel is the English child;
But I am black as if bereaved of light.

My mother taught me underneath a tree,
And sitting down before the heat of day,
She took me on her lap and kissed me,
And pointing to the east, began to say:

"Look on the rising sun; there God does live,
And gives his light, and gives his heat away;
And flowers and trees and beasts and men receive
Comfort in morning, joy in the noon day.

"And we are put on earth a little space,
That we may learn to bear the beams of love,
And these black bodies and this sun-burnt face
Is but a cloud, and like a shady grove.

"For when our souls have learned the heat to bear,
The cloud will vanish; we shall hear his voice,
Saying: 'Come out from the grove, my love & care,
And round my golden tent like lambs rejoice.' "

Thus did my mother say, and kissed me;
And thus I say to little English boy:
When I from black and he from white cloud free,
And round the tent of God like lambs we joy,

I'll shade him from the heat till he can bear
To lean in joy upon our father's knee;
And then I'll stand and stroke his silver hair,
And be like him, and he will then love me.

The students were torn between Blake's suggestion of the protective power of blackness and his setting of the poem in a racist world. In Bedford Hills, Aisha took the view that Blake loved blacks and wanted to show how powerful and close to God they were. Niecie saw only the racism evoked by Blake. It was their first experience with a literary ambiguity that touched their own lives. Simmons drew their feelings out, asking and asking, "Do you like the poem? What does he mean by 'the heat to bear'? Who is closer to God?"

He made the dialogue like the poem, and they were aware of what he was doing, complicit. The dialogue was at once about both beauty and ugliness, dreaming and the moment, hope and anger, and no harsh word was said.

10

David Howell telephoned on a Saturday afternoon in January. "Mister Shores," he said, anglicizing my name, as many of the students did.

"Mister Howell," I responded, recognizing his voice.

"How you doin, Mister Shores?"

"I'm fine. How are you?"

"I had a little problem at work."

"Uh-oh," I thought. Bad news was coming. David is a big man, generally good-humored, but with a quick temper, according to his mother. In the classroom he had been one of the best students, a steady man, twenty-six years old, who always did the reading assignments and who often made interesting connections between the humanities and daily life. "What happened?"

"Mister Shores, there's a woman at my job, she said some things to me and I said some things to her. And she told my supervisor I had said things to her and he called me in about it. She's forty years old and she don't have no social life, and I have a good social life, and she's jealous of me."

"And then what happened?" The tone of his voice and the timing of the call—Saturday morning—did not portend good news.

"Mister Shores, she made me so mad, I wanted to smack her up against the wall. I tried to talk to some friends to calm myself down a little, but nobody was around."

"And what did you do?" I asked, fearing the worst, hoping this was not his one telephone call from the city jail.

"Mister Shores, I asked myself, 'What would Socrates do?' "

It was the first concrete example of a person thinking differently because of the course. David Howell had reflected on the situation, and made a decision that differed from his instinctive reaction. The anecdote was important, but it was only an anecdote, one case. At the end of the year, Dr. Inclán would administer the questionnaire again.

There were other moments in the classroom that gave some indication of the progress the students were making in understanding and integrating what they learned. One evening, in the American History section, which I had taken over from Tom Wallace, I was telling the students about Gordon Wood's ideas in *The Radicalism of the American Revolution.* We were talking about the revolt against classicism at the turn of the century, including Benjamin Franklin's change of heart, when Henry Jones raised his hand.

"If the founders loved the humanities so much, how come they treated the natives so badly?"

There were confounding answers to offer about changing attitudes toward the Native Americans, vaguely useful references to views of Rousseau, James Fenimore Cooper, and so on, but simply to confound the issue would have been unfair, dishonest. Henry had discovered the terrible flaw in the life of the mind, which is that knowledge does not always produce goodness.

I did not know how to answer his question. For a moment I wondered if I should tell them about Heidegger's Nazi past, confirming his view. Then I saw Abel Lomas at the far end of the table. His hand was raised. "Mister Lomas," I said, hoping that his comment would give me another moment to think about Henry's question. I had made promises about the humanities; Henry was now calling for me to defend those promises in the face of hard evidence to the contrary.

Abel said, "That's what Aristotle means by incontinence, when you know what's morally right, but you don't do it, because you're overcome by your passions."

The other students nodded in agreement. They were all of them inheritors of wounds caused by the incontinence of educated men. But now they had an ally in Aristotle, who had given them a way to analyze the actions of their antagonists.

Timothy Koranda was the most professorial of the professors, arriving for each session just as the class was to begin. He always wore a hat of many styles, part fedora, part Borsalino, part Stetson, and at least one-half World War I campaign hat. From their first encounter the students recognized in their portly, formal professor what could be said to be a kind of zen sweetness; that is, not love, but a connection in that cool, empty realm where egos have been banished and inequalities cannot exist.

He taught them logic during the appointed hours, and afterward he spoke to them of zen. When the class was over, he walked with them to the subway, chatting all the way about zen or logic or Heisenberg. They did not share intimacies; he initiated them into the incorporeal world of pure thinking.

In the classroom he filled the blackboard from floor to ceiling, wall to wall, drawing the intersections of sets here and truth tables there and a great square of oppositions in the middle of it all.

One winter night, Koranda introduced them to logic problems stated in ordinary language that they could solve by reducing the phrases to symbols. He passed out copies of a problem, which was two pages long, and then wrote out some of the key phrases on the blackboard. "Take this home with you," he said, "and at our next meeting we shall see who has solved it. I shall also attempt to find the answer."

By the time he finished writing out the key phrases, however, David Iskhakov raised his hand. Although they listened attentively, neither David nor his sister Susana spoke often in class, for she was shy and he was embarrassed at his inability to speak perfect English.

"May I go to blackboard?" David said. "And will see if I have found correct answer to zis problem."

"Please, sir," said Koranda, stepping aside and holding out the chalk to David.

"May I erase?" David asked, pointing to the phrases Koranda had written.

"Be my guest. In fact, I shall assist you." And Koranda and his student together wiped the board clean.

David began writing signs and symbols on the board. "If first man is earning this money, and second man is closer to this town . . ." he said, carefully laying out the conditions. After five minutes or so, he said, "And the answer is: B will get first to Cleveland!"

Samantha Smoot shouted, "That's not the answer. The mistake you made is in the first part there, where it says who earns more money."

Koranda folded his arms across his chest, and smiled. "I shall let you all take the problem home to think about it," he said. "Meanwhile, I shall do the same, and at our next meeting we shall review the answer."

The scene took place during one of the coldest nights of that winter. When Sylvia and I left the Clemente Center a few minutes before eight o'clock, a knot of students was gathered outside in the icy night, huddled together against the wind. Snow had begun to fall again, a slippery powder on the hard gray ice that covered all but a narrow space down the center of the sidewalk. Samantha Smoot and David Iskhakov stood in the middle of the group, still arguing over the answer to the problem. I leaned in for a moment to catch the character of the argument. It was as polite as it had been inside the classroom, perhaps more so, for now they governed themselves.

11

I do not know when the course became an avenue to college. Perhaps it was at the instigation of Candace Reyes D'Andrea, the college counselor at The Door, but I think it is more likely to have occurred after two of the students who had enrolled in community college courses reported that the Clemente Course was far more demanding. Within a few weeks after that, the students began visiting with college admissions counselors from Bard, New York University, and Columbia University.

Since Bard is two hours by train from New York City, Donna Ford, who directs the Higher Education Opportunity Program (HEOP) there, and a group of students met over lunch at my house. They were astonished by her. The associate dean for academic services was young, fashionable, and easy to be with. She gave straight answers in plainspoken English. By the end of the lunch, all the students but Samantha Smoot wanted to go to Bard. Samantha said she was afraid she could not keep up.

Five students were accepted at Bard. Hector Anderson and Jacqueline Martin could not qualify for HEOP scholarships under the federal guidelines, but Henry Jones and Susana and David Iskhakov were offered complete scholarship packages.

Laura, whose GED test score was high enough to make her a candidate for admission at either Bard or NYU, chose to apply only to NYU, because she did not want to be far from her girlfriend. As the weeks passed, she missed classes now and then. Once, after she missed several classes, I telephoned her. There had been a problem, she said; she had to look for an apartment and a job, because she had to move out of the shelter.

Late in the year, after she was accepted at NYU, she stopped coming to class. Her social worker told me that Laura and her roommate had moved out into their own apartment. "We have no more control over them," the social worker said. "She does come back to pick up her mail. That's the only time I expect to see her."

"If you have her new telephone number, I'll phone her about coming back to class. There is only one session left before the final exam, and I would hate to see her lose the course credit now."

"She left specific instructions not to give the telephone number to you or anyone else from the Clemente Course," the social worker said. "I think she's afraid of what will happen if you call there."

"When you see her, please tell her that if NYU inquires about her grade in the course, I will answer truthfully."

"I'll tell her," the social worker said.

Although I never saw Laura again, I did speak to the social worker once more. She told me then that Laura's girlfriend had been non-compliant. When I said I did not know what she meant by that, she spoke about the fire, and added that there had been other problems as well. "I saw Laura two days ago. She passed by my office on the way to get her mail. Her face was bruised. I think she couldn't come to school because of the bruises."

"The girlfriend?"

"Yes."

12

During the last meeting before graduation, the students answered the same set of questions they had encountered during orientation. Sylvia and I, the people who knew them best, believed they had been changed by the humanities, but anecdotal evidence and our own good-will toward them did not prove the efficacy of the humanities in leading people toward reflection and politics. Granted, the sample was small. Students had fallen to AIDS, pregnancy, job opportunities, pernicious anemia, clinical depression, a schizophrenic child, and even to poverty itself. In three of the seventeen instances we did not have both pre- and post-course tests; one or the other was missing.

Dr. Inclán's full report of the results appears in Appendix C of *New American Blues*. In summary, these were the significant changes he reported:

1. Improved Self-Esteem ($p<.05$)[5]
2. Decrease in Verbal Aggression ($p<.05$)
3. Improved Problem Definition & Formulation ($p<.001$)

---

[5] The letter p represents the probability that the results happened by chance. According to Dr. Inclán, when the probability is less than $<.05$, there is little doubt about the results. When p is $<.10$, the results are still useful, even though the risk of error is higher.

4. Increase in Values of
   Benevolence (p<.05)
   Spirituality (p<.05)
   Universalism (p<.10)
   Collectivism (p<.10)

The scales and inventories Dr. Inclán and his staff used are all well known and widely used. In his judgment, the quantitative results corroborated the anecdotal evidence. Something happened.

There was one last piece of anecdotal evidence. It came on the night of graduation. The staff of the Roberto Clemente Center had turned the waiting room/lobby of the center into a bar and buffet. A neighborhood restaurant delivered a Puerto Rican–style feast of fried chicken, roast pork *(pernil)*, plantains and onions, flattened and fried plantains with garlic sauce *(tostones)*. The students brought enough guests to fill every one of the eighty-five chairs we had been able to crowd into the conference room.

The registrar of Bard College had prepared certificates of accomplishment, as she called them, to be awarded by Dean Robert Martin. He was to speak briefly, as were Dr. Inclán and I. The main speaker was David Dinkins, former mayor of New York City. Halfway through the exercise, the mayor swept in, slightly out of breath, wearing a dinner jacket and looking more confident and important than he had during his years in City Hall.

He spoke for perhaps fifteen minutes, mainly offering anecdotes about himself and his friends. There was no Golden Age of poverty in Mayor Dinkins's stories; he and U.S. Representative Charles Rangel and others had all pulled themselves up by their bootstraps. But the words did not matter so much to the students as the fact that the former mayor of New York had come to the Lower East Side to the room in which they had studied. He had chosen to come there, to be late for his own law school fortieth reunion, he told them, because he thought they were important.

When it came time to conclude the exercise, I spoke a few words about each of them, congratulated them, and said finally, "This is what I wish for you: May you never be more active than when you are doing nothing. . . ." I saw their smiles of recognition. The words of Cato, which Hannah Arendt so loved, were there again, as when I had first written them on the blackboard. The end of that brilliantly constructed thriller, the *Nicomachean Ethics,* was there again, too. They could recall the moment when we had come to Aristotle's denouement, the idea that in the contemplative life man was most like God.

One or two, perhaps more of them, closed their eyes. I saw tears beginning in their eyes, I saw through tears of my own. In the momentary stillness of the room it was possible to think.

"But is this what Aristotle means by action?" someone had asked.

"Yes," I had answered. "Yes, exactly!"

After a breath, I finished Cato's thought, " . . . and may you never be less lonely than when you are by yourself.

"Godspeed."

Follow-Up

1

Dr. Inclán said that there would have to be three stages to the measurement of the effect of the humanities on the students: the pre- and post-course tests, and a follow-up "to see if the inoculation took."

Six months after graduation, only one of the students was not enrolled in an accredited college or working full time or both. The remaining student, Hector Anderson, was writing occasional pieces for a New York radio station and preparing to apply again to Bard College. Carmen Quiñones was going to school and working part-time as a counselor at Riker's Island. In October 1996, five students met in a New York recording studio to participate in a series of programs based on this book for the Public Radio International program *Marketplace.* Samantha Smoot delivered a passionate extemporaneous speech on poverty and the humanities, and she and Hector Anderson, David Howell, Jacqueline Martin, and Abel Lomas held an impromptu discussion of *Antigone*. They had not forgotten the play. If anything, their understanding of Antigone had ripened over time.

In December 1996, Henry Jones was nominated to head the black students' organization at Bard College. Henry has since left Bard College without graduating. David Iskhakov was cross-breeding fruit flies in his biology course. His sister Susana was still planning to be a chemist, but a course with an excellent professor had led her to consider biology as a possible alternative.

Only Abel Lomas had not fared well. On Mother's Day, 1996, he was arrested for drinking a can of beer on the street outside the shelter where he lived. The police ran his name through their computer system and found a federal warrant for Abel Lomas. Several months before the Clemente Course began, Abel had been in his cousin's apartment when federal agents arrested his cousin and three other men for selling cocaine.

The federal agents, who were acting on information supplied by confidential informants, knew that Abel was not part of the drug ring. They did not arrest him. But a few weeks later, two of the men who had been arrested told the U.S. Attorney they would give him the name of another member of the conspiracy in return for a lesser sentence. Both men named Abel, and he was indicted in absentia.

Under the federal guidelines Abel Lomas must receive the same sentence as the other men who were in the room, a sentence based upon the amount of cocaine found by the federal agents. Had Abel been arrested by New York City police, it is almost certain that an assistant district attorney would have charged him with a misdemeanor, if he had charged him at all, and sent him home. Because his case came up in the federal court system, neither the judge nor the U.S. Attorney had discretion. Abel Lomas faced at least ten years in prison with no chance for parole.

In a meeting with Assistant U.S. Attorney Patrick Smith arranged by Lomas's pro bono attorney, Peter Neufeld, two people from The Door and I spoke in support of fair treatment for a young man who had learned reflection and politics, asking the prosecutor to consider the case in light of the man and of justice. During the conversation I asked Abel about his understanding of law. He spoke about the decision reached by Socrates in the *Crito* and about *Antigone.*

The Assistant U.S. Attorney said he had never read the classics and did not understand the references, which caused him to be confused about Antigone's decision, even though Abel explained it. All the young prosecutor could say was that the law should be applied equally to all persons. Although he would later reflect on the meeting and what Abel had said, justice was not then the issue uppermost in his mind, and in that sense he did not participate in legitimate power, he was merely an instrument of power, like the Outside Chiefs of the Pueblos—force. And no one can engage in dialogue with force.

2

A year after graduation of the first class, two more students had been accepted at Bard College: Hector Anderson and Abel Lomas, who had avoided going to prison by pleading guilty to a relatively insignificant crime he did not commit. As I understood it—in layman's terms—a charge made in the federal system cannot be withdrawn. It was due only to Lomas's appearance as an educated man and the Assistant U.S. Attorney's extraordinary efforts that the charge was reduced to a level that permitted him to be sentenced to probation. Samantha Smoot had won a full scholarship to the Fashion Institute of Technology, and Jacqueline Martin was studying to be a registered nurse. Only one of the students who had completed the course was not either employed or attending college. Pearl Lau had been fired from her job in a fast-food restaurant for attempting to start a union.

There was, however, one irony of tragic proportion. On May 14, 1997, the parole board met at Bedford Hills Correctional Facility to hear the case of Viniece Walker. She was a model prisoner and she had served more than ten years of an eight-and-one-third to twenty-five-year sentence. That afternoon the woman whose belief in the humanities had given rise to the Clemente Course was denied parole and condemned to two more years in prison. Two years later, after another hearing, lasting less than a minute, her application for parole was denied again. Early in 2001 I will begin soliciting letters from officials, journalists, educators, everyone who might be concerned, asking the governor of New York to intercede with the parole board.

XIV.

The Bard Course

AT THE END OF THE FIRST YEAR, I began to think about the future of the experiment. If it worked, it would be a mistake to abandon it, but continuing the course presented several problems. I had proved my ability as a fund-raiser the first year, and the prospect of supporting the course year after year almost entirely alone was not a happy one. Moreover, I was not an educator. Professionals were needed, if professionals had any interest in the course. The prospects were not good: If the educational establishment had been interested in teaching the humanities to the poor, they would have done so.

Perhaps Bard was an exception. I liked Bob Martin from our first telephone conversations, and when we finally met he was open and enthusiastic, and he glowed. Fair of skin and hair, white of tooth, and apple-cheeked, he really glowed. We talked over a bad meal in a third-rate restaurant on the Upper West Side of New York; he provided more light than the dimmed bulbs overhead. His conversation was quick, he understood every point halfway through my exposition, and hurried on. The moment he revealed that he was really a cellist who taught philosophy, I thought, *allegro vivace,* and a little faster, but not so quick that the notes did not have consequence.

Later, when I turned to Martin to discuss the future of the experiment, he asked the two difficult questions: Who? And how? He suggested a friend, also a philosopher, who had been educated at Brandeis, taught at Rutgers, and later suffered as assistant to the president of Adelphi College on Long Island. His name was Mickey.

"Mickey?"

"He's a wonderful guy, just right for the course."

We arranged to meet for lunch at my house. Mickey turned out to be Martin Kempner, not merely a philosopher, but one of the best long-ball-hitting first basemen who had ever played in The Bronx. He had given up the chance to try out with a major league team in order to devote himself to philosophy. A man who had survived such an error could surely survive the failure of the Clemente Course, if the experiment turned out to be neither repeatable nor reproducible. Fortunately, he had no plans to give up his day job.

Kempner spoke softly, with a slightly talmudic delivery, meaning that he could think with laughter as well as weight. He had a shock of light brown hair that fell forward over one eye when he was speaking in earnest, which was often; it made the first baseman visible in the philosopher. Could a man so apparently contemplative by nature manage the course? He loved Socrates, he believed in the good; I believed in him.

We discussed the duties of the director of the course, which have remained essentially the same over the years. I told him that we had a site, the Clemente Center, and it could provide the social services, space for child care on premises, classroom space and along with it a table or series of tables and chairs to enable a dialogue rather than a lecture to take place. Moreover, it was not a place devoted to teaching and it was not intimidating as a university campus might be. At the Clemente Center students could begin afresh, with but few of the ghosts of hard times beside them.

Kempner had to recruit a faculty for this tiny university of the humanities, and the faculty had to be first rate. Bob Martin joked that we could not expect the "million-dollar faculty" of the first year, but he agreed that the director would have to choose people who were comfortable in their own knowledge and good teachers. There was some discussion about how to choose these people. Should they all be senior faculty? Should everyone have a terminal degree? Did we require that they be published?

Martin suggested that the best philosophy professor might be a lawyer who had studied philosophy, loved the field, but had chosen law in order to earn a living. We would have to gauge the value of a professor by how she or he knew and loved the discipline and could convey that love in the classroom. He reminded us that the constrictions of establishment academe need not affect the Clemente Course. We could concentrate on finding the best professors, those who could best educate our students.

There were to be limits, however. The professors were not under any circumstances to be the usual teaching assistants foisted upon first-year students. Our students had to have the sense that they were getting the best; it was, in truth, necessary to bring excellent, even brilliant teachers into the classroom. Moreover, there had to be a sense of the dignity of education in the classroom. It was vital, I argued, that the students and professors address each other as "Mister" and "Miss." The formality would not only add to the decorum of the discussion, it would give the students a sense of security inside the room.

We discussed the idea of a core reading list, a basic syllabus for each course, which I favor, but Kempner and Martin thought the professors should be given the freedom to develop their own courses. With no core readings as a guide, the director had to be responsible for developing the syllabus for five courses with the professors. The burden placed upon a director who generally teaches American History to evaluate an Art History or Literature syllabus is severe. To bear this responsibility, the director must either be a true intellectual, versed in several fields, or have access to experts in the field who can help to evaluate the proposed course.

As the Bard version of the course is now structured, Martin Kempner is the final arbiter in this area, which serves as a check, especially in his field, philosophy. Fortunately, Kempner is a fierce defender of the rights of the students to get the best possible education in the humanities in the limited time available. He works with the directors and professors at every site. I have been with him when he was faced with the task of telling a director that the faculty was not of the quality necessary for our students, and I was astonished and pleased by his firmness. The students who come to the Clemente Course have, many of them, never had anyone either to listen to them or to defend their rights to the wonders of the humanities. Kempner knows that, and he does not take the responsibility lightly.

On occasion new people do not understand our insistence upon rigor, but once they see the effect of it on the students, they become advocates. Only once, when Dean Peter Steinberger of Reed College raised the question, has anyone suggested that the course might not be rigorous enough.

No other single issue carries as much importance as the question of rigor in the curriculum and teaching. This rigor is the truest measure of respect for the humanity of the students, as they quickly realize. Without it, the power to think reflectively, which I believe is the means for becoming a political person, does not become available to the student. The tendency to let this rigor become attenuated by the common view of the incapacity of the poor poses the greatest challenge for the faculty. If Martin Kempner and Bob Martin were to define their management role as a single task, it would be to keep the tendency to treat the poor as undeserving of the best education from ever entering the classrooms of the Clemente Course. Given that as the sine qua non, the selection of the faculty becomes more than the evaluation of a résumé. The directors and the managers of the course must know them, and if they find they have made an error, they must be prepared to remedy it, and quickly.

With the faculty in place and each section of the course approved, the director must then recruit students. The director first contacts various organizations that work with prospective students: social services, rehabilitation services, youth organizations, churches, settlement houses, neighborhood organizations, and so on. He must then arrange a meeting with groups of prospective students from the organizations.

It is a self-selection process once the students have been exposed to the idea of the course, but the manner of presentation is all-important. Most of the prospective students will be suspicious of the course and dubious about their own ability to complete it. The director must convince them of his or her sincerity, and then, in a personal interview, judge the sincerity and capability of the prospective student.

None of the usual materials for gauging the abilities of the student will be available to the director. Virtually all of the students will have had unsuccessful school experiences. The reasons will vary from a succession of incompetent teachers to peer pressure to family problems to poverty itself. Some of the applicants will have served time in jail or prison. Young women will have dropped out of school to raise their children. Others will be first- or second-generation immigrants with language problems. The director will have to see through the veil of poverty to the real person. And he or she will have to do this as many as fifty or sixty times or more to select a class of twenty-five to thirty.

There is a tragic component to the selection process, which is that the director must accept the inevitable loss of at least one of every four students, and perhaps more, some of whom he or she will have come to care for very much.

At the same time, the director must work with the management of the site—the social service agency, university, or church—to raise money to pay the faculty and director, reimburse the students for their transportation expenses, provide child care on site, and buy the necessary books.

Once the students have been selected and letters of acceptance have been mailed to them, the second phase of the director's work begins. To build and maintain a close relationship with the students and to monitor the quality of teaching, the director of the site is expected to attend every class. Although the site should offer or have access to both counseling and crisis intervention services, the director should know the students well enough to sense that a crisis is building in a student's world. Of course, that is not always possible, but crises, as everyone knows, are more easily diffused in the making than in the fact.

A few months into the course, the role of the director shifts slightly as the faculty and the director take on the task of counseling those students who plan to continue studying at the college level after completing the Clemente Course. Since the students often have a history of troubles and never have any money at all, the director must help to make educational institutions aware of the enormous potential for scholarship that the course has unlocked in the students.

And the pay is rotten.

Kempner listened to the long list of duties and problems, the emotionally and physically wearing work that Sylvia and I described, and he said, "It sounds wonderful. I can't wait."

At The Door, Kathleen Connolly had taken some materials I had sent her and converted them into a funding proposal that she could send to foundations. She and Lynette Lauretig arranged a meeting with a group of prospective funders during the summer. We sat in a circle in one of the meeting rooms at The Door. Sylvia and I spoke about the course, but our fear was that no one believed the rigorous character of it. As proof, I had brought copies of part of the final exam, which we distributed to the representatives of various foundations, all well-educated and well-meaning people, many of them with advanced degrees. After they had glanced at the examination questions, I asked them if they would please answer the questions for the philosophy section, and return the papers to me.

Not one person was willing to take the test, saying that it had been too long since the study of philosophy or that they had never studied philosophy at all. The point was made: The Clemente Course in the Humanities did function at the university level, not high school, not even the level of most community colleges; it was a university-level course.

When the faculty for the second year had been assembled, we met at a conference table outside Lynette Lauretig's office at The Door. It was the same table at which the staff of The Door and I had argued over the intellectual level of the course. And we had most of the same arguments. Instead of the Allegory of the Cave, this one was fought over the inclusion of a Greek play. And it was no less hotly contested. Even after the experience of the first year, with the staff of The Door now on my side, and with a faculty that had been recruited by a philosophy professor rather than a writer, the idea of teaching the humanities at the university level to poor people seemed to some of the new faculty absurd, impossible. We argued until some of the faculty had to leave to meet other commitments. Perhaps it took two defenders of rigor, but the problem was solved. Martin Kempner saw to it.

Since Kempner had a business to run, with national and international involvement, and the Clemente Course required more and more of his time, a decision had to made: Would he manage the Clemente Course or continue in business? If it was to be the Clemente Course, some changes had to be made.

Bob Martin arranged a meeting with Leon Botstein, the president of Bard College, to discuss Bard's commitment, the needs of the course, and so on. We met at the Bard College Graduate Center in New York City. Leon Botstein, with whom I had had several telephone conversations, but whom I had never met, swept into the office we used for the meeting, dressed for his role as conductor of the American Symphony Orchestra. We shook hands, had a brief exchange of pleasantries, then I said, "Leon, we need three things from Bard if this course is to continue: office space, a place to call home; a salary for our executive director, Mickey; and a board of directors to oversee the course."

Botstein smiled. "Good," he said, "done. What else?"

"The makeup of the board. It should be people who have a connection to the course and who can give suggestions in the areas of academic competence, finance, and organization."

We agreed, in alphabetical order here, to ask David Dinkins, former mayor of New York City; Grace Glueck of the *New York Times;* Jaime Inclán, director of the Clemente Center; Starling Lawrence, the novelist and editor-in-chief of W. W. Norton; and Peter Sourian, a writer and Bard professor.

"Good," said Botstein, "and you'll be the chair."

With that done, Leon Botstein launched into a series of charming,

funny stories. Exhilarated, still performing after his stint before the orchestra, he gave us witticisms, comic narratives, memories—an astonishing mix of charm and intellect. At one moment during the
hour or so that we talked, he leaned over to me, and with a glance
across the room at Martin Kempner, who was briefly engaged in some
business with Bob Martin, asked softly, "Are you sure he can do it?"

"Yes."

That was all Leon Botstein wanted to know. From that moment
forward, he has been a staunch supporter of the Clemente Course and
its national director. "Leon," I said, "your response is generous, but we
will try to raise enough money to make Bard whole."

He delivered an operatic "Oooh," followed by another burst of stories, but he managed to convey his sense of relief. I liked him and the
order of his thinking: first, the good, then prudence.

The stage had been set to begin thinking about the third year. The
Door had helped us to raise some money for the second year. John R.
MacArthur; the AKC Foundation; Starling Lawrence, and W. W. Norton; and Sylvia and I had added the rest. We decided to go ahead
with a second site. The Door had been involved since the beginning;
Lynette Lauretig and her staff had helped to recruit students, coun-
seled them during the year, aided them in making application to colleges. There could not have been a better place. Fund-raising became
a more demanding part of the operation. The Door had earned the respect of the foundation world, but the staff had more than enough to
do raising money for its own needs. Kempner and Martin turned to
Judy Samoff at Bard for help. Fund-raising would always be a difficult task, but we had enough of a track record to satisfy the requirements of foundations and individuals. Sometimes people telephoned
or wrote letters, saying they were interested in helping. I sent them
to Mickey, and the program went forward.

The growth process has begun to settle into a pattern, which may
be useful to know for anyone who intends to start a Clemente Course
or other work with the poor or the humanities or both. If the events
seem to be too good to be true, it may be that a self-selecting group
has been drawn to the course, but we have met few fools or villains
during the first five years.

The growth of the course outside the New York area and the Yucatán (described in Chapter XVII) came about because Linda Capell was the program chair for the 1998 annual meeting of the Federation of State Humanities Commissions. She asked if I would travel to Washington, D.C. (she was also program director for the Washington State Humanities Council) to talk about poverty, the humanities, and the Clemente Course.

Meanwhile, my wife had been urging us to start a course that would benefit American Indians. Washington had a large Indian population and Linda Capell understood what we were doing. Why not Washington? I brought up the idea with Linda, thinking she would ponder it, talk with other people, come to some decision in a few weeks or months. I was not prepared for the burst of energy in response to my very tentative notion. In retrospect, it seems that Sylvia and I boarded the plane for Seattle the next day, but I am certain it took a bit longer, even for Linda.

The Seattle visit set the pattern for bringing the idea of the course to new cities. Linda Capell arranged a lecture at the University of Washington, a talk to a civic club, visits to possible sites, enough publicity to find and connect with interested people. A meeting with Richard McCormick, president of the University of Washington, gave the course there its financial foundation. McCormick said he had read about the course while sitting on the sidelines watching his daughter play soccer. He had decided then to have such a course in Washington. To be sure it would happen, he invited the provost of the university and the director of its large humanities program to the meeting. McCormick made it clear that he wanted them to help get the course started and funded. And they did.

Margaret Ann Bollemeir, executive director of the Washington (state) Humanities Council, has since made it one of their annual projects, contributing money, energy, and most importantly, Lyall Bush, a staff member of the commission, who is the director of the Seattle course. Bush and Mickey Kempner, along with Linda Capell, hired a faculty, chose a site, which has since been changed to Centro de la Raza, and defined a curriculum.

Kempner's work had, so far, been doubling every year. In addition to going to the West Coast to help with the organization of the Seattle course, he had started a course in New Brunswick, New Jersey, not far from where he lived, and where his wife, Carol, managed the Middlesex County Head Start program.

Kempner and Martin worked with the Fund for the Improvement of Post-Secondary Education (FIPSE) of the U.S. Department of Education, which had agreed to help support the Clemente Course, especially in the area of evaluation. And in the Pacific Northwest, conversations between Linda Capell and Steve Lindbeck, director of the Alaska Humanities Forum, had led to the beginning of a Clemente Course in Anchorage, and later in Chevak, Alaska. Lindbeck, a journalist, had taken over the Alaska Humanities Forum and made it an important influence across the state, an astonishing feat in a place that still had its frontier/pipeline roughneck image to protect.

Within a few days, he had excited people across the entire state about the program, following the Seattle pattern and adding the media. The course found a friend in Mike Dunham, arts editor of the *Anchorage Daily News*. Dunham, who had been raised in Yup'ik Eskimo country and spoke some Yup'ik, grasped the idea of the Bard College Clemente Course, shared my interest in the rich and still very vibrant Yup'ik culture, and put it all in the paper.

In Tampa at the University of South Florida, Mark Amen had become interested in the Clemente Course. He and I had a conversation, and then he and Mickey began the task of putting the course together. Robin Jones and Glen Brown worked with Amen. Although her field is urban studies (her most recent book is *City Schools and Politics*), a discipline not taught in the course, she became the director in Tampa, bringing her personal warmth to the classroom and a closer connection to the services available to the poor.

Kempner taught philosophy and managed four courses while the Bard project grew to eleven courses by the beginning of the 1999–2000 academic year. To help with the administrative burden, Terence (Ted) Dewsnap, who had taught art history and been a site director, took the job of assistant national director. Bard continued to provide support.

Although many private organizations had begun to support the course, it found a very strong ally in the state humanities councils. These councils, funded by the National Endowment for the Humanities (NEH), and in many cases by state and local money as well, provide financial and organizational help, ideas, and intellectual impetus for the humanities. They are not of uniform quality. A few seem to be content to distribute funds and sit back to see if the flowers grow, but many, I think most, function as originators, gadflies, and champions of the humanities.

Politically, they follow the same rule as the Clemente Course, which is to allow people to go their own way. Some of the state councils are timid, but none of the members that I have met seems to have an interest in mobilizing people to do anything other than enjoy the humanities. Christopher Zinn, former assistant to Diana Trilling, took over the Oregon Humanities Council and gave it the same excitement and intellectual elegance he had brought to his classes at Reed College. He and the dean of the college, Peter Steinberger, have been working at starting a Clemente Course in Portland.

In Oklahoma, the historian Anita May worked through alliances across the state from her office in Oklahoma City, where the scars of the bombing of the federal building had not yet healed. Gentle and objective, she brought the historian's sense of interconnections to her work.

Fran Carey, who had connected the humanities to the poor by bringing the humanities to housing projects in Washington, D.C., moved from there to become executive director of the Florida Commission just as we were starting out in Tampa. A year earlier, I had gone to Connecticut to talk about the Clemente Course at Connecticut College. Fran Carey had been invited to sit on a panel of respondents. After the panel, which was chaired by Sondra Meyers, former chair of the Federation of National Humanities Councils, we met with Donald E. Williams, Jr., a young state senator and the assistant director of the state welfare department, to discuss the possibility of using welfare to work money to support the course. Fortunately, I had laryngitis, and by the end of the panel was unable to speak above a whisper. I asked Carey if she would speak for the course. It has never been represented so well. Many hopes were elicited. The young legislator brought Senate Bill 849 before his colleagues, but despite Fran Carey's presentation and Martin Kempner's talk before the state Senate Education Committee, there is, so far, no Clemente Course in Connecticut.

Sarah Ritchie, a program officer at the Century Foundation, who has been a good friend to the course, introduced Mickey to Hodding Carter, who chairs the Knight Foundation. Mickey worked with the staff of the foundation to develop a course in Philadelphia, forming an alliance with Temple University, then choosing the site, the director, and recruiting faculty and students. At the same time, he worked with a group, including the state humanities commission, in Massachusetts, to start a course there.

Poughkeepsie, New York, has a large population of poor people and is within a few miles of Bard College. Bob Martin and Mickey thought it only proper that the Clemente Course be available there. The course began in 1999 at the Family Partnership Center in Poughkeepsie.

Under Kempner's direction, the course underwent some changes, almost all of them for the better. Naturally, the spontaneity and excitement of the first year have diminished somewhat, but they have been replaced by a more solidly academic approach to the humanities. A different formality has come into the Clemente Course. At the end of summer each year he meets with all of the directors, those with experience to share and the new ones, to teach the course to the teachers and to learn how to improve it. When serious problems occur—a faculty member or a director cannot complete the year, funding falls short, an issue develops with the sponsoring site—Kempner and Ted Dewsnap help the director and the sponsoring site to get through the difficulty.

The evaluation procedure begun by Jaime Inclán and his staff in the first year is in the process of becoming standardized and more specific to the needs of the course. In the first year, a series of materials from various sources was used to determine whether or not the course moved the students from reaction to reflection, toward a political life. Now, some of the language in the evaluation materials is being changed to fit the demographics of the Clemente Course. Kempner gives a good example: To ask people who do not live at home how they get along at home does not produce a useful answer.

Without a standardized evaluation, it is difficult to convey the effect of the course on the students. Even measurement of the academic effect of the course requires some standardization. The judgments of the first year or two, which were as much of the heart as of the head, may have served the students then, but they do not serve future students. An institution in twenty-first-century America may be able to survive without bricks, desks, or even paperclips, but it must have data. With Dr. Inclán on the advisory board as well as the director of the Clemente Center, now in its fifth year as a host site, the managers of the course have the good fortune to have one of the country's outstanding family therapists work with the group in developing course-specific evaluation materials.

How Socrates would have looked upon quantitative measurement of the acts of human beings cannot be a question for the Clemente Course, although it might be a fine question for the students: Is 67 percent of a form still a form? Is the good divisible into A, B, C, D, or is it strictly pass/fail?

There is something irresistibly comic about applying modern "scientific" evaluation techniques to a course that inevitably finds its anchor in the work of Socrates, whose willingness to be a philosopher as well as to do philosophy may be, more than anything, what we love about philosophy and the criterion we use to distinguish it from what we dislike about Plato's version. Nonetheless, we evaluate, making all things relative to other scales, other students, other worlds, when there is really only narrative and the pass/fail of seekers after the good. We do it, not only because it is required, but to serve as a check on our own subjective judgment and our good wishes for our students.

In the beginning, there was one course, and it was as intense as any birth must be. Managing it was not easy, but compared to the management of a dozen courses, it was not difficult. The problem for the manager of many courses is to reproduce the intensity of beginning, as all teachers know. The birth analogy remains as apt now as when Socrates first used it. In the first year at every site, this intensity appears. The curious thing is that it does not seem to diminish over time. Perhaps that is Martin Kempner's greatest accomplishment, the good that he seeks and teaches, so that over time, three or four years, as the people at each sponsoring organization learn the details of the course, the demands on the central organization decrease. The role of Bard and Martin Kempner and those who manage the course will then be to continue to teach the teachers rather than to oversee their work. And like all good teachers, they will learn from the process.

Over time, bureaucracy will become the enemy of the Bard College Clemente Course. Kempner already has the burden of arguing with me in addition to his important work. Some variations on the course, which will be discussed later, have not been well thought out. We sometimes feel like the chorus in *Antigone* when it accused her of being too autonomous. Fortunately, the people who want to help the poor to study the humanities are of goodwill. There have never been disputes over motives or ends, and within the concept of teaching the humanities as the means, the differences are small and the debate is as delicate as Botticelli's brush.

XV.

The Curriculum

THE CLEMENTE COURSE in the Humanities has no core curriculum, although perhaps it should. The general curriculum originally followed Petrarch: Philosophy, Literature, Art, History, and Logic. This venerable approach to the humanities has undergone some changes over the first five years, mainly in the last-mentioned area, logic. Robert Martin and Martin Kempner, both philosophers by training and trade, opposed the idea of teaching logic, preferring instead to divide the Literature section into its two constituent parts: prose and poetry. In Seattle, Lyall Bush developed an alternative to logic that he called Critical Thinking. Other course directors, among them Susan Weisser, have substituted a Writing section for logic.

Ideally, the course should include Critical Thinking, which is devoted partly to writing, a writing section, and a logic section. But then world history as well as American history should also be part of any humanities course. And how we can claim to teach the humanities without sections on music, dance, and theater puzzles many people, especially devotees of those arts. Choices must be made when the students have only one academic year, 110 hours in the classroom.

If the goal were to prepare students to enter college, one set of disciplines would be indicated. Those would be reading, mathematics, science, composition, and history. The pedagogy would include frequent multiple-choice tests to prepare the students for that method of measurement. The course would take on much of the character of an SAT cram course, and it could be evaluated by how well it prepared the students to be evaluated.

The aim, however, has never been simply to prepare students for college entrance requirements, although it has often done so. Nor are the suggestions here appropriate to a standard four-year university liberal arts curriculum. There is no language component in the Clemente Course, nor does it offer studies in the social, physical, or biological sciences. It is a humanities course, taught with the assumption that the study of the humanities will lead to a citizen's life. The most common error we make in presenting the course to students, funders, and so on, is to describe its success or failure in terms of the percentage of students who enter colleges. The second most common error is to promise a political life to the students, a change from reaction to reflection, from private to public life. If and when that change occurs, it will be a byproduct of taking possession of some significant part of the riches of the humanities. The end of the course, in the Kantian sense, is dignity, which, as Kant said, "has no price." In this case, not even a price or a prize called college.

Robert Maynard Hutchins once told me that universities in the United States are judged by the number of Nobel Prize laureates they produce instead of the number of intellectually well-rounded men and women. The idea produced a sadness in him; he wilted momentarily at the thought of what it had done to his vision of education. His composure returned in a few sentences, and the brisk, biting enfant terrible, who had become in his retirement a grand symbol of American educational reform failed, was once again in command of the conversation. His admission that the wish for prizes had been largely responsible for the collapse of his idea of a liberal education cannot be dismissed. Hutchins knew what should have been. Prizes, even the prize of college admission, must not rule the Clemente Course.

Socrates won no prizes, started no academies, wrote not a word; he was a philosopher, the one who connected philosophy with the public world. If it can be said that Socrates bears the true responsibility for the Clemente Course, we shall not be able to measure its effect upon our students until after they are dead, to borrow an old Greek view of evaluation. As winning the Nobel is not the only mark of accomplishment, going on to college is not the only route to the examined life, the pursuit of virtue, a habit of good actions, acting according to a maxim which could become a general law, understanding the happiness of others as the greatest good. Although it is seldom mentioned in Cambridge, Massachusetts, Abraham Lincoln did not attend Harvard College.

The goal of the Clemente Course requires a curriculum that may prepare students to go on to college, but aims mainly to repeat the pattern of reflection, autonomy, the public world, that we see in ancient Athens. Petrarch's vision suits that goal; the vision of the Educational Testing Service of Princeton, New Jersey, does not.

1

Why teach a course in logic? How is a student helped by understanding that P and not P cannot both be true? The questions seem to me rhetorical. How can one reflect upon propositions without being able to analyze them? The student who lacks the tools to examine the ideas that flow at him or her in this world, who cannot distinguish between an appeal to emotion and an appeal to reason, will be confused and defeated or repelled by the public world.

Logic has yet another value in the Clemente Course. Learning it does not require a middle-class upbringing. The purity of logic is as available to a poor person as to a rich one. A T. S. Eliot poem may not be immediately available to a person brought up in Appalachia or the South Bronx or East Los Angeles, but set theory has neither race nor gender, and it does not shop at Harrod's. In the study of logic, the students enter as equals. Imprecise language and faulty reasoning, the nemeses of successful reflection, are no more the province of the poor than the rich.

2

To be able to write well requires the precise language of a logician, the aesthetic sense of a poet, and the organizational genius of a storyteller. The students should learn to write, must learn to write. But who should teach them? I favor learning to write in very small groups with volunteer tutors who are writers or editors at magazines, newspapers, or publishing houses. The alternative is to recruit graduate students to teach academic writing, which is the literary equivalent of bringing smallpox-laden blankets to indigenous peoples.

Working with a tutor rather than learning to write in a large class has the added advantage of close and continuous dialogue with an accomplished person, which the students have rarely, if ever, experienced before. The tutorials should take place in the tutor's office or in some neutral place, even a coffee shop, to break away from the rigidity of the classroom. While the students must learn the rules of composition, they must also gain some understanding of the limitless possibilities of language.

An important distinction between writing and academic writing for the students arises over the question of voice. Academic writing should have the academic voice, not the personal voice. Literary or creative writing, in its many forms, should encourage the development of the student's personal voice. Academic writing has no relation to autonomy, while literary writing encourages the measured expression of the self.

Academic writing has all the characteristics of tribalized work, while literary writing liberates the self-governing aspect of the person. At some later time, if they choose academic careers, the students will have to learn to work within the routinized forms of academic writing; but for now, the critical and personal essay, for example, will have the greater effect in the journey from poverty to the public life.

I do not have the faintest idea how to teach people to write other than to ask them to write about something that interests them, read what they wrote, discuss how to make it better, and then ask them to write it again. If the material taught in the Clemente Course does not fit into the category of things that interest the students, a problem even worse than bad grammar and clumsy syntax will have been uncovered.

3

Petrarch did not have to draw a clear distinction between world history and the history of Greece and Rome. Unfortunately, we do not have such parochial comforts. A choice must be made between the United States and the world, a choice made more difficult by the demands of multiculturalists, each of whom wants the history of a particular foreign country to be a key part of the curriculum. The multicultural position carries the seeds of absurdity for a course that pays no heed to ethnicity in selecting students. But mere continents might not satisfy the multiculturalists. People of African ancestry might demand greater specificity—Nigeria, for example. But which Nigerian view of history? Would the Ibos be defeated again?

People of Russian ancestry should, of course, know something about Russia. Zulus should know about South Africa, Cantonese should know China, and the Maya should know Mexico or Guatemala, whichever applies. The history of the United States, a nation of immigrants, implies the history of the world. The question comes down to what we mean by teaching history and which country's history will contribute most to the goal of the course.

History can be taught as a progression of events, piling one on top of the next, like building a wall of bricks. The successful student of this form of history will then know that the Fall of Rome preceded the Battle of Hastings, which preceded the invasion of Europe on D-Day. It is certainly useful to know this order, but it presents a problem of inferences. Without knowing something about the ideas of John Locke, one might think that the imposition of a tax on tea by the British crown gave rise to the Declaration of Independence. The history of events without the history of ideas leads to a stream of *post hoc ergo propter hoc* errors, for one can only assume that succession and causation are somehow synonymous.

For the student who undertakes to gather in the riches of the humanities in the course of entering the world of reflection and citizenship, history as a succession of events offers little help; ideas are better catalysts of reflection. To separate the United States from the history of the world is also an error, a loss of both ideas and events. Fortunately, that error can be mitigated somewhat in the study of art, literature, and philosophy.

The history of the United States has two potential effects upon the student, if the ideas behind the events are taught. First, history should lead to reflection upon the present and one's place in the present; and second, it should enhance the student's practical ability to act as a citizen, knowing the concepts of civil rights, participatory democracy, and so on. Although history should not be taught as a tool for mobilization, it can have the effect of directing the student's newly learned reflection toward the public life.

Once the decision has been made about the value of history in the course, the selection of a textbook poses no problem: It must be a book containing basic documents; nothing else will do. In dialogue with the professor, the students should be able to understand and assess the effect of the documents. In eleven sessions, the students should read certain basic documents: Locke, the Declaration of Independence, selections from *The Federalist,* the Constitution, the Bill of Rights, de Tocqueville, Thoreau, *On Civil Disobedience,* Sojourner Truth, the *Dred Scott* decision, Lincoln, the XIV and XV Amendments, Chief Joseph, FDR on the Four Freedoms, Martin Luther King, Jr. Although it does not appear in many collections of documents, Ruben Salazar's *What Is a Chicano?*[1] will help to round out the civil rights issue. To help the students put the ideas of American history in social and economic context, a standard history text should accompany the documents: Morrison, Brinkley, or Zinn, or anything in between,

---

[1] Reprinted in Shorris, *Latinos: A Biography of the People.*

depending upon how one wants to view the development of the nation.

Every professor who teaches the history section of the course will want to vary the list of documents above, adding or subtracting here and there, but American history has a foundation in these documents; they cannot be ignored.

4

The purpose of studying art is to learn to see. Only then can one reflect upon the beauty we make in the physical world. An alternative to learning to see is learning to do, as in fingerpainting or making baskets according to prescribed patterns. For artists, doing implies reflection; for dilettantes, doing implies paint. It may be therapeutic for some people to paint flowers or make mudpies, but these activities substitute for reflection; they require time, crowding out the leisure in which reflection takes place. Since the Clemente Course has the encouragement of reflection as a goal, there is no place in it for doing, only for learning to see.

The Art section of the course invites several approaches. It could be organized following the various principles of art: balance, perspective, representation, abstraction, and so on. Subject matter might also be an organizing principle: nature, the human form, pre-Christian religion, Christianity, non-Christian religion, daily life, satirical or critical visionings, form and color, art itself, and so on. Art could also be considered by region: the Mediterranean, Asia Minor, Northern Europe, Asia, Africa, the Americas.

Historical organization of the course may not be the best way to learn to see, but it offers two advantages: First, the professor may organize the course so that the students learn how the principles of art were discovered and how the application of them changed over time; second, it conforms to the structure of most of the other sections of the course, enabling the professors to integrate the disciplines in their discussions. For example: Plato's forms and the idealized figures of Greek sculpture.

In the syllabus for this course, selected readings should be included so that the students integrate the disciplines, learning to see and at the same time reflecting on what they see. Another method for bringing the student to reflect on the work while seeing it uses comparisons of works of various periods as the exciting device. A more or less Hegelian progression becomes the focus of the course, with the antithesis used to illuminate the thesis. The professor who teaches in that fashion must be careful, however, because the student can come to the conclusion reached by the critic Arthur Danto, who saw art arriving at an end. Unlike Danto, the student may not be able to solve the Hegelian conundrum by arguing that art now relinks with the past.

Grace Glueck taught the section chronologically, from the cave at Lascaux forward, integrating the works with the ideas of the time in which they were produced, but also asking the students to see the formal changes. No matter how the course is taught, the experience of viewing art in a reflective manner over an academic year opens the eyes of the students to beauty. When at last, in another section of the course, they say aloud, in a way that no one else can hear, Keats's Ode on a Grecian Urn, these readers of Plato who have also learned to see know exactly what the poet means.

5

In 1980, while reporting on the Republican National Convention for *Harper's,* I chanced to ask one of Ronald Reagan's closest friends what the governor read. The man, a car dealer, swelled to full bloat at the opportunity to represent the best side of Governor Reagan to the readers of a serious magazine. "Well, I can tell you for one thing," he said. "He doesn't read books or magazines; he reads reports." If we hope to teach literature in our time, we must ask ourselves, Why would anyone read stories, novels, plays, or poems when they could be reading reports? Or not reading anything at all?

It seems to me that we should begin with words, not as lexicographers—well, perhaps as lexicographers—but more as poets in the guise of readers of poems. The first thing we might say to the students would be a borrowing from Valéry: "Poetry is to prose as dancing is to walking." Then the teacher must help them to give birth to their own understanding of language. The great dancers of the art of words can be employed to help. Perhaps they could waltz with Poe or take some stately step with Donne, do a turn with Shelley or a quick-step with Emily Dickinson. In a moment or an hour or two, it will come to them that poems do not go from here to there, like walkers, but are arranged in sound and sentiment, reflections played out in thoughts upon the music, each word a step, each phrase a turn, every stanza a stage arranged with sentences, words all in order, beautiful as they are, with no other dress, no intentions beyond the moment.

No beginning but poetry will do, and they should take pleasure in it, because it is not work. Sooner or later, they will hear of Plato's desire to ban poets from his Republic. It may be important to tell the students of Plato's fears at the very beginning; then they will know that poetry is not simply sweet stuff, but dangerous, a knife at the throat of repression.

Stories should follow poems, if the first stories have to do more with words than actions. A Hemingway story appears to be about action, but really is about words. A Richard Wright story appears to be about action, but really is about ideas. Flannery O'Connor stories appear to be about action, but really are about feelings. John Cheever stories appear to be about action, but they really are about fears. Some stories are not about action or anything else at all; the students should learn that there is no pleasure in such stories, because they cannot be taken at their words.

The students should read *Billy Budd* and *Heart of Darkness* and a Gabriel García Márquez story, probably *The Handsomest Drowned Man in the World* or *An Old Gentleman with Enormous Wings,* because they will need to know that former worlds and unknown worlds and worlds that never were or will be can be made of words. Shakespeare deserves a turn, but not *Hamlet* or *Romeo and Juliet;* I would suggest one of the comedies so the students find out that words do not lose their laughter over time.

They should make the acquaintance of the Greeks, if for no other reason than to try to understand Hume's definition of a classic as a work that lasts over time. They should investigate the lasting power of Thucydides when he puts words in the mouth of Pericles, and they should have a taste of Homer to know that beauty and brutality have always lived side by side in the world of words. I insist, too often without effect, that the Literature section conclude with the reading of *Antigone.* Every student should learn from her travails how close literature can come to the human core. And to read *Antigone* after listening to Pericles cannot help but teach that the best rhetoric is no more than a simple hill compared to the ranges of mountains contained in a work of art.

No movies should be shown to the student of literature, because they could very well confuse the student into thinking that a series of moving pictures is the equal of one word dancing.

6

Viniece Walker advised me to begin the course with the Allegory of the Cave from Plato's *Republic,* and I have yet to find a good argument to the contrary. The trouble with that beginning, of course, is that the students will have to take a try at understanding what Plato means by the forms, and as we know, the definition did not come easily to him. The students will prefer to think of the journey up from the Cave as prefiguring the journey they have embarked on. It may be a simplistic, even erroneous reading of the allegory, but it does serve to encourage the very people Plato would not have admitted to his academy.

Taught properly, that is, elicited properly from the students, the Allegory of the Cave can serve to make an ally of philosophy. Socrates will do the rest, but in the beginning, the students will need to know that even in Plato's rigid world anyone may seek the truth in its ideal form.

Given the general correctness of Whitehead's view that all philosophy after Plato is but commentary on Plato and the foundation of the course itself in the method, thought, and life of Socrates, the course should begin from its beginning. The students should read the *Apology,* enough of the *Crito* to understand the offer to avoid death and the responses Socrates makes about the law and death itself. They will want to know what happened, of course, and that is told in the *Phaedo.*

I did not teach the sections on morality in *The Republic,* but Kempner does, and I think he has a good idea, as usual. The students will need to know something about morality and about relativism. Plato offers the best of opportunities to discuss the distinction between cultural and moral relativism. In some instances, the students will have to teach the professors, lest they find themselves trapped, like Allan Bloom, in the cage of ethnocentrism, unable to discern the difference between the familiar and the good.

To teach moral philosophy without moving from Plato to Aristotle may leave the students without the understanding that philosophy may be built upon Plato but does not come to an end, in any argument, with Plato. By reading some of the *Nicomachean Ethics,* they find out how philosophers build upon each other's work through a process of criticism and development. Aristotle teaches them the difference between discoursing upon virtue and the habit of good actions. Best, perhaps, is that the *Nicomachean Ethics* has a lively structure, with a startling conclusion in the idea of the contemplative life. It affords the professor the opportunity to discuss the idea of the unmoved mover and the relation of the wonder of the action of contemplation by humans to the effect with no imaginable cause. No moment in the teaching of philosophy will equal that of the decision by Socrates not to take Crito's offer of escape from death, but the end of the *Nicomachean Ethics* leaves the students awed at the discovery of their own possibility as reflective beings.

Kempner gives the students the chance to talk about Hobbes on morality after reading selections from *Leviathan,* and then to discuss portions of Kant's *Groundwork of the Metaphysics of Morals,* and to think of Plato again. Thus, he organizes the section around Moral Skepticism and the answers of three philosophers to the skeptics. Like the response of Aristotle to Plato, the answers of Hobbes and Kant give the students the chance to experience differing ideas in a thoughtful rather than violent atmosphere. They learn from Kant that each of them has dignity and that they are, rich or poor, no matter where they have been or what they have done before, an end in themselves. In philosophy, as in art and literature, and of course history, they come to know that the humanities always speak of beginnings and suggest new beginnings, not beginnings by cataclysm, but in the thrill of dialogue or the action of contemplation.

These thoughts on carrying out Petrarch's view of the humanities in a single, five-part course over one academic year should not be construed as a plan for a liberal arts education or a design for anything other than a Clemente Course in the Humanities. The course was developed and continues to develop with the backgrounds and needs of the students in mind. It is a survey course, but it should not be entirely so. The students must also have the chance to learn the pleasure of close reading, examining a poem here, a paragraph of Plato or Aristotle there, embracing a Tintoretto or inhaling the scent of a Cézanne, wondering how to reconcile the *Crito* with Thoreau's civil disobedience. This last represents one of the most important aspects of the course, which is the integration of the disciplines—a task that must be aided by the professors, who should read each other's syllabi and adjust them, one to the other, to build toward wonder at the interrelated whole of human culture over time and the limitless possibilities for yet other beginnings through art and reason.

Sample Syllabi

Since no standard core of readings and discussions has yet been devised for the course, it will probably be useful here for the reader to see in some detail how professors in the Clemente Course have developed syllabi. All the syllabi have unique characteristics, which means, of course, that they are not of uniform quality.[2]

---

[2] Directors and professors at the various Clemente sites should not understand the choice of syllabi here as a comment on the quality of their work. Deadline pressure made it impossible for me to look over more than a few of the 1999–2000 academic year syllabi. Some site directors and professors chose for whatever reason not to offer their work for inclusion in this book.

The syllabus designed by Martin Kempner for his course has been refined over several years. It is probably no accident that the syllabi for the Moral Philosophy section of the course are all outstanding, given Kempner and Martin's passion for their work. The pleasant surprise comes in the quality of the syllabi for other sections.

Kempner's syllabus here is followed by one of the handouts he gives to his students to help them read and prepare for class discussion. It will help to make clear the level of the course and the quality of mind of the man who directs it.

Moral Philosophy Syllabus
Dr. Martin Kempner
Socrates and the Moral Experience

Morality is one of the central elements of human experience. Three major sets of issues about morality will be explored in this course: (a) What is the ultimate source or basis of morality? Is it God, or Man, or something else? (b) Which moral principles should guide our behavior and what, specifically, do they require of us? And, importantly, are these principles the same for all people in all cultures, or is morality "relative" to a particular time, place, and culture? (c) Why should we be moral? Is there any special benefit that comes from being moral? Does it pay to be moral or is it foolish to forego the advantages that immoral behavior can bring? The exploration of these issues offers you a chance to achieve an in-depth understanding of a vital area of human experience.

Our approach to these issues will be to spend the first part of the course learning about Socrates as he is portrayed in Plato's dialogues *Euthyphro, Apology,* and *Crito.* Socrates is one of the key figures of Western culture. Our study of Socrates will not only introduce you to his life, teachings, and contributions (which is an essential element of any humanities education); it will also help define a central concept of moral philosophy and of this course—the concept of a moral person or moral agent. And it will shed light on the questions mentioned above.

We will then read selections from the second most famous book of Western culture, Plato's *Republic* (the Bible being the most famous). Additional readings will be drawn from Plato, Hobbes, Kant, and other great figures in the philosophical tradition. Class handouts will also form an important part of the reading for this course.

In order for you to fully benefit from this course, you must come to classes, do all the readings and complete the short written assignments. [Editor's Note: The written assignments are not included in the syllabus.]

Part One: The Life, Trial and Death of Socrates
    Class 1 Overview of the Course and Short Essay
    Class 2 Socrates' Service to Athens
        Please read: The *Apology,* pp. 21–42, and Handout One*
    Class 3 Socrates on Trial
        Please read: *The Apology* and the *Crito*, pp. 43–54, and Handout Two
    Class 4 Socrates and the Decision Not to Escape
        Please read: The *Crito,* and the *Phaedo,* pp. 55–58, and Handout Three
    Class 5 Socrates' Contributions to Humanity
        Please read: The *Euthyphro,* pp. 91–105, and Handout Four

Part Two: Moral Skepticism—Three Challenges to Morality
    Class 6 Morality Is a Fake: The Discussion with Thrasymachus
        Please read: *The Republic,* pp. 2–18 (especially 7, 9, 13, 14, 18), pp. 25, 26, and Handout Five
    Class 7 It Doesn't Pay to Be Moral: The Discussion with Glaucon and Adeimantus
        Please read: *The Republic,* pp. 42–53 (especially 43, 44, 45, 46), and Handout Five

---

* Immediately following this syllabus.

Class 8 Morality Is Relative/Subjective: There Are No Objective and Universally Valid Moral Standards: where two cultures/individuals disagree, neither is mistaken
  Please read: Handout on Relativism

Part Three: Three Answers to the Skeptics
  Class 9 Plato's Answer: Why Morality Pays—it makes true happiness possible
    Please read: *The Republic,* pp. 129–143 (pay particular attention to 139–143), pp. 227–235 (The Allegory of the Cave), and Handout Six
  Class 10 Hobbes's Answer: Human Beings Invent Morality to Avoid a "War of Each Against All"
    Please read: Selections from the *Leviathan,* pp. 31–42, especially pp. 31–36
  Class 11 Kant's Answer: Morality Is Objective and Universal Because It Derives from Reason and Rests on Respect for Persons
    Please read: Selections from *The Groundwork of the Metaphysics of Morals,* pp. 112–123

Handout One: Socrates' Service to Athens

Introduction
The story of moral philosophy begins with Socrates (469–399 B.C.) He is one of the most famous people who ever lived—thousands of books and articles have been written about him, almost from the moment he died until the present day. One thing that all those who have studied Socrates agree upon is that he eludes complete understanding. No one can totally figure him out. He is a puzzle, and when all is said and done, no one can put all the pieces together.

But though Socrates is a puzzle, a person who strikes us as odd in many ways, we can't simply dismiss him as a peculiar guy. For when we consider his beliefs and behavior in the context of his life, we come to see that he made monumental contributions to humanity, in such vastly important areas of human life as religion, morality, rationality, and personal wisdom.

Our study of Socrates will provide us with the opportunity to join the long line of human beings who have tried for themselves to understand the meaning of Socrates' life and the lessons it holds. Our study of Socrates will not only introduce you to his life, teachings, and contributions (which is an essential element of any humanities education); it will also help define the central concept of moral philosophy and of this course—the concept of a moral person or moral agent.

Most of what we know about Socrates derives from dialogues written by his student Plato. We will piece together the central aspects of his philosophical life from the *Apology* and *Crito.* During the next four classes we will focus on his trial, defense, conviction, sentencing, and shortly after the trial, his response to the opportunity to escape from prison and avoid the death penalty. Finally, we will consider the lasting contributions Socrates has made to humanity. Tonight, we will begin with a strange incident that changed the course of Socrates' life.

The Oracle's Riddle

We learn in the *Apology* that the central feature of Socrates' life is that he is a man with a divine mission. As a young man, Socrates had been active in the intellectual life of Athens and had achieved a reputation for being especially acute and insightful. In fact, he was so impressive to his inner circle of associates that when he was about forty, his friend Chairephon asked the Delphic Oracle (through which the god Apollo spoke to the Greeks) whether there was any man in Greece wiser than Socrates.

> You know Chairephon. He was my friend from youth, and the friend of most of you . . . You surely know the kind of man he was, how impulsive in any course of action. He went to Delphi at one time and ventured to ask the Oracle . . . if any man was wiser than I, and the Phythian replied that no one was wiser. Chairephon is dead, but his brother will testify to you about this. . . . (p. 25, 21B)

The Oracle's reply marked a turning point in Socrates' life. He did not know what the god, speaking through the Oracle, could mean by this. The Oracle was known to speak in riddles, and Socrates felt it was incumbent upon him to figure out the meaning of the Delphic Oracle's pronouncement.

> When I heard of this reply I asked myself: "Whatever does the god mean? What is his riddle? I am very conscious that I am not wise at all; what then does he mean by saying that I am the wisest? For surely he does not lie. . . ." (p. 25, 21B–C)

Thus, Socrates set out to unravel the meaning of the god's puzzling utterance. His approach was to go about Athens, cross-examining many of his fellow Athenians who had a reputation for being wise. This would enable him to compare himself to them, and to see if any significant difference emerged which shed light on the Oracle's pronouncement. Socrates discovered that what was true of his very first interview was true of all the following ones:

> For a long time I was at a loss as to [the Oracle's] meaning; then I very reluctantly turned to some such investigation as this: I went to one of those reputed to be wise . . . when I examined this man—there is no need for me to tell you his name, he was one of our public men—my experience was something like this: I thought that he appeared wise to many people and especially to himself, but he was not. I then tried to show him that he thought himself wise, but that he was not. As a result, he came to dislike me, and so did many of the bystanders. So I withdrew and thought to myself: "I am wiser than this man; it is likely that neither of us knows anything worthwhile, but he thinks he knows something when he does not, whereas when I do not know neither do I think I know; so I am likely to be wiser than he is to this small extent, that I do not think I know what I do not know. After this I approached another man, one of those thought to be wiser than he, and I thought the same thing. . . . (p. 25, 21B–E)

Socrates believed that the insight he gained through this experience—that human wisdom begins with an awareness of our own pretenses and ignorance—was one the god wanted all mankind to have, and that he had bestowed upon Socrates the job of "spreading the word."

> What is probable, gentleman, is that . . . the [god's] oracular response meant that human wisdom is worth little or nothing, and that when he says this man, Socrates, he is using my name as an example, as if he said: "[That] man among you, mortals, is wisest who, like Socrates, understands that his wisdom is worthless." So even now I continue this investigation as the god bade me—and I go around seeking out anyone, citizen or stranger, whom I think wise. Then if I do not think he is, I come to the assistance of the god and show him that he is not wise. (p. 26, 23B)

It was as though the god had said to Socrates: "You have led the examined life and so are aware of the difficulty of gaining true knowledge. You do not pretend to have knowledge when you do not. This is an important insight for all of mankind to have. As you have seen in your efforts to understand my riddle, your fellows Athenians are not like this; in fact, just the opposite seems to be the case. They are ignorant of what is truly important but don't know that they are. Set them straight on this point, and by so doing, help them to become seekers of wisdom. It is important to me that you do this for your city. For the rest of your life, I am stationing you in Athens to perform this service. This is your duty to me. I command you to do this. I charge you with this mission."

The Socratic Mission
Thus, after Socrates discovered the meaning of the Oracle's riddle, he continued to go about Athens, as the god commanded, cross-examining Athenians. He was ready and eager to help each and every Athenian launch his own personal search for wisdom. Socrates' divine mission resolves itself into four important components, which I shall now describe.

(i) Socrates as Gadfly
First, like a gadfly, he was going to sting others into an awareness of

their own ignorance. Doing so was the first step in helping them begin their own search for wisdom. Socrates explains this aspect of his divine mission in the following passages:

> I was attached to this city by the god—though it seems a ridiculous thing to say—as upon a great and noble horse which was sluggish because of its size and needed to be stirred up by a kind of gadfly. It is to fulfill some such function that I believe the god has placed me in the city. I never cease to rouse each and every one of you, to persuade and reproach you all day long and everywhere I find myself in your company. (p. 33, 30E)

(ii) Socrates as Fellow Searcher

Once someone is convinced of his/her own ignorance through Socrates' sting, and can no longer pretend to have wisdom, they are ready to search for wisdom. At that point, Socrates was prepared to help that individual as best he could, by joining forces, by searching together like two fellow travelers helping each other on the same journey. This journey was one of dialogue, a give and take between individuals jointly and sincerely seeking wisdom. It is through such a venture, Socrates believed, that the truth would emerge. Thus, Socrates says to Critias:

> Critias, you act as though I professed to know the answers to the questions I ask you, and could give them to you if I wished. It isn't so. I inquire with you . . . because I don't myself have knowledge. (*Chrm.* 165D)

And Socrates says to Protagoras:

> . . . Don't think that I have any other interest in arguing with you, but that of clearing up my own [questions] as they arise. (*Prt.* 348C)

And Socrates says to Crito:

> I am eager to examine together with you, Crito, whether we are to abandon . . . or believe this argument [that it is wrong to harm the state by breaking its laws]. (*Crito,* p. 47, 46E)

Thus, Socrates believed that—as we might say today—it was through direct "existential" contact with another human personality that the truth would emerge.

But what, ideally, is the sort of truth to which such a collaborative effort is supposed to lead? Socrates believed that by trying to define the key concepts that played a role in thinking about how to behave (concepts such as justice, piety, courage, friendship, etc.), we could gain an insight into the overall end or goal of human life. That is, he believed that through an examination of key moral concepts, we could gain an insight into the nature of what later philosophers would call the "supreme good," that is, the true or proper end or goal of human life. Then, with this insight, we would be in a position to make wise decisions about how to properly conduct our lives and thereby achieve fulfillment during our brief time on this planet. In attempting to explain the kind of insight or wisdom Socrates sought, the scholar Francis Cornford has written:

> This question—what is the end of life?—is one that, then as now, was rarely asked. When a man becomes a doctor, he has settled that his business is to cure the sick. Henceforward he lives mostly by routine. When he has to pause and think what to do next, he thinks about means, not about the value of the end. He does not ask: "Ought this patient to be cured, or would it be better if he died? What is the value of health, or of life itself, in comparison with other valuable things?" Nor does the tradesman pause to ask: ". . . What is the value of riches?" So we go on from day to day, contriving means to settled ends, without raising the question whether the ends are worth living for. That is precisely the question Socrates did raise, and forced others to consider, thereby causing a good deal of discomfort. Taking life as a whole, he asked which of the ends we pursue are really and intrinsically valuable, not mere means to something else we think desirable. Is there some one end of life that is alone worthy of desire?
>
> Now it would not be hard to convince a tradesman that money is not an end in itself. He would agree that he wants money for the sake of something else that he might call pleasure or happiness. And a doctor might admit that health is valuable only as a condition of happi-

ness. In that way human happiness emerges as a common end, to which other aims are subordinate. But what is happiness [that is, a truly satisfying way of life for Man]? From Socrates' time onwards, this was the chief question debated by [moral philosophers and theologians]. (From *Before and After Socrates,* pp. 33–35)

Now, when Socrates says that he is ignorant, that he doesn't know anything worthwhile, this is what he is referring to. Neither he nor anyone else knows (they are unable to define) the true or proper goal of human life. Yet this knowledge is what is needed to make wise decisions about how to conduct our lives. It is this that is the object of the quest for wisdom. And this quest is of the highest importance, for as Socrates says in *The Republic* (section 352), the question of how to live is "not a trivial question."

(iii) Socrates as Social Critic

Third, Socrates' search for wisdom led him to examine the conventional wisdom of Athenian society. Did the conventional wisdom of the day have something important to offer, or did it merely enshrine centuries' old prejudices? Socrates subjected many of the prevailing beliefs, values, and practices to intense examination. For example, as we will see in *The Republic,* he challenged one of the central ideas of the morality of the day, that "justice" is "giving everyone his due," where this is taken to mean "doing good to your friends and harm to your enemies." Socrates challenges this conception of justice by asking the disarmingly simple question, "Can it really be the just man's obligation to harm anyone?" (section 334) Further, he calls into question the then current religious conception of "piety" as doing "what pleases the gods," where this meant, primarily, praising the gods and praying to them. Socrates begins his examination of this conception of piety by pointing out that any voluntary "transaction" between two parties (in this case, a human being and the god) should benefit both, and then goes on to ask how the gods could possibly benefit from human praise.

Socrates also challenged the cardinal tenets of most people's personal morality; that is, he called into question the materialism of his day. He questioned whether the way to a truly fulfilling life consisted in securing as much wealth, fame, power, and material possessions as one could. Are these really the things that make life worthwhile? Is securing these things consistent with the true end or goal of human life? Or do material values and the way of life they give rise to constitute an obstacle to true satisfaction?

In the next section, we will see more specifically how Socrates challenges the materialism of his day. The important point for now is that Socrates thought that traditional values, beliefs and practices should not be unthinkingly accepted, but rather should be subjected to intense rational examination, so that we can see for ourselves if there are any good reasons for adopting them. By joining together with his fellow Athenians in a dialogue aimed at assessing the respective strengths and weaknesses of conventional beliefs, practices and values, Socrates thought that he was further helping his compatriots (and they him) in the search for wisdom. He believed that such scrutiny of the received wisdom of the day is also a part of "what the god orders me to do, and I think there is no greater blessing for the city than my service to the god." (p. 33, 30B)

(iv) The Socratic Gospel

The fourth important aspect of the Socratic mission, and another vital way in which Socrates believed he was assisting his fellow Athenians to search for wisdom, was his insistence that it is not materialism but the care and improvement of one's soul that is the true road to human satisfaction or fulfillment.

In Socrates' view, material possessions, wealth, honor, and reputation were external things, and while they had their place in life, they paled in comparison to what was truly important, the care, improvement and perfection of the soul. Yet most people believe precisely the opposite, and base their lives on a materialistic set of values. But according to Socrates this is a costly mistake on their part, for the overriding importance that most people ascribe to a materialistic set of values is itself a roadblock to the pursuit of wisdom and the satisfaction that it promises. Socrates believed that it was a part of his mission to help people to see past this materialism, to realize that they have gotten their values backwards, and that true fulfillment comes from spiritual excellence and not material well-being.

In the most famous passage of the *Apology,* Socrates says,

> Good Sir, you are an Athenian, a citizen of the greatest city with the greatest reputation for both wisdom and power; are you not ashamed of your eagerness to possess as much wealth, reputation, and honors as possible, while you do not care for nor give thought to wisdom or truth, or the best possible state of your soul? Then if one of you disputes this and says he does care, I shall not let him go at once or leave him, but I shall question him, examine him and test him, and if I do not think he has attained the goodness that he says he has, I shall reproach him because he attaches little importance to the most important things and greater importance to inferior things. . . . Be sure that this is what the god orders me to do, and I think there is no greater blessing for the city than my service to the god. For I go around doing nothing but persuading [that is, offering reasoned arguments to] both young and old among you not to care for your body or your wealth in preference to or as strongly as for the best possible state of your soul, as I say to you: "Wealth does not bring about excellence, but [on the contrary] excellence makes wealth and everything else good for men, both individually and collectively." (pp. 32–33, 29D–30B)

Now if what is truly important in life is to improve one's soul, to bring it to excellence, how can this be done? According to Socrates, it is done in two ways, by behaving honorably and by seeking wisdom, the latter of which is exactly what he is trying to help his fellow Athenians do. In fact, according to Socrates, a life that does not involve the search for wisdom, whether or not it ultimately yields wisdom, is not worth living. Seeking wisdom, whatever results it may yield, is itself a spiritual pursuit of the highest importance:

> . . . if I say that it is the greatest good for a man to discuss virtue every day and those other things about which you hear me conversing and testing myself and others, for the unexamined life is not worth living for man, you will believe me even less. (pp. 39, 38)

The view that the truly important aspect of life is spiritual, that the care of one's soul is more important than power, fame, and the possession of material goods, has been called the "Socratic gospel." Scholars have noted that it is not dissimilar to the Christian gospel, "What shall it profit a man, if he gains the whole world, and lose his own soul?"

Thus, there arises with Socrates (as was later to happen with Jesus) a new set of values under the rubric of "the care and improvement of the soul." As the scholar A. E. Taylor has written, this is Socrates' real significance in the history of Western culture.

> What is the real significance of Socrates in the history of European thought? . . . At bottom the answer seems to be a very simple one. . . . It was Socrates who, so far as can be seen, created the conception of the soul which has ever since dominated [Western] thinking. For more than two thousand years it has been a standing assumption . . . that man has a soul, something which is the seat of his normal waking intelligence and moral character, and that, since this soul is . . . the most important thing about him, his supreme business in life is to make the most of it, and do the best for it. (From *Socrates the Man and His Thought,* pp. 131–133)

Conclusion

Socrates' life work involved not just stinging his fellow Athenians into an awareness of their own ignorance; it involved joining forces and working together with them as fellow seekers of wisdom, and this included among other things subjecting the moral beliefs, values and practices prevalent in Athens to rational scrutiny. Socrates' mission also involved urging people to go beyond their materialistic values and to "care for their souls." He regarded all of these things as necessary preliminaries to helping each and every Athenian search for wisdom. This was the mission the god had given him; he would do no less.

Yet it was precisely these activities that were to cost Socrates his life, for these activities did not sit well with the political authorities of Athens. Socrates' activities, which obviously were not politically motivated, consisted in such apparently innocent pursuits as engaging his fellow Athenians in discussions about the values that should guide their lives. Yet the authorities claimed that those discussions, because of their subject matter, constituted criminal behavior. They formally charged Socrates with the "crimes" of being "impious" and "corrupting the young," and brought him to trial. And while Socrates undertook to answer these specific charges, he considered his indictment as calling into question the meaning and value of his whole way of life, the so-called "examined life." True, by his own admission, he led a life that had a large "downside" to it.

> Because of this occupation, I do not have the leisure to engage in public affairs to any extent, nor indeed to look after my own, but I live in great poverty because of my service to the god. (p. 27, 23B)

And now, to top things off, it appears that the life he has led may bring about his death. Shouldn't he be ashamed of having lived such a life, so lopsidedly devoted to the quest for wisdom? At his trial, he imagines a member of the jury asking him just this question:

> Are you not ashamed, Socrates, to have followed the kind of occupation that has led to you being now in danger of death? (p. 31, 28B)

Next time we will take an in-depth look at the trial of Socrates and the answer that he gives to this powerful and poignant question about the value and significance of his own life.

Here is a representative syllabus for the Art History section of the course. It does not include the background information and the connection to other aspects of the course provided by the professor during class discussion.

Art History
Professor Tom Wolf
    1. Introduction: Defining the subject matter of art history—painting, sculpture, architecture

Aspects of Prehistoric, Egyptian, and Greek art

2. Roman and Medieval art: Sculpture and architecture—Colosseum compared to Romanesque and Gothic cathedrals

3. Late Gothic into Renaissance: Giotto, Van Eyck, Donatello, Botticelli

4. High Renaissance: Leonardo, Raphael, Michelangelo

5. Mannerism into the Baroque
Short paper comparing two works reproduced in the text due

6. Seventeenth-century painting, sculpture, and architecture: Rubens, Bernini, Rembrandt

7. Eighteenth- and nineteenth-century art: Baroque into Rococo, Rococo into Neo-classicism; Romanticism and the Realist reaction in France

8. Museum trip to the Metropolitan Museum

9. Impressionism and Post-Impressionism
Outline of final paper due: Comparison of two works seen in the museum

10. Symbolism into Fauvism and Cubism

11. Dada, Surrealism, Abstract Expressionism, and Pop Art
Final paper due

Although some of the American History syllabi use textbooks rather than original documents, the majority use the documents and supplement them either with a textbook or lectures by the professor to set the context for the documents.

American History
Kevin Mattson
Course Description: This course will study America from two different perspectives: what *ideals* America has stood for (democracy, equality, freedom, etc.) and the *reality* of American society and politics. In order to do this, we will examine the major eras in American history, from the colonial period up until the 1960s. The course will combine lecture (to provide students with background understanding of key events) with critical discussion of historical documents. What follows

is a class meeting description, with the reading assignment for each class. Paper assignments will be announced at our first meeting.

Session I Beginnings: Colonial America

John Winthrop, "A Model of Christian Charity"

Thomas Jefferson, "Notes on the State of Virginia (Query XIX: Manufactures)"

Session II Revolution! And Then Putting the Country Back Together Again . . .

Declaration of Independence (read in class)

To be read prior:

The Constitution (up to Amendment Ten)

The Federalist (#10)

Session III Jacksonian America: What Should America Be?

Tocqueville, *Democracy in America* (selections)

Session IV Slavery: What Is America in Reality?

Frederick Douglass, *Autobiography* (selections)

Session V Secession and Civil War

Lincoln, Selected Speeches

Session VI Reconstruction: Putting the Country Back Together (Again)

Booker T. Washington, Atlanta Exposition Speech

Session VII Industrialize and Revolt!: The Gilded Age

Andrew Carnegie, "The Gospel of Wealth"

The Populist Party Platform

Session VIII The Birth of Modernity in Intellectual Thought and Reform: The Progressive Era

William James, "Pragmatism"

Session IX From World War I to the Great Depression

F.D.R. Speeches

Session X World War II: The Rise of America Beyond Its Borders and the Beginnings of the Cold War

George Kennan, "The Sources of Soviet Conduct"

Session XI Revolt (Again): The Civil Rights Movement and the 1960s

Martin Luther King, *Selections*

Here follows the entire Seattle, Washington, curriculum, including the syllabus for each course. The reader will be able to gather from this complete curriculum a general overview of a course outside the East Coast (the preceding examples having come from New York, New Jersey, and Florida). In Seattle, a relationship between the center at Bard and the site has grown and matured, with contributions flowing back and forth between the two coasts, enriching both.

Bard College Clemente Course in the Humanities, 1999–2000

Critical Thinking and Writing
Lyall Bush
CLASS 1 November 28, 1998
Kinds of Non-Fiction Writing
   Examples from Genesis, Freud *(The Interpretation of Dreams),* Frederick Douglass *(My Bondage and My Freedom),* Gibbon *(Decline and Fall of the Roman Empire)*
Introduction to Arguments
   I. Speaking vs. Writing
   I. WRITING
      Narration
      e.g., Thucydides, *The Peloponnesian Wars* excerpt, "The Plague in Athens"
      excerpt, Warren Commission Report
      Description
      e.g., Frederick Douglass, excerpt from *My Bondage and My Freedom*
      Exposition
      e.g., Sigmund Freud, excerpt from *The Interpretation of Dreams*
      Argument
   Many different forms, including: magazine prose, philosophy, editorial writing in newspapers, political speeches. But usually thought of as academic argument-making. It involves:
      • a Thesis

- a Combination of inductive and deductive reasoning
- Proofs
- Quotation
- Citations of other authorities
- Footnotes

CLASS 2 December 21
Styles of Argumentation
    Reading assignments:
    1. Thucydides, from *The Peloponnesian Wars* (pp. 334–343)
    Pericles' Funeral Oration
    2. Aristotle, from *Nicomachean Ethics* (pp. 442–454 and
        529–537)
    Writing assignment:

The passages from Aristotle take up "continence" vs. "incontinence" and, in the second excerpt, happiness. Write one page about a choice you made in which you had before you both continent and incontinent roads, as Aristotle defines them.

Which did you choose? Explain why you chose that. What were the short- and long-term consequences of your choice? Which would you choose today? Why?

CLASS 3 January 21, 2000
Arguments and Thesis Statements
    Reading assignments:
        1. Seneca (pp. 106–113)
        2. Hobbes, *Leviathan* (pp. 329–349)

Class 4 February 8
Compare and Contrast
    Parallelism and Elegant Variation

Class 5 February 25
    —Tone
    —Using analogy
    —The Ciceronian sentence

Class 6 March 4
Quotation/Supporting your ideas

Class 7 March 22
The Art of Persuasion

Class 8 April 8
Research Paper I
    What is research?
    Using sources, quotation,
    style, tone

Class 9 April 26
Research Paper II

Class 10 May 13
The final draft (or, How do I know I'm done writing?)

Class 11 June 7
Review of styles
Closing writing assignment

United States History
Lorraine McConaghy
Welcome! Our class will explore issues and ideas of U.S. history through discussion of critical documents and images—sometimes music and film. Students will prepare for most meetings by reading and thinking about the Selections in their photocopy packets. Your thoughts are important to us all.

Please use your textbook as general background for the Selected Readings—it is meant to be read for your enjoyment or reference.

There will be two written assignments, fully described on separate handouts.

Briefly, the first assignment will ask you to think and write about a topic raised during our first five meetings, and the second assignment will ask you to think and write about a current issue, using evidence from our class. The first assignment will be due at our seventh meeting; the second assignment will be due one week following our final meeting.

Learning about the past helps us to understand the present and make good choices for the future. I love studying history, and I hope you will, too. Don't hesitate to be in touch by e-mail or telephone with questions or comments.

Meeting 1 Getting Started
November 1, 1999 What is history? How do we find evidence for history? How do we understand it? Presentation, photos, political cartoons, documents
Reading and discussion:

    1.1 Opening lines, Homer, the *Iliad* ca. 850 B.C.

    1.2 Selections, Genesis story of Noah ca. 550 B.C.

    1.3 Opening lines, Thucydides, *The Peloponnesian Wars* ca. 420 B.C.

    1.4 "The Young Man's Ascent of Mount Rainier"—A Nisqually tale recorded in the 1920s

Meeting 2 Contact and Conquest: Two Old Worlds in Conflict
November 15
Reading and discussion:

    2.1 Christopher Columbus's letter to Queen Isabella, 1493

    2.2 Selection, Bartolome de Las Casas, *Destruction of the Indies,* 1542

Meeting 3 Colonial America: The Making of Americans
December 6
Reading and discussion:

    3.1 "The Liberties of the Massachusetts Colonies," 1641

    3.2 Selection, *The Diary of Michael Wigglesworth,* 1653

    3.3 Selection, Michael Wigglesworth, "The Day of Doom," 1662

    3.4 Benjamin Franklin, "The Way to Wealth," 1757

    3.5 Selections, Thomas Jefferson, *Notes on the State of Virginia,* 1782

Meeting 4 Revolution: Breaking Colonial Ties, Making a New Nation

January 6, 2000
Reading and discussion:

    4.1 Selection, Tom Paine, *Common Sense,* 1776

    4.2 The Declaration of Independence, 1776

    4.3 Constitution of the United States, 1787

Meeting 5 Slavery and Racism: Africans in America
January 27
Reading and discussion:

    5.1 Selection, Frederick Douglass autobiography, 1845

    5.2 Selection, Harriet Beecher Stowe, *Uncle Tom's Cabin,* 1852

    5.3 George Fitzhugh, "The Universal Law of Slavery," 1850s

    5.4 James Henry Drummond, "In Defense of Slavery," 1858

    5.5 Jourdon Anderson, "To My Old Master," 1865

    5.6 Black Code, St. Landry's Parish, 1865

    Submit paper topic

Meeting 6 Westward Ho!: American Frontiers
February 17
Reading and discussion:

    6.1 Selection, Lewis and Clark, *Journals,* 1805

    6.2 Selection, Owen Wister, *The Virginian,* 1903

    In-class selections, classic American western movies

    Receive paper topic back, with suggestions and comments

Meeting 7 Immigration, Cities, and Industry
March 9
Reading and discussion:

    7.1 Selections, Jacob Riis, *How the Other Half Lives,* 1901

    7.2 Selection, Upton Sinclair, *The Jungle,* 1906

    Selected Riis photographs, political cartoons

Meeting 8 The Great Depression and New Deal: Been Down So
Long It Looks Like Up to Me
March 20
Reading and discussion:

8.1 Selection, John Steinbeck, *The Grapes of Wrath,* 1939

8.2 Selections, Studs Terkel, *Hard Times* (oral histories, first published 1970)

8.3 Selections, James Agee, *Let Us Now Praise Famous Men,* 1939

In-class selection, *The Grapes of Wrath*

Hand in paper

Meeting 9 World War II: Internment, Arsenal of Democracy, the Good War

April 6

Reading and discussion:

In-class *Daffy Duck Goes to War* selections, wartime newsreels

Selection, *Visible Target*

Selection, *Best Years of Our Lives*

Case Study: *Seattle's War*

Meeting 10 Vietnam, Counterculture, and Civil Rights

April 24

Reading and discussion:

10.1 Selection, David Halberstam, *The Making of a Quagmire,* 1965

10.2 Selection, Tom Wolfe, *The Electric Kool-Aid Acid Test,* 1968

10.3 Martin Luther King, Jr., "I Have a Dream," 1963

10.4 Selection, Malcolm X, *Autobiography,* 1964

Meeting 11 Contemporary Issues: Living in America, 2000

May 15

During Meeting 9, the class will have chosen three issues that have historic dimensions to research and explore on our last night together. Students may collaborate. After class, each student will prepare a two-page paper, which may take the form of an op-ed essay or a letter to the editor on the contemporary issue they've chosen to research. This final assignment is due on May 18, in Professor Opperman's Art class.

Moral Philosophy

Liz Lyell

Students may contact me by e-mail or telephone

Brief Course Description: Greetings to everyone. Philosophy is a curious and fascinating subject, which takes a little getting used to! However, if you are open and willing to try, philosophy can give you the very best tools for examining your life, and to discover new meaning in much that you may have taken for granted around you.

There have always been people who believed it was important to ask questions about life, and who have tried to answer them or explain why they couldn't be or haven't yet been answered. In this course, we will be looking at different philosophical writings which pertain to ethical issues, questions about what is the right and wrong way to behave, to live, to treat others. These are some of the most intimate matters our lives can be engaged with, yet they are often ignored, even denied outright. In this course, we will jump right in and attempt to look them in the eye!

Please be prepared to work hard, struggle with readings which are often difficult to fathom, to discuss ideas, and of course maintain a good sense of humor. There is no better time than now to converse together about these matters, and to contemplate the strange and unfathomable nature of human life. What is important is not a person's abstract intellect but rather the vitality of their curiosity, their mental application, their desire to know more about who and what they are, and their willingness to live in the question of things, in a passionate and balanced way. If you apply yourself in the consideration of this subject, you will reap great rewards.

Here's to a good year together, pursuing truth, meaning, and other vital matters!

Text for the Course:
Gary E. Kessler, editor, *Voices of Wisdom*

Class 1 October 25, 1999
Territory: The Beginnings of Philosophy
- general introduction to course . . .
- what is philosophy?
- basic questions and reasonings

- why is it important to philosophize?
- what does it mean to philosophize about values?

Readings: A handout read together in class

Class 2 November 11
Territory: The Pursuit of Wisdom
- Socrates vs. the Sophists
- the problem of relativism
- the search for universal values
- why is it important to "know thyself"?

Readings: Socrates, *Apology* (in our text)
Abba Mika'el, *The Book of the Philosophers* (handout)

Class 3 November 29
Territory: How to Live [part 1]
- Indian thought
- Chinese thought

Readings: *Bhagavad-Gita* (Ch. 2, in text)
Buddha, *The 4 Noble Truths* (Ch. 2, in text)
Confucius, *The Analects* (Ch. 2, in text)

Class 4 December 20
Territory: How to Live [part 2]
- Greek thought
- Native American thought

Readings: Aristotle, *Nicomachean Ethics* (Ch. 2, in text)
Eagle Man, *We Are All Related* (Ch. 2, in text)

Class 5 January 20, 2000
Territory: Getting a Sense of the Overall Picture
- are we living a shadow reality?
- if so, do we have a responsibility to find out what's real?
- do we have a responsibility to help others find out what's real?
- what is "The Good"?

Readings: Plato, *The Republic*, Book VII (Ch. 7, in text)

Class 6 February 3 FIRST PAPER DUE!
Territory: How to Know What Is Right
- how do we distinguish right actions from wrong actions?
- is there a method by which we can tell?
- is an act, in and of itself, right or wrong?
- or is it my motive that makes it so?
- or is it the consequences that make it so?

Readings: Kant, *Groundwork of the Metaphysics of Morals*
Mill, *What Utilitarianism Is*

Class 7 February 28
Territory: Are We Determined?
- does heredity and environment determine everything we do?
- if we are determined, does this mean we are not responsible?

Readings: Robert Blatchford, *Not Guilty* (Ch. 6, in text)

Class 8 March 13
Territory: Are We Free?
- is the human a free agent, free to choose, whatever their past?
- if we are free, does this mean we are completely responsible?

Readings: Sartre, *Existentialism* (Ch. 6, in text)
Radhakrishnan, *Karma and Freedom* (Ch. 6, in text)

Class 9 March 27
Territory: What Makes Society Just? [part 1]
- why is there a need for law?
- are there moral and immoral ways of governing?
- what is justice?
- how do we discover which societies are more just?

Readings: Confucius, *The Great Learning* and *Ruler as Moral Model*
(handouts)
Plato, *The Philosopher King* (handout)
Arendt, *Against Conceiving Politics as the Ruler and the Ruled*
Havel, *Trust in Leaders* (handout)
Golding, *Lord of the Flies* (excerpt, handout)

Class 10 April 13 SECOND PAPER DUE!
Territory: What Makes Society Just? [part 2]
  • is liberty a right?
  • are there just and unjust laws?
  • is the majority always right?
Readings: Mill, *On Liberty*
  Martin Luther King, *Letter from Birmingham Jail*
  Paul Wallace, *The White Roots of Peace*

Class 11 May 1
Territory: To be decided . . .

Art History
Hal Opperman
Students may contact me by e-mail
Visual expression, or the purposeful shaping of the matter of the physical world around us as a means of communication, is as old as humankind. There were painters and sculptors, designers and planners, tens of thousands of years before written languages ever developed. Even today, works of visual art influence and reflect our values, our beliefs, our judgments, our desires, and the way we live our lives, every bit as powerfully as does the written word.

In our eleven sessions, we will examine together several of the most significant works of art in the Western tradition, from Ancient Greece to Seattle in 1998, associating them with other works of art, literature, and speculative thought. We will read about them. We will look at them in slide lectures. We will discuss them and analyze our reactions to them. What are they communicating? How do they work on our minds and our emotions? Why do they look the way they look?

Your textbook is *The Visual Arts: A History,* by Hugh Honor and John Fleming (5th edn). This book offers a thorough introduction to the history of the arts as an essential part of the development of humankind. Certain parts of it are required reading (see below), and you may find it valuable and interesting to read other sections of the book even when not specifically required. In addition, an Art History

Packet containing a few supplementary readings will be handed out during our first class meeting. Come to class each time having done ALL assigned readings for that unit, whether from Honor and Fleming or from the Packet.

Sessions 1, 2, 3—The Ancient World
  1. Thursday, October 28, 1999. DISTRIBUTION OF TEXT-BOOK AND SYLLABUS
  Introduction to the Art History component of the course
  2. Thursday, November 4. Come to class having read Honor and Fleming, pp. 126–172, "The Greeks and Their Neighbours." Pay special attention to the section on naturalism and idealism (pp. 148–153), which includes the *Doryphoros.*
  Also, be sure you are ready to discuss the long passage from Plato's *Phaedo* in your Art History Packet. Focal Artwork: *Doryphoros* by Polykleitos.
  Presentations will also include additional works of Greek sculpture, and a piece or two from Egypt.
  3. Thursday, December 2. FIRST PAPER TOPIC ASSIGNED. Come to class having read Honor and Fleming, pp. 173–221, "Hellenistic and Roman Art." Pay special attention to the sections on Roman architecture and sculpture (pp. 193–215). In addition, be sure you are ready to discuss the excerpts from the *Meditations* of the emperor Marcus Aurelius in your Art History Packet. Focal Artwork: *Column of Trajan.* Presentation will also include additional works of Greek and Roman sculpture and architecture, and a smattering of material from Egypt and the Near East.
Sessions 4, 5, 6—The Medieval World
  4. Thursday, December 16. FIRST PAPER DUE. Come to class having read Honor and Fleming, pp. 296–340, "Early Christian and Byzantine Art." Pay special attention to the sections on Christian art in northern and western Europe (pp. 328–340). Focal Artwork: *Lindisfarne Gospels.* Presentations will also include the early history of the illustrated book.
  5. Monday, January 10, 2000. PAPERS RETURNED; SHARING OF IN-

SIGHTS. No assigned readings from Honor and Fleming this time. Be sure you are ready to discuss the excerpts from Bede's *Life of St. Cuthbert* in your Art History Packet.

6. Monday, January 31. SECOND PAPER TOPIC ASSIGNED. Come to class having read Honor and Fleming, pp. 364–421, "Medieval Christendom." Pay special attention to the sections on Gothic architecture, sculpture, and painting in France (pp. 383–395). In addition, be sure you are ready to discuss the excerpts from Medieval Latin poetry in your Art History Packet. Focal Artwork: Chartres Cathedral. Presentation will also include highlights of Christian architecture and sculpture throughout the Middle Ages.

Sessions 7, 8, 9—The Early Modern World

7. Thursday, February 24. SECOND PAPER DUE. Come to class having read Honor and Fleming, pp. 464–513, "The Sixteenth Century in Europe." Focal Artwork: *Death of the Virgin* by Caravaggio. Presentation will also include a few key examples of European painting and sculpture, 15th–17th centuries.

8. Thursday, March 30. PAPERS RETURNED; SHARING OF INSIGHTS. Come to class having read Honor and Fleming, pp. 574–613, "The Seventeenth Century in Europe." Pay special attention to the sections on new beginnings in Rome, and Baroque art and architecture (pp. 575–598).

9. Monday, April 17. THIRD PAPER TOPIC ASSIGNED. Come to class having read Honor and Fleming, pp. 614–639, "Enlightenment and Liberty." Focal Artwork: *The Harlot's Progress* by Hogarth. Presentation will also include some other examples of European painting and prints.

Sessions 10, 11—Recent Developments

10. Thursday, May 4. THIRD PAPER DUE. Come to class having read Honor and Fleming, pp. 706–739, "Impressionism to Post-Impressionism," and pp. 772–800, "Art from 1900–1919." Pay special attention to the section on Impressionism, pp. 707–718. In addition, be sure you are ready to discuss the excerpts from the poetry of Walt Whitman in your Art History Packet. Focal Artwork: *Lun-*

cheon of the Boating Party by Renoir. Presentation will include an overview of Impressionism.

11. Thursday, May 18, PAPERS RETURNED; SHARING OF INSIGHTS. Come to class having read Honor and Fleming, pp. 801–833, "Between the Two World Wars," and pp. 834–861, "Post-War to Post-Modern." Focal Artwork: Fin Project by John Young (field trip to be arranged outside class). Presentation will include a look at selected tendencies in the art of the last hundred years.

Literature
Lyall Bush
Students may contact me by e-mail or telephone
This class will introduce you to some of the great works in European and American literature, from lyric poetry in sixth-century Greece to poetry and fiction in our own century. We will discuss and interpret the poems, plays and stories that you read, emphasizing the skills of interpreting literature. By the end of the year, you will be able to talk comfortably about a poem's figurative language, a poet's "voice," and his or her use of rhythm and meter. You will be able to describe a short story's characters and dialogue and a play's gathering of passions into ideas. Some of the themes we will discuss have survived more than 2,500 years, including the passage of time, nature, fate, love, the imagination, death, and the dream life.

BOOKS: Kinko's Packet (KP); Shakespeare, *Othello;* Sophocles, the Oedipus Cycle

October 25, 1999 HISTORY AND LANGUAGE
    Introduction to Reading: Poetry
        T. S. Eliot, "Preludes"
        Tennyson, "Lady of Shalott"
        Yeats, "Leda and the Swan"
        Hughes, "The Weary Blues"; "The Negro Speaks of Rivers"

November 18 1st Paper Assigned
    Introduction to Reading II: Prose
        Chekhov, "The Lady with the Dog"

James Joyce, "The Sisters"
Raymond Carver, "Neighbors" (KP)

December 9 All Readings in KP
   First Paper Due
   Greek poetry: Sappho, *Fragments*
               Theognis, "Best of all . . . "
               Ibycus, "In spring time . . . "
               Praxilla, "Finest of all . . . "
               Hesiod, "Pandora"
                     "Summer"
                     "Winter"

January 3, 2000
   Sophocles, *Antigone* (Oedipus Cycle)

January 13 KP
   Roman Poetry: Ovid, "Europa"
               "Cadmus"
               "Acteaon"
               "Apollo and Hyacinthus"
               "Pyramis and Thisbe"
               "Tereus, Procne and Philomela"
               Virgil, "Orpheus and Eurydice"

February 10
   Shakespeare, *Othello* (Signet Classic)

March 2 KP
   Elizabethan Poetry: Shakespeare, Sonnets: II, XV, XVIII,
                     LXXIII, CXVI, CXXX
                     Michael Drayton, "The Parting"
                     Christopher Marlowe, "The Passionate Shep-
                     herd to His Muse"
                     Sir Walter Raleigh, "Her Reply"
                     Robert Herrick, "To the Virgins, to Make

Much of Time"; "The Funeral Rites of the
Rose"
Edmund Waller, "Go, Lovely Rose"
Thomas Gray, *Elegy Written in a Country
Churchyard*
Marvell, "To His Coy Mistress"

March 16 2nd Paper Assigned KP
Romantic Poetry: Wordsworth, Ode: Intimations of Immortality
John Keats, "On First Looking into Chapman's Homer"
"When I Have Fears . . . "
Emily Dickinson, "There's a Certain Slant of Light"
"I Heard a Fly Buzz"
"A Bird Came Down the Walk"
Percy Bysshe Shelley, "Ozymandias"
William Blake, "O Rose"
"Little Black Boy"

April 3
Later 19th Century: Robert Browning, "Porphyria's Lover"
Matthew Arnold, *Dover Beach*
Robert Frost, "Mending Wall"
Charles Baudelaire, "The Albatross"
"Giantess"
"Lethe" from *Fleurs du Mal*

April 20 2nd Paper Due
Modernism: Robert Frost, "After Apple Picking"
"Stopping by Woods"
"Desert Places"
Wallace Stevens, "Thirteen Ways of Looking at a
Blackbird"
W. C. Williams, "The Red Wheelbarrow"
"This Is Just to Say"
Ezra Pound, "A Pact"
"In a Station of the Metro"

May 11
    20th Century: Stories
                James Joyce, "Araby"
                Bruno Schulz, "Sanitorium Under the Sign of the Hour Glass"
                Franz Kafka, "A Hunger Artist"
                Samuel Beckett, "Stirrings Still"
    20th-Century: Poetry
                T. S. Eliot, "The Love Song of J. Alfred Prufrock"
                Octavio Paz, "In the Middle of This Phase"
                Rita Dove, Selections from *Mother Love*

In truth, the adjustments to my suggested syllabi made by most of the professors were good ones, because they brought the section closer to their own interests and to their conception of the intersection of their interests, the interests of the students, and the reason and beauty of the humanities. No part of the course is perfect, but all so far have held to the simple proposition that our students merit the humanities as an entrance to the public life of citizens in a democracy.

XVI.

Variations and
Self-Criticism

T HE CLEMENTE COURSE in the Humanities, in its Bard College version, is not the only such course. Other versions have sprung up in various places, sometimes very much like the Clemente Course and sometimes almost in opposition to it. There are brief courses, like the eight-week version for homeless people started by the University of Notre Dame, and long courses, like the one in the Yucatán (discussed in the next chapter), that last for two full years.

Three of these variations will give some idea of how the course can be extended, emended, or opposed. The first two have proved themselves; the third is less than two months into the academic year at this writing. The extension has no goals other than those of the original course. The second course, which I hope to visit and study in 2000, grows out of community work. It has been built, so to speak, from the community rather than from the academy. The third course was conceived along the lines of radical educational notions first made popular at the end of the 1960s. Several other variations are only in the very earliest stages of development.

Is there a point at which a program for educating the poor based on the Clemente Course deviates so far that it is in error, actually harmful to the students? How rigorous must a course be to bring the students to the point of reflective thinking in their daily lives? Can a course partly in opposition to the classical notion of the humanities have the same effect as a course in the humanities?

There are two dangers in varying from the model of the Clemente Course. One is falling into nonsensical academic vogue. The other is the desire to mobilize the students. That said, Bob Martin, Mickey Kempner, and the members of the Advisory Board all understand that it is our obligation to constantly seek better ways to convey the benefits of the humanities to the poor. As every Clemente Course informs every other, so every variation can inform the original. Perhaps one of the variations will turn out to be better than the original. One can only hope so.

Variations

1 A Bridge Course

In 1999, Stuart Levine, the dean of Bard College, told Martin Kempner that he feared the effects of education would begin to fade unless those students who had completed the course but had not gone on to college could find some way "to sustain the advantage they had gained."

The question had been raised earlier by Jaime Inclán, when he asked if "the inoculation would take." Inclán, the psychologist, was interested in longitudinal studies, or if we didn't have the money for formal studies, he wanted at least to keep a file of anecdotal information. Levine, who also holds a doctorate in psychology, saw the same issue. For Inclán, as for me, it was a question of how the students chose to live after attending the course: Would they become part of the public world? Citizens? Would they exercise their legitimate power? Would they continue to live reflectively rather than reactively?

For Levine, who had been the dean of the college for twenty years, the answer a priori was to continue the education of the students. In virtually every instance it is the *best* answer, although it may not be the only answer: good citizens sometimes have good jobs, start unions, raise children, and so on. Were it possible for all the graduates of the course who want to go on to college to do so, the Levine/Inclán question would have been moot. But we all knew by then that economics, family situations, past records, citizenship issues, a vast number of possible barriers bar some of the students from going on even to a community college. And we had not even begun to formalize our college counseling work.

Levine was not to be denied a solution to the problem he had pointed out. He said there ought to be what he called a "bridge" course between the Clemente Course and further education. He then offered to design and teach a bridge course on a once-a-week basis in New York City at the Roberto Clemente Family Guidance Center. Moreover, he offered to do it without pay. We had only to provide the place and the students from among those who had graduated but had not continued their studies.

Levine's offer raised a delicate issue. If there were enough students in that situation to form a class, it meant that we had failed some of the very students we had motivated to continue their studies. The dean, of course, was too gentle to put his case in such terms. Instead of pointing out our failure, he offered to solve the problem.

He is a social scientist, and there are no social science courses included in the humanities curriculum; what would he teach? It did not matter to him. His interest was in teaching the students how to read a text closely, to understand it deeply. He compared it to Bard, where in their second semester, students are required to attend a seminar in which they read something closely. As Levine put it, the students in the bridge course, like those at Bard, would "experience mastery of something."

"When I first came to Bard," he said, "I was taught to be tough, to assign a thousand pages a week to win the respect of students and the faculty. Never mind that they got to only eight hundred of the thousand pages. But then I realized that the students soon begin to skim the tough parts. Early on, I gave an assignment to the students: 'Read five pages, but read them deeply, as if you were the author. Come in and tell the class about the article, but know it as if you were the author, so that if someone asks a question about why you cite this instead of that, you can answer the question.' "

Levine, who has been teaching close reading at Bard for more than thirty-five years, has very much the demeanor of *the dean:* tall, professorial, with a slightly pedagogical manner; he is a handsome man, pleased at having been the dean for twenty years, but powerfully unselfish as a teacher, so much so that he can afford to be critical of his students while still desperately wanting to find success in their work.

"My hope," he said, "is that over the semester one of the students will have the insight that I (the student) know this well and understand that for the first time in my life I know what mastering something is all about. This may happen to some of them."

His approach to the classroom is what one would hope for from a teacher: "I said to myself, 'Mister Dean, why are you doing this? You're no longer a young man.'

" 'I'm doing it because there's something to learn from this experience. Do you want to teach? Ask yourself what new idea you gained from teaching.' I now have eight to ten ideas that came to me over the semester." And he smiles. The students who come to his class every Thursday evening from 6:30 to 8:30 on the Lower East Side of New York are as he had hoped: They are invigorating the dean as much as he is teaching them.

The true founder of the Clemente Course would be pleased that the dialogue works for both. Like the 2,500-year-old inventor of the teaching method, Levine brooks no sloppy thinking in the class. His students will not revert to the methods of argument of the streets outside the classroom. The question that comes to mind when listening to him talk about the teaching of close reading, his belief in the importance of mastery, is how well can the dean of twenty years relate to the twenty-three students who come to his course? For him, it is not an issue: "I don't feel a social gap. I don't see the way they dress, the rings, et cetera. I see struggle to learn." He likes being with young people. While most people age along with their friends, he says, he finds himself always in the society of nineteen-year-olds, and it has served him well.

Perhaps a more important question is how the students see him. "What is the outcome?" he would ask. The manner, the close reading of difficult texts in the social sciences, seven- to ten-page articles that require hours even for the dean to master, and then two hours or more of discussion of seven pages—fewer, five—would seem difficult, even offputting for young people struggling to keep themselves afloat in their quotidian lives. The answer came from Lynette Lauretig, the educational director at The Door. Near the close of the first semester of Levine's Bridge Course, some of the students who were Door members told her they were upset: The course was coming to an end. What would they do? What could they do? Was it possible that the dean, who brooked no sloppy thinking, who demanded they read as if they were the authors of the work under consideration, would continue to teach the course?

It was possible, but Levine had other ideas, too. He wanted to teach the course more intensively; he was thinking about how to get the students up to Bard for a month in the summer.

2 Vancouver

One need not have been the dean of a fine liberal arts college for twenty years to devise an interesting variation on the Clemente Course. The Clemente Course in Vancouver, Canada, was started by Am Johal, who was twenty-five years old at the time.

Who is this audacious young person? "I would characterize myself as a community organizer rather than an academic. My undergraduate background in human kinetics and commerce would only qualify me to sell running shoes rather than talk about philosophy. I have volunteered with non-profits and front-line community people and believe strongly in community-driven approaches to help mitigate the profound hardships imposed by a life in poverty.

"Too often, university students come to the Downtown Eastside, study poverty, write their Master's thesis, and leave without that research having any net benefit to the community. We were interested in an approach that benefitted everyone: the academics, the student volunteers, and the students who took the class."

Johal applied to a joint University of British Columbia (UBC) and student union fund for innovative projects, and won a grant of $15,700. He and Allison Dunnet, then twenty-three years old, looked for volunteers and lecturers from the university. With the help of Jim Green, a Downtown Eastside community organizer in Vancouver and a lecturer in anthropology at UBC, they worked through a series of debates about a site for the course, as well as a curriculum that they thought appropriate to their student population.

Johal and Dunnet settled on a three-month pilot project to be known as Humanities 101, with the first month of classes to be held in an art gallery downtown and the rest on the UBC campus. "The idea," said Johal, "was to foster a sense of community in the classroom and then to go as a group to the university so it wouldn't feel uncomfortable."

When the professors thought about the course, according to Johal, the debate was over teaching the traditional canon or works they thought more personally related to their student body. As with the mix of campuses, they reached a compromise. "A Seattle cop who was working on his Ph.D. in philosophy taught Plato and Aristotle." American history included a comparative look at Martin Luther King, Malcolm X, and Angela Davis. Literature ranged from Edgar Allan Poe to Wayson Choy's *Jade Peony*. Students were able to audit Green's course on the Downtown Eastside of Vancouver. Johal and Dunnet arranged visits to the Museum of Anthropology, the Vancouver Symphony Orchestra, and a performance of *Tosca,* as well as a screening of *When We Were Kings,* the documentary about Muhammad Ali.

Their students were older than those in the standard Clemente Course, like the students in the brief and very successful course for homeless people that had been worked out by Notre Dame. The Vancouver Course recruited twenty-five students, and began with twenty-three on the first day; at the end of 1998, "eighteen students crossed the floor in the rustic Old UBC Library and received their certificates of completion from the Dean of Arts at the university," said Johal.

In the 1999–2000 academic year, the course has expanded to a full eight months. UBC has put it on the front page of its Web site, and Johal has moved to Victoria to develop a course there, again based on the Clemente model. Johal has secured a $15,000 grant from the provincial government, and begun working with community organizations. Again, he will start in the downtown area and then move to the University of Victoria campus.

3 Antioch

The course in Los Angeles began after Shari Foos read an article in *The Family Therapy Networker* about the Clemente Center experiment. Her initial interest was in seeing the Clemente Course operate in conjunction with Antioch College, her alma mater. Antioch, however, has devised its own version, which is called CHE (Community Humanities Education). The students range in age from eighteen to seventy, the faculty is from Antioch, and the director of the course is the chair of the college's B.A. program, David L. Tripp.

Although he has not had the time to read any of the magazine articles or *New American Blues,* Mr. Tripp wrote:

> When Shari Foos first approached us with the . . . idea and Bard materials, I rejected the opportunity to start up such a program here. My reasons could be briefly summed up as feeling very uncomfortable with the idea of teaching the Western tradition of the humanities to the poor as toward some ameliorative end. I could hear colonial bells going off in my head. . . .
>
> The traditional content of the humanities marks a powerful discourse, which stands at the core of Western culture. Its place has been secure both because it has been useful to Western culture in seeking to raise and wrestle with important questions, and as representative of valuable and meaningful achievements of that culture. But it also holds this place of privilege because the humanities have functioned successfully as a means of defining and maintaining coercive power,

privileging particular views of the world and personhood while marginalizing others.

He goes on to say that teaching the humanities can "be understood as reinscribing hierarchies of power through a false inclusion into the discursive community of the powerful."

Of the CHE course, he writes: "First, we must labor to situate the humanities within their particular social, economic and political contexts, bringing attention to both the positive and negative functions of these discourses, and always raising anew the question of whose interests are served. This, of course, is part of the work of critique. I am reminded, however, of [Henry A.] Giroux's claim that the project of radical education involves both a language of critique and a language of possibility. So the project of contextualization is not one only given to critique, but one which also opens unprecisely because it underscores the constructed nature of the discourse of the humanities' new horizons of possibility.

"A second task of my ideal CHE would involve participating in the cultivation of resistance in our students."

The Antioch course is divided into three sections, each of which is broken down into five sections: philosophy, literature, art history, history, and writing. The sections are taught as follows: two weeks on each subject, followed by a week of writing. The three sections, called projects, are Ancient Greeks; Modernity; and (mainly contemporary) Marginalized Voices, "which bring the tradition of the humanities into question." Graduate and undergraduate students serve as writing tutors.

It is interesting to compare the Antioch CHE—which opposes the Clemente Course from a point of view based on the ideas of Foucault and Marxist educational notions that first became popular a generation ago—to the criticism offered by *New York Times* cultural critic Edward Rothstein, who stands with Allan Bloom and the Leo Strauss school. Rothstein complains that the Clemente Course expects the humanities will lead students to become political, the public life of the citizen in a democracy, the *vita activa* so treasured by the Greeks, to his mind being somehow a debasement.

Despite our differences, I embrace, albeit gingerly, Mr. Tripp and the Antioch Course, for we hold the same ethical views about poverty, education, and democracy. And as long as we are doing the work that *ought* to be done, we are allies.

Self-Criticism

The Clemente Course has many flaws, although the general conception seems, so far, to have been sound. First, or, less comfortingly, worst among these flaws is the retention rate. Students drop out of the course for many reasons, most of them not directly related either to the content of the course or the quality of the teaching. Several students drop out of almost every course after the first or second class. In those instances, the error usually came in the recruiting procedure: The student did not understand the rigorous nature of the course.

That error dates back to the original course when the students were qualified simply by asking them to write a few lines and to demonstrate the ability to read a daily newspaper. When the entrance requirement is changed to reading a page of Plato, as Martin Kempner has suggested, both the student and the director of the course learn something about the match.

Retention rates can be improved by recruiting older students, people in their fifties, sixties, and seventies who are more settled in their ways, and it is a fine idea to teach the humanities to older people, although not in the same classroom with people in their late teens.

One year, Dr. Jaime Inclán formed a group headed by a therapist at the Roberto Clemente Family Guidance Center to see if a more cohesive unit could be formed of the class. Not a single student who attended the group dropped out of the class, but too few students could get away from jobs or family responsibilities to attend the group sessions.

Another way to improve retention may be to form small groups of two or three students to work with a writing tutor. In that way, the students can support each other while attending to their academic needs. The tutor also becomes a mentor, who may be able to help the student through a crisis by directing him or her to the proper source of aid.

These are all means to ameliorate some of the dramatic attacks on the students from the surround of force in which they live. Students suffer from abuse by a spouse or partner, eviction from their apartments or rooms, problems encountered by their children, the loss of the low-paid job that enabled them to pay the rent and put food on the table, past problems with the law, pregnancy, victimization by criminals, the sudden catastrophic loss of food stamps or other benefits; and more than anything else, they suffer from ill health. No other problem affects the retention rate as much as the inability of poor people to deal with health problems, many of which arise from poverty itself.

There is another issue which we do not yet understand. After about three months in the course, many of the students face a crisis of worldview. This could be described as the change from reaction to reflection, or simply a new outlook, but I think the former is more accurate. By the time people reach their late teens or twenties without having encountered the humanities, and I imagine this applies to people of all classes, not merely our students, some sort of intellectual agoraphobia sets in. They find the constant beginnings fomented by the humanities somehow unsettling. Stuart Levine, for example, describes his students occasionally reverting to the conversational tactics they knew before they came to the class.

Reversions are comforting; it is a commonplace that newfound freedom can be terrifying. The humanities, contrary to the views of some critics of what they refer to as "the canon" or the works of "dead white European males," generally comprise the works of troublemakers, artistic and intellectual dissidents, those who were both critics and builders. When the study of the humanities leads students to understand that the world, including the world they recognize as "the establishment," is as protean as gifts of mind can make it, they suffer a new and unexpected terror. I believe it is the terror of the newly free.

Three interesting possibilities for improving retention are in use now. One, which has been successful in the course in Yucatán described in the next chapter, requires the faculty to know the students so deeply that they are aware of most facets of their lives and able to intervene when problems, including health problems, arise. In that course, which has a retention rate of about 90 percent over more than eighteen months of continuous twice-weekly instruction, the familiarity is such that one student's ailment was discussed regularly by e-mail between New York and Yucatán.

At The Door, which has long experience working with young people without money or resources, Lynette Lauretig and the staff have designed a new procedure that has, so far, greatly reduced the attrition rate. An experienced counselor at The Door, in this instance Stan Adamson, meets with the class at Orientation and stays with it. He is introduced to the students as a part of the team that will be working with them (director, faculty, and college counselor) rather than as a counselor who deals only with troubled people. In other words, Lauretig said, "he is non-threatening. Speaking with him about problems becomes natural."

The counselor/team member meets with the academic director every week to discuss the students. He (or it can as well be a woman) attends some classes, now and then speaks briefly with the class. As problems arise in the lives of the students, they naturally come to talk with him. During the first months of the 1999–2000 course at The Door, Adamson has already dealt with one serious problem, helping the student to remain in the class.

According to Lauretig, who has been working with the Clemente Course from its inception, the involvement of the counselor replaces the more or less familial situation of the first year of the course.

In Tampa, Florida, where the University of South Florida is the intellectual locus of the Clemente Course, the academic director, Robin Jones, does not teach one of the sections. Her discipline is urban sociology, which is not part of the curriculum, but she has brought other qualities to the course, not the least of them her own personal warmth. In setting up the course in Tampa, she arranged a meeting with a large group of social service providers, including the director of the Crisis Center, who agreed to make the center's services available to students in the course.

Jones is concerned with what she calls the "humanity as well as the humanities," helping the students to cohere into a group in which they strengthen each other. When a student had to leave Tampa to resolve a spousal abuse problem, Jones helped her get settled in Pennsylvania. The student was lost to the course, but the course did not fail a student in crisis. Jones and Mark Amen, who began the process of bringing the course to Tampa, have joined the skills of social scientists to the humanities. The structure is different from all of the other Bard College Clemente Courses. Is it ideal? It works in Tampa.

Like many of their peers from all economic classes, Clemente Course students do not write well when they enter the course. In several instances, as in Academic Director Susan Weisser's course at The Valley in New York City (Harlem), writing holds an important place. In Tampa, Professor Carolyn Ellis tells the students that the purpose of a writing course is "(1) To demonstrate the value of writing for understanding what's going on in your life, for figuring out how to live a meaningful existence and cope with the problems life throws your way, and for deciding what you want in the future and how to achieve it; (2) To assist you in developing papers required in your other Clemente classes." As one would expect, her students do not write only academic papers, but interviews, autobiographical exercises, and so on.

Having a Writing section means giving up another part of the course, usually Logic. When the Writing section is a tutorial apart from the other sections of the course, it enriches the students' educational experience and enables them to establish a relationship with someone who lives outside the surround of force. If taught in a very small group, the tutorial contributes to Robin Jones's notion of "humanity as well as the humanities."

Patricia Chui, the young editor at W. W. Norton, described the methods she used as a tutor in the original course: "When Samantha Smoot [a student] showed me one of the first papers she had written for the Clemente Course, it was clear that she had little concept of writing as a step-by-step process, or as a means for exposition. We had to start at the beginning. It is a fairly standard process, focusing on getting the student to brainstorm, come up with a thesis, and form an outline before writing the actual paper. Also, Samantha's grasp of grammar was far weaker than I had experienced with other students I had tutored, so we spent a fair amount of time doing grammar exercises.

"Each time Samantha came in with a new assignment, we began by discussing the work she had been assigned to write about: what she thought the major themes of the work were, which characters or scenes engaged her most, how she related to the issues presented; and so on. Then we turned to the question itself and attempted, through both conversation and her jotting down of pertinent insights, to formulate a cogent thesis that was interesting to her. Since the tutor's job is merely to ask questions, not to answer them, I did not ever suggest a thesis or line of reasoning; it all had to come from her.

"After we looked at what she had brainstormed, I asked her to identify the main points supporting her thesis and draw up an outline. At our next session, she usually brought in a draft, which I asked her to read aloud, then we discussed how she felt about what she had written. If there were problems with organization or holes in the logic, or if Samantha was unhappy with the way things were going, we broke the paper down paragraph by paragraph, or even sentence by sentence, to make sure her work had a central point that was backed by textual evidence.

"Despite some setbacks, Samantha progressed amazingly well in both her writing and analytical skills, although I did give her one assignment that I never asked to see. To help her think differently about writing, I suggested that she start keeping a journal. She had mentioned to me at one point that she had written a few poems, so I thought she might get some use out of free-form writing that had no purpose aside from self-expression. From what she told me, she enjoyed the exercise a great deal, because it gave her a new emotional outlet. I believe it also stimulated her considerable creative powers."

To offer this kind of opportunity to other Clemente students, we will have to find ways to involve writers, journalists, editors, and perhaps attorneys, as well as teachers, wherever the course is taught.

Scholarships for students who want to go on to college but have no money at all pose another problem that is solved only partially by a bridge course like that devised by Stuart Levine. The conjunction of the American academic and economic systems prohibits scholarship help to students who have suffered the wounds of the surround of force and then through some extraordinary act of resilience—the Clemente Course or some alternative—choose to be educated. Unlike students who come from poverty, but choose education early on, our students do not have sterling academic records to present to those who give scholarships. Nor are they like those students who have enjoyed (or suffered) a series of social promotions and arrive at the doors of academe as hapless products of corrupted systems in which the rewards for scholarship do not differ markedly from the rewards for showing up (most of the time).

By definition, no Clemente Course student can enter a university through the portal of "legacy." But neither can they ordinarily find scholarship money to help them get through a year or two at a community college, where they can establish strong academic records. They are outside the system, which must learn to bend to accommodate these students. Admissions committees and those who grant scholarships will have to know enough about these students to recognize their possibilities.

The aims of the course are not thwarted when students choose not to go on to college; but when the desires of the students to continue their education are frustrated, the course has failed them. We will have to do far better at telling the post-secondary educational establishment about the course and the students. If colleges and universities truly seek diversity in the student body as a way to enrich the educational experience, Clemente Course graduates are ideal candidates: They have experienced the surround of force and taken a major step toward overcoming it. They have much to teach and much to tell.

XVII.

Other Countries, Other Cultures

1

I HAD NEVER CONTEMPLATED teaching the Clemente Course in any language but English, nor had it occurred to me to allow it to move away from its roots in the work of those "dead white European males." In a book which drew its title from the "DWEBs," Bernard Knox had given the best reason for the primacy of the Greeks in a humanities course: " . . . it is simply a reflection of the intrinsic worth of the material, its sheer originality and brilliance." There had been a serious argument during the second year of the course when one of the professors suggested a curriculum that did not include a Greek play. Fortunately, the life and thought of Socrates had never been challenged as the foundation of the course. In fact, Martin Kempner had brought it into even greater focus on Socrates. But when I went to the Yucatán, and Raúl Murguía Rosete and I began to talk about a Clemente Course there, a new question arose.

Surely the same course could not be taught in a Maya village as on the Lower East Side of New York City? We would teach the course *mutatis mutandis,* but what changes would have to be made? What did the Maya merit? How would the Greeks have looked upon such a problem?

Setting aside his reputation for stretching the truth in his efforts to interest the Greeks in his travels, I turned to Herodotus. Poor Herodotus, so desperate to become an Athenian, only to be refused all the length of his life. He was a man of Asia, a lover of Athens, who found the concept of equality in Otanes of Persia, and the grandeur of high culture in Egypt. His adventures as an explorer or anthropologist and as a historian were denounced as fables by Plutarch, among others, but the concepts have generally been proved true and the exaggerations not so bad as the Johnson and Nixon administrations' reports from Southeast Asia. If nothing else, Herodotus, the somewhat inaccurate historian, brought to the Greek world the idea of the value of other cultures. If he preferred Athens, he did not dismiss Egypt or Asia. Was he a moral as well as a cultural relativist? He was not the sort of fool who equated moral and cultural relativism; he did, after all, ask to become a citizen of Athens.

And Homer? Perhaps it was merely for the purpose of telling a story well that Homer gave his audience both the Greek and Trojan sides of the story, but it appears to have been more than that. Objectivity? Surely, there had never been such a tale before, one in which there were heroes on both sides. Moreover, in the character of the Trojans, he gave us the other, and not dismissively, as a tribalized writer would have done—Hector was not Grendel, or a dragon, nor were the Trojans mere "ba ba ba ba" barbarians, so primitive their speech was limited to incomprehensible babbling. Homer chose to write about enemies who were enough like the Greeks to be respected as human. If Achilles was the partly divine hero, Hector was the great human.

Homer set the Trojans apart; he made them different from the Greeks, but not so different that they lost their humanity. Priam's pleading for the body of his slain son Hector is as tender a moment as one can find in Homer. Even the epithets applied to Troy, with its wide streets, give it a position of equality. And although Homeric

morality should not be compared to modern Judeo-Christian thinking or the morality of the fifth-century B.C. Greek philosophers, it is
clear that Homer gave the Greeks and the other a similar moral code.
In fact, from a Judeo-Christian point of view, the Trojans could be
considered morally superior.

What then were the proper changes to be made? Language, of
course. One could not teach people who spoke Spanish and Maya except in Spanish or Maya. But that did not solve the problem of culture. Was it the purpose of the Clemente Course to make Europeans
of the Mayas or to bring the poor into the public world through the
humanities? And if it was the latter, how could one instill reflective
thought in people by conquering them?

To adopt the role of cultural conqueror would be to inhibit reflective thinking, to destroy the political life of the students. No, *mutatis
mutandis* in this instance meant substituting the Maya language for
English, and Maya history, art, philosophy, and literature for the European humanities. Moreover, I was to learn from the faculty we assembled in the Yucatán that the Mayan humanities were grounded in
the culture of the *milpa* (the small farm).

More difficult, there was no tradition of democracy in Mayan history or culture. The monarchies had fallen hundreds of years ago.
Whatever was left of their social organization was destroyed by the
Spaniards. The Maya held out longer than the Mexica on the high
plateau, but not as long as the roaming Chichimeca and Yaquis and
isolated Raramurí of the north of what is now Mexico. For the Maya
on the Yucatán-Campeche border, the Clemente Course had two steps
to take: First, they had to become Maya again; and then they had to
enjoy the effect of the humanities. Murguía, director of the Programa
de las Naciones Unidas para el Desarollo in the Yucatán (PNUD),
and I met with various groups to talk about establishing a Clemente
Course.

On a rainy night in Valladolid, which is near the place the Maya
call the "center of the world," we talked with a group that intended
to save Maya culture. It was headed by Pedro Pablo Cocom Pech. The
meeting was a disaster. Pedro Pablo was hours late and insufferably ar-
rogant. He said that his current project, which had to take prece-

dence over all others, was the translation of Aesop's Fables into Yucatecan Maya.

Murguía was disappointed, but undaunted. If there is an ideal person in the field for the United Nations, it is Raúl Murguía. The man is physically imposing, yet modest, impatient with the abundance of fools and crooks in Mexico, but never with the Maya poor whom he serves. When Pedro Pablo failed us, we went to a small village to meet with José Chim Kú and a group of young people who had begun to work together under Murguía's direction.

It turned out that the arrogance of Pedro Pablo was the best thing that could have happened. In the village of San Antonio Sihó, there were about 1,400 people, 120 of whom had more or less steady work in the *henequen* (sisal) fields and the small processing plant. Other than that, people raised crops in the fields, foraged for food in the woods, or traveled to distant cities or resorts to do menial labor or domestic work. Among the young people, the use of the Maya language had deteriorated, very few could read or write Maya, and the great culture existed in a curious fashion—an unknown, almost secret controller of behavior, but not one that inspired reflective thinking.

Murguía and I met with some of the prospective students in a small building used as a sort of clubhouse. It had no proper windows, the door was a large iron plate that covered the opening, and inside the one room it was hot and breathlessly humid as it can be in the afternoon in the interior of the Yucatán. José Chim Kú and I shook hands in a most formal way. He is a thickset man who wears a baseball cap, like every other male in the village, but there is something distinctive in the way he carries himself: He has not been defeated.

Murguía is more than a quarter of a century older and a foot taller than Chim Kú. He arrived in a spare but sturdy van, and he did not wear a baseball cap, but he addressed Chim as his equal. It was the way they both wanted it. Chim smiled more frequently, laughed more easily, but there was no sense of fealty in his good humor: They were two tireless men and they had work to do.

Chim and Andy May Cituk, one of whose ancestors was a Korean or Chinese who had been brought to the Yucatán to help build the railroad, along with several other young men and women, had formed a group, Coox Baxa Ha, and it was this group that came to hear what I had to say about the Clemente Course. *Coox,* the verb in the name, means "go" or "let's go," which was the sense of the group. The problem is that there is hardly anywhere to go in the village.

They listened to my description of the course in the United States, and they agreed to give it a try. I will never know whether they really comprehended this utterly Greek idea as I explained it to them, but they knew Raúl Murguía. He was the pillar of hope, not a shaman, but a *halach uinic,* a "true man," as the ancient Maya had said of those who led.

After the first conversation, I asked the prospective students to bring a long table or two and chairs, enough to seat twenty people, for the next meeting. There would be no lectures. We would teach high Maya culture as we taught high European culture in New York City. The form of teaching we would use was called the Socratic method, and in this method I would serve as their midwife. I cannot remember people ever laughing quite so fully as the young Maya students did when I told them I would be their *partera* or midwife. Raúl intervened, saying it would be maieutic dialogue. But it was not necessary: The students knew what I meant. The importance of the moment was that I laughed, too.

The next day, Raúl Murguía and I returned from Mérida to the small building, now the schoolroom. I had told the students the course was known in the United States as the Clemente Course, but they had already given it their own name: *Curso de Alta Cultura Maya—Hunab Ku* (Course of High Maya Culture—One God). Murguía and I stopped at the largest bookstore in Mérida on the way to the village and bought twenty copies of the *Popol Vuh,* the single most important Maya work, sometimes called the Maya Bible.

When we arrived at the school, the students were waiting for us. They had followed my suggestion exactly: there were sufficient tables and chairs, but there was not one table or two, there were many small wooden tables all lined up in a row, and the seats were every manner of worn, torn, patched, wooden or metal and plastic chairs. Where the tables and chairs had come from was obvious, but Raúl took care to be sure I understood. The students had taken the tables and chairs from their houses. They had a choice between having a place to eat at home or a place for midwifery in the school, and they had chosen the school.

At that first meeting, we read aloud a section I had chosen from the *Popol Vuh,* the story of the people of wood. It is about one of the first creations, the one in which people are made of wood, and resemble humans, except that they cannot think. They are the makers of many things, but they have no powers of reflection, nor do they venerate the gods. They are destroyed when their things, their cooking utensils and household items, turn on them and tear them apart. The *Popol Vuh* even includes the sound of this destruction of people by their things.

We read the brief section of the book aloud, and then discussed the meaning of it. A young woman, Sandra del Carmen Chuc Kú, the possessor of one of the quickest minds I have ever encountered, brought the story into modern context. She said it was about technology, which was destroying us now, fouling the air so that when it rained, the acid in the air damaged the crops. From that conversation forward, the young people of Coox Baxa Ha were students of the humanities.

Late that night, after Raúl dropped me off at my hotel, I telephoned my wife in New York to talk about the day in the village. When I came to the part about the tables, she asked how the families of the students would eat when their tables were in the classroom. I said I didn't know. She had a suggestion.

Two days later, when Murguía and I went back to the village, we had loaded long wooden tables with folding legs and two dozen white plastic garden chairs, a blackboard, and so on, into the back of his van. The students took the equipment for an indication of what they had to do. A year later, they had put up a new building, complete with shutters for the windows and a real door.

Meanwhile, in Mérida, Raúl was putting together a faculty. We gathered in a meeting at his office so that I could explain the course and the Socratic method. The president of the faculty and professor of history was to be Dr. Alejandra García Quintanilla of the Autonomous University of Yucatán, whose work on the history of hunger and disease in Yucatán at the close of the nineteenth century involved the study of the Maya codices, especially the Dresden, to which she had brought a new understanding of some of the non-glyphic drawings.

To teach the Maya language and then the reading and exegesis of the great Maya documents in Maya, Raúl had invited Miguel Angel May May, whose stories and criticism were appearing in periodicals and collections of the work of indigenous writers. He served on the board of the Casa de los Escritores en Lenguas Indígenas (the House of Writers in Indigenous Languages) and taught at the Academy of Maya Languages. He was young, a Mayero (Maya speaker), educated, self-confident, and as I was soon to learn, a charming and imaginative teacher.

Silvia Terán, whose degrees were in anthropology, and who had collected and translated the three-volume *U Tsikbalo'obi Chuumuk Lu'um (Stories from the Center of the World)*, a Maya/Spanish edition of stories from Xocén, as well many other works, was to teach the history and culture of the *milpa* (the small farm). Roger Arellana, a professor of ecology, was to teach the science of the Maya as it related to the literature and life of the people. Art was soon to be more real than I could have hoped for. Pyramids had been discovered near the village, and some of the students were to work on the restoration.

As the curriculum developed, I found myself in serious argument with the faculty. My interest in the *milpa* was mild, at best. Although there has long been speculation about the ability of the larger Maya sites to feed the population, I had found those ideas about the sudden decline of Maya classic civilization unconvincing and uninteresting. I insisted that the course be taught in Maya as it was in English, that we look at the world from the point of view of the great literature.

The most vehement argument to the contrary came not from Miguel May or the anthropologist or ecologist, but from the historian. Alejandra García Quintanilla has the face of goodwill. On the hottest afternoon in the Yucatán, she is as elegant as any matron on Madison Avenue in New York: perfectly made up, never a hair out of place. And at the same time she looks as if she might at any moment break into tears over the suffering of the world. But there were no tears in this conversation. She said that I was wrong about how the course should be taught, that I failed to understand this essential of Maya culture, because I was too involved with the ancient Nahuas (Aztecs and others who speak Náhuatl), influenced by my friend and co-author Miguel León-Portilla, who was himself far too knowledgeable to make such an error about the Maya. And she would not be moved from that view.

I did not realize how much in error I was until some months later, when she and I took our students on a field trip to the anthropological and historical museum in Mérida. A museum guide led them through the first ten minutes or so of the tour before Alejandra and I saw that we knew far more about the subject, and took over the tour. When we arrived at a depiction of the corn god, Alejandra told them about the relation of the god to the corn cycle and the idea of Xibalba, the Maya underworld, and then it was my turn to talk about the story of the hero twins in the *Popol Vuh*. As I spoke, I found myself telling of the origin of the story of the descent of the twins into Xibalba. It was the corn cycle! Of course. The *milpa* was the proper place to begin the study of the culture. It was not the gods who made the *milpa*, but the *milpa* that made the gods.

But I am getting ahead of the story. On our visit to the village to introduce the faculty, we encountered a problem. Instead of the usual noise of goats or pigs complicating conversation, there was a backhoe outside, digging a trench along the road in front of the schoolhouse. The noise was fearsome as the metal teeth tore into the limestone under the thin Yucatecan topsoil. The machine chugged and clanked, and spat foul, oily smoke into the air. José Chim looked at me, and with his brotherly smile in full bloom, he said, "It's the men of wood."

Each member of the faculty spoke briefly to the students. Alejandra was nervous; Silvia was stern; and then it was Miguel's turn. He had come to the school dressed in a fine white *guayabera*. Although he was a young man, still in his thirties, there were flecks of gray in his hair. He was taller than any of the students by a few inches, but in profile unmistakably Maya, and when he spoke to them, which he did entirely in Maya, they were immediately in awe, for Maya is a difficult language, both tonal and accented, and as the students told me later, they had rarely heard the language spoken so beautifully. He made them laugh, they took pleasure in the success of him as a Maya, they listened to him. When he had completed the introduction of his part of the course, I explained to the students that he spoke Maya so well because I had been his teacher, and they waited for Miguel to laugh, to be sure of the comfort in the room, and then we all laughed at our ease with each other.

When I returned home, it was with some trepidation. I did not know whether the course would last, nor could I be sure how it would affect the students. It was a long and difficult trip from Mérida, where the professors lived. There was little money available. Raúl had started the course with miraculous speed and efficiency, but he had more than fifty other projects spread across Campeche, Quintana Roo, and the state of Yucatán; he was constantly traveling across the whole of the Yucatán. And the students had other issues; there was always the problem of having enough to eat.

There was yet another issue, the one that keeps the name of the village out of anything that might be read in Yucatán. The local members of the Partido Revolucionario Institucional (PRI) had attacked the village once. If they misunderstood the course as some sort of revolutionary activity or any activity that threatened their hegemony, no one could predict what they might do.

I returned to the little village a few months later, along with Miguel Angel May May, who taught that evening. He began the class by concentrating on the difficult sounds of Maya. To demonstrate the ups and downs, stops and starts, of the language, he used coins dropped on stone, bricks banged together, blocks of wood. The students followed his example, they made the sounds; the corrupted speech of the *henequeneros* cleared, they spoke Maya.

On another visit, after a group of the students and I had come from a visit to the *henequen* plant, we began to speak about work. One of the young women said she had worked in Mérida, in the home of a mestizo family, as a domestic servant. She spoke of the pittance they paid her, the scraps they gave her to eat, the occasional slaps and frequent scoldings. It had been a dreadful and debasing time.

"Will you go back to that job after the course?"

It had been six months since the Maya version of the Clemente

Course began; she looked at me as if I were mad. "I am Maya," she said.

Raúl and Alejandra reported the visit of a group of Europeans to the village. Alejandra was to present the course to them as potential funders. They were from such organizations as the World Bank and the International Monetary Fund. When they arrived in the classroom, they were greeted by José Chim, who spoke to them in Maya. It was, so far as we know, the first time in five hundred years that a group of Europeans arriving in a Maya village in the Yucatán had been greeted by a Maya who spoke proudly in his own language.

At the end of the first year, the attrition rate was zero; the students read and wrote in Maya, and were working on a translation of the *Popol Vuh* (written originally in Quiché Maya, which is unintelligible to Yucatecan Maya speakers) into Yucatecan. The popular name of the course in the area was "El Rescate," meaning the rescue, and other villages were asking why they did not have such a course.

José Chim Kú gave his view of the course to a meeting of students and faculty in late summer of 1999: "The course brings us back to our origins; it permits us to recover this from the ancient ones so that we can live better with our family and our community. A community that loses its roots is like a body that goes about without a soul.

"The course has brought me knowledge; it has made it possible for me to come closer to the people that I did not value, like the old ones and children. The school has given me courage as a Maya. It has given me a new life. It is something that must continue for many generations. You [professors] have given us a place. Many communities want to have this course, but we have it."

Then Andy May Cituk added: "I feel glorious because of this course."

Ruby Esmeralda Chay Chuk said, "At first I did not like the course. Soon it came clear to me that we had something very beautiful, and that is our history. To speak Maya is to feel strong. Now we know that we are Mayas, but when we were born, we did not know it."

José Chim became ill during the second year of the course, and could not be cured by the *h-meen* (healer) of the village. He went to a medical doctor who said he thought Chim, whom we all know by the name PepeChim, spoken as if it were one word, had cancer. Studies were necessary, perhaps an operation. Money was raised and given to PepeChim for his medical bills, but instead of using the money for doctors, he spent it on the needs of the village. Fortunately, the medical doctor's diagnosis was far too dire. PepeChim had a serious medical problem, but he has fully recovered.

2

In the beginning of the second year of the course, I went to Alaska to help start a Clemente Course in Anchorage and to speak about poverty and education at the state Democratic Convention, which was being held for the first time in "the bush," in Bethel, a town of about five thousand, some four hundred miles west of Anchorage in the midst of the Yukon-Kuskokwim delta and accessible only by air. Steve Lindbeck, executive director of the Alaska Humanities Forum, had arranged the trip as a way to get the course started in Anchorage. We held meetings at the University of Alaska there, as well as with the Rotary Club and so on. At the end of the trip I visited with Mike Dunham, the editor of the arts section of the *Anchorage Daily News,* and one of the most ardent supporters of Alaska Native language and culture. He did a long piece about the course and the conversations I had with the Yup'ik* Eskimos in Bethel and upriver in Akiachak. As it turned out, he would help to begin the course in indigenous languages in the United States.

Bethel serves as the center of the fifty-six Yup'ik Eskimo villages, with a federal hospital, a community college, stores, Snowmobile and four-wheeler dealerships, and so on. On my first evening there, I had dinner, arranged by Lindbeck, with Elsie Mather and Lucy (Uut) Sparck, two Yup'ik scholars and college-level teachers. The next day, at the convention, I met Mike Williams (Qurcaq), best known perhaps for his participation in the Iditerod, the annual 1,000-mile

---

* The common spelling is Yupik, without the apostrophe; Yup'ik is more accurate.

dogsled race. He is one of the young leaders of the Yup'ik Eskimos, a member of the Alaska school board and the Humanities Forum, and so on.

The next day, we all went up to Akiachak, a village of about six hundred people, traveling on a Hovercraft that was used mainly to carry the mail over the ice-filled water of the river in late spring. On board the Hovercraft, Elsie Mather and I spoke about language. We spoke, or rather shouted over the roar of the engine, about the word "horizon." "In Maya," I said, "it's *siyan kan,* which really means 'birthplace of the sky.' How do you say it in Yup'ik?"

"Qiliim menglii," she began, and continued with what appeared to be a kind of story. She translated: "It means the place where one falls off the edge of the world and passes through a star hole."

"We should have a Clemente Course in Yup'ik," I shouted.

In Akiachak, the group aboard the Hovercraft met with Willie Kasayuli, Joe (Ariss) Slats, and Qurcaq's uncle, the former chairman of the fifty-six villages and one of the elders of the Yup'ik Nation, Joe (Uyaquq) Lomack.[1] On the way back down to Bethel, in one of the few places where the roar of the engine permitted conversation at only two or three times normal volume, Qurcaq, Steve Lindbeck, and I discussed the possibility of a Clemente Course in Yup'ik. When Lindbeck, a Native Alaskan and former Boston Globe reporter, said he would help with the course, Mike Williams said, "Then there will be a Clemente Course here."

The next day, in the small conference room at the Pacifica Inn, the prospective faculty and I met for several hours. The third member of the group, Cecilia (Tacuk Ulroan) Martz, was destined to become the driving force behind establishing the course, although I did not know it then. I had thought it would be Elsie Mather, although her very

---

[1] I have used Yup'ik Eskimo names here as well as the English-language versions. It is not an affectation. The Yupiit (pl. of Yup'ik) and I speak to each other often via e-mail, and Yup'ik or Cup'ik (a dialect spoken in two villages on the western edge of Alaska near the Bering Sea) names are used. The names used here are shortened versions in common use: Uut for Utuan, Tacuk for Tan'gaucuaq, and so on.

close relationship with the Moravian Church and its schools seemed as if it might be a problem.

It was Mike Williams (Qurcaq) and Steve Lindbeck, however, who moved the course forward. Williams wanted to meet this fellow Miguel, the Maya teacher, and Lindbeck said he would finance the trip through the Humanities Forum. Diane Carpenter, the owner of the Pacifica Inn in Bethel, had a house in Mexico where she went for the winter, and she had invited a Mexican fellow to run the lodging part of the inn for her. He could translate for Miguel.

On his way north, Miguel stopped in San Francisco. "I am not going with you," I said. "We do not want the shadow of the white man over this meeting." Miguel agreed, as had Mike Williams and Steve Lindbeck, that a meeting between the Maya and the Eskimos was best without my presence.

The Yucatán–Yukon/Kuskokwim connection was established. Miguel and Cecilia (Tacuk) discussed the curriculum, teaching methods, and so on. Tacuk and Ariss (Joe Slats, deputy superintendent of the school district headquartered at Akiachak) began putting proposals together. Bob Martin at Bard said he could not grant credit for the course, which he thought was far outside the Bard Clemente Course project; we had to seek it elsewhere.

By then, I had learned to look to Steve Lindbeck to understand and resolve problems in Alaska. He suggested Ted Kassier, Dean of Arts and Sciences at the University of Alaska at Anchorage, a Spanish scholar and a man who had become deeply interested in Alaska during his few years there. As usual, Steve was right. Kassier took on the task of bringing the course and the university together. Tacuk prepared a draft of the curriculum, and Ted, giving nights and weekends to the project, restated it in a form his academic committee would accept without corrupting it.

This is the version that the University of Alaska approved:

School/College: CAS   Date: August 14, 1999
Course Number and Title: HUM 194, Introduction to Alaskan Native Humanities Studies

I. COURSE DESCRIPTION

A year-long, multidisciplinary approach to Alaskan Native culture specifically focused on the Cup'ik tradition. Study includes Cup'ik Language, History, Art History, Music (Song and Dance), and Literature, with the involvement of selected Native elders. Published and unpublished texts.

II. COURSE DESIGN

A. Readings, lectures, study, writing and composition in Cup'ik Language. Art, Song, Dance, History, and Literature, including comparative study with European traditions. Multidisciplinary strands interwoven to provide an integrated representation of Cup'ik culture.

B. Number of course credits: 6

C. Total time of student involvement
   (1) Class attendance hours/week: 3 (total 90 hours)
   (2) Laboratory hours/week: 0
   (3) Class preparation, writing: 6

D. Fulfills electives requirements for Associate and Bachelor's degrees

E. Lab fees: none

F. Offered in two semesters, standard timeframe

G. Cost of materials: None

H. Coordination: None required

III. COURSE ACTIVITIES

Readings, translations (English/Cup'ik/English, with English-language and Cup'ik texts), writing practice in the Cupi'k language; introduction to Alaska Native oral historical and literary tradition and works; examination, explanation of, and reasoned exposure to Alaska Native dance, music, and art; presentation by and interaction with Native elders; oral and written evaluation, conferences, quizzes, final examination.

IV. COURSE PREREQUISITES

Novice Oral Proficiency level in the Cup'ik language.

V. EVALUATION

A. Course grade is Pass/No Pass
B. Grade basis is as follows:

Attendance and participation	(30%)	
Graded assignments and quizzes	(30%)	
Oral readings		(25%)
Final Examination		(15%)
		100%

VI. OUTLINE (NB: MULTIDISCIPLINARY SUBJECTS ARE INTERRELATED AND PRESENTED SIMULTANEOUSLY THROUGHOUT THE COURSE, NOT CONSECUTIVELY)

1.0 Cup'ik Language
1.1 Orthography
    1.11   alphabet
    1.12   vowels
    1.13   double vowels and clusters
    1.14   stop consonants
1.2 Word formation
    1.21   syllables
    1.22   lengthening
    1.23   gemination
    1.24   apostrophe
    1.25   beginning oral reading
1.3 Phonetics
    1.31   fricatives (single and double)
    1.32   nasals
1.4 Skills development
    1.41   oral reading
    1.42   written assignments
    1.43   beginning translations
2.0 Cup'ik History
2.1 Creation stories

2.11   world creation stories
2.12   stories of first man, woman, and Panik
2.13   Qiuryam nallii
2.14   formation of the Yukon/Kuskokwim Delta
2.15   rivers. Elluarutait
2.2 Creation of people(s)
2.21   history of the Quissunamiut (Chevak people)
2.22   famous historical figures
2.3   Ceremonies, rituals, festivals
3.0 Cup'ik Literature in the Context of Other Literary Traditions and Cup'ik Literary Creation
3.1 Comparative Cup'ik literature
3.31   philosophy of Cup'iks
3.32   memorization: "Ciuliaqatuk," "Qiuryam Nalii," "Qurvik"
3.33   readings: "Make Prayers to the Raven: Principles of Koyukon World View"; "Wisdom of the Elders: Mathew King, Unto the Seventh Generation"; "Dreamkeepers: Dreamtime Is Now, The Healer's Touch"; Plato, *Republic,* "The Allegory of the Cave"
3.2 Cup'ik Literary Creation
3.21   creation stories
3.211   oral presentations
3.212   documentation
3.22   tapes of elders (e.g., epics, proscriptions, prescriptions, history, traditions, values, spirituality, ceremonies, Cuuyaraq)
3.221   transcriptions
3.222   discussions
3.223   reflections
3.224   meanings
3.23   Comparisons and contrasts
3.24   Students' creative work presented to elders
4.0 Cup'ik Art History
4.1 masks
4.2 dance accoutrements
4.3 fancy parkas' designs
4.4 clothing, artifact designs

4.41   women's items
   4.411   Kakivik
   4.412   Qalutamirun
   4.413   Issran
   4.414   woven items
4.42   men's items
   4.421   tools
   4.422   weapons
   4.423   clothing
4.5 ceremonial, festival objects
5.0 Cup'ik Music
5.1 Song
5.2 Dance

VII. TEXTS (NB: SOME MATERIALS ARE UNPUB-LISHED)

"Dreamkeepers"
"Last Days of Okak"
"Make Prayers to the Raven"
"Wisdom of the Elders"
Steven Jacobson, *Yup'ik Eskimo Dictionary* (Fairbanks: University of Alaska Press, 1984)
Reed Miyaoka and Elsie Mather, *Yup'ik Eskimo Orthography*
Plato, *The Republic*
Miyaoka Reed, Steven Jacobson, and Krauss Afcan, *Yup'ik Eskimo Grammar* (Fairbanks: University of Alaska Press, 1977)
Anthony Woodbury, *Cev'armiut Qanemciit Qulirait-lly* (Fairbanks: University of Alaska Press, 1992)

Perhaps the most astonishing aspect of the course, one that Mike Dunham thought worth mentioning in the *Anchorage Daily News,* was the reversal of the historic flow of culture. Tacuk had sent the curriculum to the University of Alaska and Ted Kassier had accepted it.

By early fall of 1999, Tacuk, Uut, Ariss, Uyaquq, and I, sometimes in the company of Steve Lindbeck and Mike Dunham, went from village to village, explaining the course on tiny local radio stations and in town meetings, gathering the consensus required to start such a venture among the Yupiit. At times, the intellectual level of the public conversation was astonishing. In Akiachak, we spoke of the meaning of *Ellam Yua,* which generally means "world person," but has far more complex overtones, for *Ella* can also mean "consciousness" or "house" or "sense." We compared this Yup'ik idea of something like God to the Nahuatl epithets, such as Tloque Nahuaqe (the Close and the Near) and Ipalnemoani (Giver of Life). Soon it became clear that one might also be speaking of "the seen and not seen" when referring to Ellam Yua.

The Clemente Course in C/Yup'ik was called *Yaaveskarniyaraq,* which meant the study of Yaaveskaryaraq, the C/Yup'ik Way. A loose translation had been made and presented with apologies for "the limitations of the English language":

We, the C/Yupiit are raised according to the original directions of our forefathers.

We love one another, our belief is strong, and we continue to better our lives.

We know that our way of life has been grounded in traditional values and customs since time immemorial.

Those who follow the teachings of respect understand that everything has a spirit with rewards of gratitude.

Those who follow the teachings of our ancestors are intelligent, self-assured and prosperous.

All through the conversation the Yupiit listened to the elder, whose speech was so eloquent in Yup'ik (which becomes subtle by the addition of postbases or suffixes, often more than one, sometimes as many half a dozen) that they murmured *ii-i* (yes) in appreciation of his inventive and nuanced use of language.

When we flew to Chevak, a Cup'ik-speaking village of about eight hundred people, mainly children, a few miles inland from the Bering Sea, the elder and I spent most the time together. I did not attempt even a word in Yup'ik, for I had learned my lesson at dinner a few days earlier. In the course of conversation, I used the word for shaman, *angalkuq,* and each time I did, the others at the table, all of them Yupiit, burst out laughing. Finally, they told me that I had been mispronouncing the word so that what I was actually saying was "an old piece of shit."

In Chevak, I spoke in English, and the C/Yupiit faculty translated. But there was really very little use in my being there. It was a Cup'ik project by then. Everyone in this village where 92 percent of the people lived on some kind of federal aid was just being kind to the *kass'aq* (white person, from the Russian, cossack). Two days after I left, the Clemente Course began in Chevak. Tacuk and three elders taught for five hours each day two days running. At the end of the second day, the students did not want to go home.

The course outline done by Tacuk had already been sent to Howard Meredith at the University of Science and Arts of Oklahoma, who was working with his Kiowa graduate students to develop a Kiowa version of the Clemente Course. Dr. Meredith is the author of many books, including *Dancing on Common Ground* and *The Cherokee Vision of Elohi.* He and I had met in 1998 in Oklahoma City, when I was invited there by the Citizens League to talk about poverty and the Clemente Course. By summer of 1999, Emily Satepauhoodle, Jay Goombi, and Jackie Yellowhair had put together a paper on the Kiowa culture and the humanities, to which Howard Meredith had added an illuminating foreword.

Anita May, executive director of the Oklahoma Humanities Council, had made a grant to hold a planning session for the course. This time, it was Dr. Alejandra García Quintanilla who came from Mérida on November 8 to speak to the North Americans. Her lecture was attended by a large number of Kiowas, students, tribal leaders, scholars, and elders. Two Cherokee faculty members from the Sequyoah School in Tahlequah who heard Alejandra's lecture talked with Howard Meredith and his wife, Mary Ellen, who has recently been in charge of the historical museum at Tahlequah, about the possibility of a Cherokee course. Their response was to talk with Chad Smith, principal chief of the Cherokee Nation, and members of the tribal council. (See the Appendix for a trial Cherokee curriculum.)

Alejandra said she was awed by Meredith's books and by Meredith himself. The meeting of the Chichimeca professor from Mexico and the Indians of Oklahoma had not only an intellectual content, it became deeply emotional for everyone. The sense there, as it had been in Yucatán and Chevak and Akiachak, was of the continuance of the life of a people through the humanities.

With the Kiowa Course progressing quickly, our attention turned to Tahlequah, where Mary Ellen Meredith was working out details of the course. Mrs. Meredith left no doubt about the future of the Clemente Course in Tahlequah. "There will be a course," she said, as her husband, Howard, had said a year earlier that there would be a Kiowa course. Funding was an issue, although the intellectual power and effectiveness of the Merediths seemed capable of overcoming virtually any problem. Even so, it pleased them to hear that Chairman William Ferris and many members of the senior staff of the National Endowment for the Humanities had expressed an interest in both the Kiowa and Cherokee courses. At the same time, Raúl Murguía Rosete in Yucatán suggested a meeting in a year and a half or two of the faculty and students of all the courses in American languages. With a smile, Alejandra García defined the reach of the idea, "From Mesoamerica to Frozenamerica."

The question of relativism, which had been a concern from the beginning of the courses in American languages, finally was answered in Alaska in conversation about Ellam Yua (world person/universal consciousness), but not God, as in the Judeo-Christian, which is another Yup'ik word, *Agayun*.

Yuk, the word for person, becomes *Yua* when it is possessive. In the Yup'ik worldview, everything has a *yua,* whether that thing is animate or inanimate, animal or human. If one kills a seal for meat and oil, one must give the seal a drink of fresh water to prepare its *yua* for the trip through other worlds. Then it will return in another seal to give food to the Yupiit as its way of thanking them for the fresh water. If one sees a piece of wood in the snow on the tundra, one must turn it over to give its other side to the air and the light, and the perhaps the *yua* of the wood will return the favor to the person.

The metaphysical notions of the Yupiit produce their ethics. If one were an Enlightenment philosopher rather than a Yup'ik or Cup'ik Eskimo, the idea of the *yua* would lead to something like "Act according to a maxim which can become a general law."

If Kant's categorical imperative can serve as a grounding for European ethics, can we argue that there is a question of moral relativism when teaching the Yup'ik humanities? To complain about cultural relativism, of course, is ridiculous, except in the case of a certain culture in which people eat frogs and snails and the mashed livers of fatted geese.

The issue of moral relativism becomes more difficult when considered from the indigenous American point of view. They are expected to accept the ethics of a culture which had conquest and genocide as its avowed purpose. What is the *yua* of such a culture?

In Mexico in 1998, at a conference sponsored by a Norwegian-backed group, Comparative Research on Poverty (CROP), studying the problem in Latin America, several North Americans, among them the economist John Roemer, along with jurists, philosophers, and many social scientists, presented and discussed papers. There was one public meeting held at the Universidad Iberoamericana (Ibero), at which the Mexican philosopher Luis Villoro and the prominent Mexican economist/legislator Ifigenia Martínez, and I spoke, among others. The speakers were introduced by Jesús Luis García, director of research and graduate studies at the Ibero, as it is known. At the end of the meeting, he asked if I had more information about my ideas on poverty and the Clemente Course.

García, who was by far the youngest of the directors at the Ibero, moved rapidly. By summer of 1999 he had arranged a seminar at the Ibero for senior faculty, with the end in mind of starting a Clemente Course in Mexico. Two members of his department arranged the seminars: María Estela Eguiarte, the historian, and arts scholar José Luis Barrios.

My friend José Romero Keith, of the Pan-American Health Organization, whom I invited to the seminars, asked if he might also invite Dr. Herlinda Suárez, of the National Autonomous University of Mexico (UNAM). It was a marvelous idea: Suárez, who holds degrees in both mathematics and social science, energized the room. The seminars were open and interesting, raising serious questions about the difference between a rich country like the United States and one such as Mexico. We compared Mexico's two levels of poverty, the second of which is known as *pobreza extrema,* and the problems of poverty and education in the United States.

Ibero determined to move ahead with establishing a course. Eguiarte and Barrios were to take the lead, with the director, García, to back them up. We visited possible sites in the nearby community of Santa Fe, which had at one time been the garbage dump for Mexico City. Questions of culture and deracination among these internal immigrants had to be considered and understood. A new curriculum was discussed, one that would include Cervantes and the Aztec poets as well as the Greeks and Shakespeare.

The problem for Ibero remains a problem for any institution: funding. But it is a special problem in Mexico, which has no tradition of private philanthropy, although one is beginning now. Contributions have always been made to the Catholic Church, but not for projects that do not include religious education, and it had been agreed very early on that the Ibero version of the Clemente Course would not include religious studies. María Estela Eguiarte, to whom the main task of organizing the course had been given, would have to search very diligently to find the money to pay the faculty.

Meanwhile, Herlinda Suárez arranged a meeting with Humberto Muñoz, who was one of the two sub-rectors of UNAM, responsible for everything but the hard sciences and technical training. Muñoz broke away from the negotiations over the long student strike at UNAM to eat a quick lunch and discuss the idea. "We will do it in Morelos," he said. "We already have a project there. It will fit perfectly." Moreover, he and García of Ibero thought it would be a good idea if the private and public universities (Ibero is a Jesuit institution) could work together on the project.

In Cuernavaca, in the state of Morelos, Dr. Gustavo Valencia, Suárez's husband, professor of mathematics at the Morelos campus of the Instituto Tecnologico y de Estudios Superiores de Monterrey (ITESM) and director of Extension and Development, said he wanted to begin Clemente courses in Morelos, but on two levels: one, a course that required a tuition payment for those who could afford it, and another for people at the lower end of the middle class *(clase media baja);* that is, the poor who can read. By late autumn of 1999, his project was moving forward.

He had worked out most of the details for his two-year version of the course. It would follow the curriculum of the original course, adding a section on contemporary Mexico. One section of the course would be located in an area of Cuernavaca known as Lagunilla, which had been settled by internal immigrants, the squatters who were among the poorest urban residents in Mexico, those who were said to live close to *pobreza extrema* (extreme poverty). ITESM would give faculty release time to teach in the course, students would come from both the middle-class residential areas and Lagunilla. A new version of the Clemente Course, this time with the humanities in the Mexican tradition, rooted in two of the world's five basic cultures, was about to begin. The energy and goodwill that emanated from a single household in Morelos was remarkable, and the quality of mind was extraordinary.

Mutatis mutandis, the utterly Athenian pattern—the humanities, reflective thinking, *auto nomos,* and the public life of citizens in a democracy—seems to survive the particularity of culture; we are indeed as different as snowflakes, as similar as snow.

XVIII.

Conclusion:

A Dangerous Corollary

THE SUCCESS OF THE UNITED STATES has always rested on the certainty that the poor are not dangerous. If that seems an overstatement, said for shock value or merely to gain the reader's attention again at the end of a long book, that was not my intention. I want only to show that poverty and the blues, the feeling that "you can't get out of it," live in the same house.

They have lived there for generations, since the founding of the country in a revolution different from any other in history. In all the others, the people, mainly the poor, took power away from the rich. The lesson of those revolutions was simple and memorable: The poor can be dangerous. Watch out for the poor.

In the British colonies in America, it was not the poor but the aristocracy who revolted. The poor fought and died in the war—they always do—but they did not make the revolution. They were not dangerous. When it came time to write a constitution, it did not have to address the problems of the poor. With its Lockean origins, the U.S.

Constitution had great concern about property rights, but no interest at all in distributing the wealth of the nation in some way that included the poor.

The dominant view of the poor in the young nation, and still the view in many quarters, was that of Herbert Spencer, who coined the phrase "survival of the fittest." The Social Darwinists, following Spencer, believed that the only reason to give charity to the poor was to improve the character of the donor. That took care of the moral question. And with no reason to fear a violent uprising, it made no sense to those in power even to consider sharing the wealth of the nation with the poor. There were dissenting voices, of course, socialists and do-gooders, but they had no power; they were not dangerous either.

In the South, slaveholders worried about runaways but not about revolt, even when blacks vastly outnumbered the whites on plantations in isolated areas far from any town or military installation. On the way west, the Indians offered some resistance, but their destiny was manifest. William Graham Sumner expressed the popular view: Either the Indians became "civilized" or they became extinct.

When civil war did come to the United States, it was not between the rich and poor, although the immediate cause of the war was economic. The poor did not ever gain anything in the United States by threatening to overthrow the established order.

The poor are timid, conditioned by life within a surround of force; they kill each other. Even during the morally and politically tumultuous sixties, when McGeorge Bundy of Harvard and the National Security Council returned from seeing the American dead on the battlefields of Vietnam and said to send more Americans to die, the poor shouldered their rifles and went. And died. They did not want to die. The unfairness of rich men choosing to send the poor to die enraged them, so in Watts, in Detroit, and in Chicago, they burned down their own houses and killed their brothers.

Americans do not like such civil disorder, even when it does not touch them, but the response to disorder has not been to close the income gap between rich and poor. The gap is, in fact, far greater now than it was during the riots of the sixties. The response to public disorder among the poor is not to end or even to alleviate poverty. It is more like the sentiment expressed by Lieutenant David I. Harris of the Riviera Beach, Florida, Police Department, who said, "If we don't do something about poverty in the next twenty or thirty years, my job will be to shoot people down in the street." Lieutenant Harris does not fear the overthrow of the government by the poor so much as he fears the effect of killing people on his own character. Herbert Spencer again, but in a mirror image.

Poverty is a problem in America because exposure to it may coarsen the rest of the population. That is why the poor are generally kept hidden and why the homeless and the mendicants, who wander among the affluent, are both feared and detested.

The fear of mendicants and other visible poor has to do with the only real danger the poor have ever posed in America, which is to our sense of our own moral worth. Franklin Delano Roosevelt, for all that he is said to have wanted to save capitalism, also sought to salvage the nation's sense of itself as capable of goodness. A generation later, Lyndon Johnson and the War on Poverty, misguided and underfunded as it was, took the same path.

It was not until the rise to moral dominance of Ronald Reagan that the poor ceased to be a danger to our sense of our own moral worth. Reagan dismissed all moral questions in his own life and that of the nation through the deceits of charm. Now, at the end of the century, under cover of being a Democrat, Bill Clinton has acceded to Congress, and turned the nation's attitude toward the poor back to the time before Roosevelt. He has made them morally and politically inconsequential. Only the poor are not covered by the quilt of political correctness that intends the protection of all persons who are, in truth or imagination, deprived of their natural or civil rights.

Since no one will help them, the poor have no alternative but to learn politics. It is the way out of poverty, and into a successful, self-governing life, based upon reflection and the ability to negotiate a safe path between the polar opposites of liberty and order. But to learn politics may also be a way for the poor to become dangerous at last.

Coming into possession of the faculty of reflection and the skills of politics leads to a choice for the poor: They may use politics to get along in a society based on the game, to escape from the surround of force into a gentler life, and nothing more. Or they may choose to oppose the game itself. It it is the latter, if the poor enter the circle of legitimate power and then oppose the cruelty of the game, they will pose a real danger to the established order.

No one can predict the effect of politics, although we would all like to think that wisdom goes our way. In their newfound autonomy, people may turn to the left or right or choose to live smugly, disinterestedly, in the middle. That is why the poor are so often mobilized and so rarely politicized. The possibility that they will adopt a moral view other than that of their mentors can never be discounted. And no one wants to run that risk.

Tens of thousands or even millions of poor people entering the public world may not endanger the established order at all. But the possibility that it could must perforce change the view of the poor held in America since the eighteenth century: The rest of the citizens would have to pay heed. Then the remaining poor might be spared some of the forces that make misery of their lives. And that, in turn, would make it easier for more of the poor to move out of the private life and into the public world, where all persons may think of themselves as having effect.

If the poor who learn politics do not become dangerous, if they choose to survive modestly in peace and comfort, that is surely good enough. The goal is to end poverty, to consign the blues to history and romance, to make citizens of the poor. If that can be accomplished, the question of danger changes, for then the poor will be dangerous in the way that all citizens are dangerous in a democracy—they will *be* power.

In one way or the other, politics will make dangerous persons of the poor. The certainty of that has worried the elites of this earth since politics was invented. But Plato was wrong about politics then and his fundamentalist followers are wrong now. The happiness of others is a goal worth pursuing, and the method for achieving it, democracy, is a risk worth taking.

Appendix
Cherokee/Clemente Course

Summer Session 2000

1. Goal:

The course of study will examine the expansion of Cherokee thought and practice. In doing so, it will compare traditional Cherokee identity and characteristics of Classical and Modern European modalities.

2. Outline:

Session 1 (5-9)—Introduction
   a. Registration
   b. Concept of Cherokee/Clemente Course
   c. Course Outline

Session 2 (5-16)—Identity and Recognition: Multicultural Societies and Democratic Constitutional Nations
   a. Multicultural Curricula
   b. Talking Points in Cherokee Policy and History
   c. Civilizations, City-States, and Empires
   Reading: Cherokee Photo Timeline; Beginning Cherokee Timeline: Cherokee, U.S., and World History
       Sappho, *Lyrics;* Sophocles, *Oedipus;* Euripides, *Medea*

Session 3 (5-23)—Leaders and Thinkers
  a. Honored Cherokees: Attaculaculla, Nancy Ward, Oolateeca, Sequoyah, David Vann, Elias Boudinot, Major Ridge, John Ridge, John Ross, Stand Watie
  b. Ancient Athenians: Draco, Solon, Cleisthenes, Themistocles, Socrates, Plato, Aristotle, Pericles, Thucydides
  c. Contemporary Leadership: Chad Smith, Hastings Shade, Harold DeMoss, Barbara Starr Scott, William Smith, Jack Kilpatrick, Anna Gritts Kilpatrick
  Reading: Early Treaties
  Transitional Government
  Plato, *Apology*
Session 4 (5-30)—Military Affairs
  a. Clan Organization
  b. Greek Training, Tactics
  Reading: "Voluntary Removal"; Clan Organization
  Legal Characteristics of Cherokee Nation
  Plato, *Republic;* Aristotle, *Ethics*
Session 5 (6-6)—Spatial Concerns
  a. Origin of the World and Migration Stories
  b. Geography: Colonies and Alliances
  Reading: State's Rights and Cherokee Nation
  Forced Removal
  Aristotle, *Politics* and *Poetics*
Session 6 (6-13)—Commerce
  a. Economic Interdependence
  b. Agriculture and Manufacture
  c. Service
  Reading: Federal Erosion of Criminal Jurisdiction
  Cherokee "Golden Age"
  Livy, *The History of Rome from Its Foundation*
  Plutarch, *Lives: Marcus Cato*
  Virgil, *Aeneid, Ovid,* and *Metamorphoses*
Session 7 (6-20)—Urban Life
  a. Chota, New Echota, Tahlequah
  b. Towns, Architecture, Interiors, and Exteriors

Reading: Civil War
  Civil War Retributions
  Augustine, *The City of God* and *Confessions*
Session 8 (6-27)—Literature
  a. Cherokee Syllabary and Cherokee Writers
  b. Greek Alphabet, Writing, Education, Greek Writers
  c. Roman Alphabet, Grammar, Logic, Roman Writers
  Reading: Territorial Status
  Cherokee Outlet
  Maimonides, *Guide to the Perplexed*
  Avicenna, *Psychology*
Session 9 (7-4)—Review
  Reading: Allotment; Termination
Session 10 (7-11)—Art and Architecture
  a. Cherokee Etching, Basketry, Pottery, Visual Art
  b. Classical Greek and Roman Design and Style
  c. Art of the Renaissance
  Reading: Resistance; Oklahoma Statehood
  Dante, *Comedy*
Session 11 (7-18)—Medicine
  a. Ritual, Plants, and Disease—Swimmer
  b. Religion, Philosophy, and Physicians—Hippocrates
  Reading: Restriction Acts; Federal Policy
  Machiavelli, *Prince*
  Montaigne, *Essays*
Session 12 (7-25)—Politics
  a. Clan Law and Constitutional Governance
  b. Democracy
  Reading: Tribal Revitalization Law
  John Locke, *Civil Government* and *An Essay Concerning Human Understanding*
Session 13 (8-1)—Alliances
  a. Federal Relationships
  b. Ethnicity
  Reading: Modern Federal Law
  Jean Jacques Rousseau, *The Social Contract*

Session 14 (8-8)—Participation
    a. Self Determination
    b. *Polis* and Nation
    Reading: Cherokee Country
        Adam Smith, *The Wealth of Nations*
Session 15 (8-15)—Conclusion
    a. Self Governance
    b. Republicanism
    Reading: Present Status of the Cherokee Nation
        Alexis de Tocqueville, *Democracy in America*

3. Texts:

    Chadwick Smith, compiler, *Cherokee Nation History Course* (Tahlequah: Cherokee Nation, 2000)

    Sarah Lawall et al., editors, *Norton Anthology of World Masterpieces,* Volume I (New York: W. W. Norton & Company, 1999)

4. Assessment:

    a. Active Class Participation
    b. Mid-term Oral Review
    c. Final Oral and Written Examinations

Index